SACRED MARRIAGE

Sacred Marriage

THE WISDOM OF
THE SONG OF SONGS

Words by

NICHOLAS AYO

and Paintings by

MEINRAD CRAIGHEAD

CONTINUUM · NEW YORK

1997
The Continuum Publishing Company
370 Lexington Avenue
New York, NY 10017

Printed in the United States of America

Library of Congress Cataloging-in-Publication Data

Ayo, Nicholas.
    Sacred marriage : the wisdom of Song of songs / words by Nicholas
Ayo and paintings by Meinrad Craighead.
      p.   cm.
    Includes bibliographical references.
    ISBN 0-8264-1030-8
    1. Bible. O.T. Song of Solomon—Commentaries. 2. Marriage—
Biblical teaching. I. Title.
BS1485.3.A86   1997
223.9077—dc21   97-17744
                                                CIP

Excerpt from "Ash Wednesday" in *Collected Poems 1909–1962* by T.S. Eliot, copyright 1936 by Harcourt
Brace & Company, copyright 1964, 1963 by T.S. Eliot, reprinted by permission of the publisher.

    Excerpt from "Little Gidding" from the *Four Quartets* in *Collected Poems 1909–1962* by T.S. Eliot,
copyright 1936 by Harcourt Brace & Company, copyright 1964, 1963 by T.S. Eliot, reprinted by permission
of the publisher.

    Excerpt from "I Knew a Woman," copyright 1954 by Theodore Roethke, from *The Collected Poems
of Theodore Roethke* by Theodore Roethke, reprinted by permission of Doubleday, a division of the
Bantam Doubleday Dell Publishing Group, Inc.

    Excerpt from "Sewing Lesson" by Lizabeth Lennon, reprinted by permission of the author.

    Excerpt from "The Poet" by Leanne Ponder, reprinted by permission of the author.

    Excerpt from John of the Cross, translated by John Dunne, in *Love's Mind: An Essay on the Contemplative Life* by John Dunne, copyright 1993 by John Dunne, reprinted by permission of the author.

Dedicated to the many friends
who have shown me wisdom and love.
"It is only a matter of time to embody
an eternal present."

Contents

Acknowledgments

I AM MOST GRATEFUL to Meinrad Craighead, a visual artist, whom I hold as a co-author of this commentary on the Song of Songs. Our work was done in collaboration but independently, although there was a prior presumption that we shared common values. Her paintings are not a reflection upon my writings. Her work is a visual commentary upon the biblical text itself. Her painting complements my writing and I hold her contribution crucial to the overall endeavor of this book. I am also thankful to Sharon Toffey Shepela and Miriam Therese Winter for leading me to the work of Meinrad Craighead.

I owe a debt of gratitude to Mary Catherine Rowland, who was a missionary in Ghana during the writing of this book. She has given the spiritual dimension much support. I owe a debt of gratitude to Sharon Toffey Shepela, feminist scholar and professor. In reading the text in more than one version, she has given the woman's point of view constant consideration. I owe a debt of gratitude to Henry Weinfield, poet and critic, as well as a colleague of mine at the University of Notre Dame. He has given valuable suggestions for revision, and he was especially attentive to my English rendition of the verses of the Song of Songs. David Burrell, colleague and friend for forty years, read the whole manuscript and gave me assurance the overall rhetoric was acceptable. His enthusiasm for the work gave me hope. Mary Louise Gude and Gretchen Reydams-Schils read parts of the manuscript and made comments for its improvement. William Dohar was a personal support to me in moments of keen discouragement. Laura Zawadski, my student assistant, proofread the manuscript and checked the references. The Institute for Scholarship in the Liberal Arts at Notre Dame assisted me with a semester leave of absence. The

Program of Liberal Studies at the University of Notre Dame has always been encouraging of my writing and also provided me travel funds.

Roland Murphy's published works were for me a bible of scholarship on the Song. Marvin Pope's "Song of Songs" in the *Anchor Bible* series has been an encyclopedia of useful information. Gene Gollogly and Frank Oveis at Continuum Publishing Company gave continual assistance, and they are skillful editors and publishers indeed. In particular, I thank Gene Gollogly for a very prompt and encouraging phone call when the manuscript was first submitted.

Though many people have been a part of this work, I want to say that the responsibility for any shortcomings in the final version remains mine alone.

Preface

· I ·

IN ONE OF THE EARLIEST Jewish commentaries Rabbi Aqiba writes: "for the whole world is not worth the day on which the *Song of Songs* was given to Israel, for all the Writings are holy, and the *Song of Songs* is the Holy of Holies." In one of the earliest Christian commentaries, Origen proclaims his appreciation: "This little book is an *epithalamium,* that is a nuptial song, which it seems to me that Solomon wrote in a dramatic form, and sang after the fashion of a bride to her bridegroom, who is the word of God, burning with celestial love. Indeed, he loves her deeply, whether she is the soul, made in his own image, or the church." In one of the earliest medieval commentaries Saadia Ben Joseph puzzles over the Song of Songs, which resembles "locks to which the keys have been lost." According to legend Saint Thomas Aquinas was asked to explain the Song of Songs when he was dying, and the Song was read to him by his request on his deathbed.

An early twentieth-century commentator, Morris Jastrow, Jr., urges the reader "to take the book for what it clearly is, a continuous ecstasy on the theme of sexual love." Artist Eric Gill speaks of the Song as "a poem of which atheists can see the beauty, even when they cannot see the meaning, of which moralists can see the meaning, even when they cannot see the beauty." Michael Fox writes of the Song as a gem of many facets, a meandering river with a different vista around every bend, a book "full of fun, erotic allusions, sensual word-painting of the lovers and their worlds, and heart-warming sentiments." Marina Warner calls the Song "that most languorous and amorous of poems," which leaves the reader "spellbound by its sensuality and drowsy voluptuousness." Karl Barth calls the Song of Songs a "Magna Carta of humanity." And the *New Jerusalem Bible* concludes: "No book of the Old Testament has been subjected to more diverse interpretation."

This book is intended for lovers. I have particularly in mind a man and a woman betrothed to be married. I have written this book to provide what might be helpful for an initial reading of the Song of Songs as the love poetry of sacred scripture. My hope remains to draw the reader through the Bible's words into the heart of this song as the everlasting word of God. In this biblical song the reader is invited to see how human love and divine love do kiss. The divine "love that moves the sun and stars" finds tender and poignant human voice in the Song of Songs. This book might well be seen as a betrothal gift to celebrate that love greater than all of our hearts and more than the lyric poet can ever sing.

In the verse by verse commentary I offer first-time readers of the Song both the classical King James version and beneath it my own poetic version of the text. Both English versions can readily delight. Culling the wisdom of many ages, both drawn from and laid upon the lines of this ancient song, I then add succinct reflections upon each verse in order to amplify the reader's appreciation of this exquisite love poetry of the Hebrew Bible. Finally, I present some meditative insights of my own upon each verse of this remarkable poem, so clear and so opaque, so secular and so sacred.

In the verse commentary I have tried to include only those details that explain and enrich the poetry. I am interested less in the Song of Songs as ancient biblical literature than I am in the Song as poetry affective even to this day. The meaning of the poetry and its religious implication remain more valued than the complete exegesis of every detail. The view of the forest through the trees I hope to secure. The verse commentary, therefore, seeks not to overwhelm the text with the arcana of botanical lore, clinical body parts, exhaustive rhetorical analysis, elaborate historical speculation, labored allegorical correspondences, or any other exhaustive reading of this text so charged with pure and rich imagination. I hope to deal with the text as a love song, with enough judicious exposition and commentary to assist readers to understand the Song of Songs and to maximize their enjoyment of the literary delights of this ancient love song of love songs.

In this commentary I hope also to give a spiritual interpretation, but not one that takes the text as an occasion or prompt in order to read into the words whatever exposition, however valuable, the commentator wishes to impart. On its own the Song stands as a text worthy of close reading, which should also disclose its spiritual values. My commentary tries to bring out a plausible and germane spiritual reading, one that allows the least disregard of the biblical text and the author's intent insofar as it may become known. This commentary will be eclectic yet not without discrimination, poetic but not without justification.

Allusions to sexual intimacy in the Song are nuanced and always covered with an appropriate veil, and so should the commentaries be. Spiritual wisdom is equally hidden, and the text should not be stripped for understanding before the more overall sensuality of the Song is fully explored. The focus centers on what the Song of Songs says as well as what it means. This book is thus a binocular critique—physical and spiritual, erotic and mystical, profane and sacred, realistic and romantic, an integrated literary and theological critique. My writing hopes to be an irenic synthesis of the various fruitful ways to read the Song. After all, the Song of Songs is love embodied, the word of God made human language, and in that vein so would the commentary be.

· II ·

In my reading of the Song of Songs I hold the text as a sacred inspired revelation and I assume a hidden wisdom in the text to be explored but never exhausted by any commentator past, present, or future. I hold the songs in the Song much as the psalms in the Psalter. As the psalms were read through an understanding of the Torah (the central Hebrew Scriptures) so the Song should be read through the eyes of the whole Bible, and with a particular focus upon the tradition of the wisdom literature. In the Song the man and woman celebrate human embodiment, just as in the psalms the human condition is sung. The Song of Songs is a book of the Bible, and it looks backward to the literature that gives origin to this love story and forward to the literature that fulfills the deepest meaning of God's revelation. In some ways the Song is a focus of the Bible, for God's love story is the focus of salvation history. Indeed, the Bible is God's own loveletters, telling of God's perduring courtship of humankind.

God's love story begins *in the beginning* when the father of the bride presents Eve to Adam, who takes such delight in her, saying "this at last is bone of my bones and flesh of my flesh" (Gen 2:23). The marriage imagery between the Lord God and Israel can be found throughout the prophets, and especially in Hosea, Jeremiah, Isaiah, and Ezekiel. In Jesus, the word of God made flesh, the love story reaches a unique consummation. "God so loved the world that he gave his only Son" (Jn 3:16). The beginning of the public ministry of Jesus is situated in a marriage feast in Cana where the festive wine must not run dry (Jn 2:3). And the ending of the life of Jesus centers upon the hardwood marriage bed of the cross, where the love of Jesus, his body given for us, becomes eternal love.

The Bible concludes *in the ending* with the marriage in heaven, where the heavenly Jerusalem is prepared for the nuptials with the Lord God "as a bride adorned for her husband" (Rev 21:2). One could well argue for the Songs of Songs as the very center of the Bible, a pivot point around which other more weighty texts revolve, for the Song does present the human love story in an incomparable way. It has ever been read in the believing community as a courtship that ultimately speaks of God's love for humankind, which in the physical and spiritual love of woman and man in this world but mirrors the divine nuptials "in a glass darkly."

· III ·

The Song of Songs presents love poetry of high quality, and at times it is similar to the poems with exotic imagery and erotic allusion in the writings of the Sumerian, Mesopotamian, and Egyptian cultures surrounding Israel. Israel borrowed in many ways from them. Comparable love songs abounded in the near east, especially in Egypt, and in the far east in Tamil love poetry found along the coast of India. The spice trade may have facilitated a literary exchange with the Mediterranean world. The erotic and cultic poetry of pagan cultures was significantly changed, however, in the biblical songs. Hence the limitation in trying to explain the Song of Songs in a comparison with the tradition and analogs from which it may have borrowed but which it also transformed.

The Song of Songs was probably compiled or edited in the form we now enjoy about the same time as the psalms of the Bible, themselves a high mark in Hebrew poetry. That time frame most likely centers on the late sixth and early fifth century before Christ in the early decades of the period after the Babylonian exile (587–537 b.c.). Several words in the Song are borrowed from the Persian, which would indicate that at least parts of the Song date from the exile or later, when many of the Hebrew scriptures were finalized in the form that the Bible now contains them. As with the psalms, many of the elements of the Song of Songs would stem from an oral or written tradition that goes back another five hundred years to the time of David and of Solomon (circa 1000 b.c.). There may have been some preexilic written versions of the Song, but the completed biblical book would seem to require later dating.

An even more speculative matter remains with the question of authorship. Who wrote the Song of Songs will probably never be determined. The themes of the Song are universal and it would seem, despite references to Solomon in the poems, that human nature is being sung rather than the experience of a particular historical person. If Solomon or the Jerusalem court poets of the period of the Davidic kingdom wrote or collected some of these songs, they probably did not write the majority of them. The arguments advanced for an overall unity of theme and metaphor in the Song of Songs suggest at the least one final poet-editor who fixed the text as we now have it. There are no further internal clues to the name of the author(s) or last redactor of the Song of Songs.

One might ask the question how the Song of Songs became incorporated in the canon of inspired biblical books, where it is included as such in the Hebrew scriptures and in the Christian scriptures as well. The poems in the Song of Songs were probably at first an oral collection of secular love poems of exquisite devotion and especial regard for the integrity of human courtship love. Subsequently, these poems were probably sung in their preliterary form at festivities, such as weddings, betrothals, and perhaps gatherings particularly of women. The best of these song-poems were adopted into various ceremonies that enjoyed religious implications. A written literary form emerged. The written text yoked to the liturgical ceremony encouraged a more spiritual reading of the songs. A certain sacred status of the text followed upon this development. Gradually the Song of Songs became a part of the canon of the Bible, according to the aphorism, *lex orandi, lex credendi* (the way of prayer is the way of faith).

The Hebrew Masoretic text is the basis of most biblical translations of the Song of Songs. The Greek Septuagint is also generally judged to have been faithful to the original texts used in the establishment of the Masoretic text. The Latin Vulgate testifies to the consolidated proto-Masoretic text, even though the Vulgate does not now serve well as the overall text for the Song of Songs.

In 117 verses and some 1200 words the Song of Songs employs a vocabulary of about 500 Hebrew words out of some 8000 words in the general vocabulary of the Hebrew scriptures. About one-third of the vocabulary in the Song consists of words that are not common in the Hebrew Bible, and most of the verses of the Song contain at least one of these words. Some thirty or more words or phrases in the Song are found nowhere else in the Bible. A third of these are found nowhere in extant Hebrew writings. Hence there has been considerable variety in how some passages have been translated, and several verses are so obscure as to defy a widely accepted construal of the Hebrew, much less a translation.

· IV ·

The unity of the Song centers upon the wonders of youthful human sexual attraction and the passionate love of a woman and a man. My conclusion, shared by many commentators, is that the argument from thematic and linguistic commonalties supports an underlying unity, however imperfect. Thus the poems in the Song are interrelated in a more profound way than poems in an anthology devoted to one theme, such as love poetry. It is most probable that the Song was originally a collection of similar poetic material. A subsequent poet-author or poet-editor configured the biblical Song of Songs in a thematically and rhetorically unified text that does not obliterate the outline of some of the original and disparate songs gathered over the centuries from oral or written sources. It is further judged that the Song is not history, though it may contains fragments of history. Despite these conclusions there is no definitive resolution to the question of what genre of literature embraces the Song of Songs.

The *Revised Standard Version* of the Bible proposes that the Song is a collection of some twenty-five separate poems. Many other divisional schemes have been proposed by commentators, as few as five and as many as fifty. Most of the critical opinion suggests a number of poems from five to ten. Within each poem there may be several subsections. As always there are the lumpers who see common ground and the splitters who see particular differences. Breaking the Song into five to ten major divisions or poems does not neatly follow the biblical eight chapter arrangement, but it does present roughly a corresponding pattern. Roland Murphy divides the Song into ten units with twice that number of subdivisions. Murphy accepts unity in the Song wherever it can be found and allows diversity where it can hardly be avoided. His major demarcations follow the biblical chapter pattern more or less. In a matter that allows no absolute precision, his scheme provides a plausible division of the text convenient for purposes of discussion, and I have adopted it in this book.

The Song of Songs presents a quilt of many colors and of a rich texture, a variegated mosaic made of many-splendored fabrics. Here is an intimate family album of courtship days made up of many candid photos arranged to allow the viewer to see the picture quickly. Here is no well-wrought novel from beginning to end, but rather a collection of epistles and episodes, moments of lovetalk and snapshots beyond description, a love story line as old as woman and man and as fresh as the ineffable yearning for divine love that wells up within the human breast today as yesterday. The Song of Songs is thus a patterned quilt with pieces of poetry that are pieces of the life of a woman and a man in love:

> Watermarked waves of briney, sea foam taffeta lapping up against plaidly faded flannel. Delicate rosebuds sprawling across working class calico. An uneven polygon of striped pillow ticking and a perfect square of white linen from an old dinner jacket. Tears and snags of raw silk, vulnerable, pocked and painfully made beautiful; all at once. Jungles of tropical flowers, reclining in the chintzy heat of summer under awninged patios. Wide wale corduroy. The slender yet surprisingly tough blue of chambray. Innocent, pure white eyelet. Swiss: properly seductive in black translucence; strategically and masterfully dotted with opaque dabs (in all the right places). Organza, grosgrain, oxford cloth, double-knit polyester.
> (Lizabeth Lennon, *Juggler,* spring (1994), 53)

The Song of Songs is not a woven piece of whole cloth. It is a hand-stitched quilted pattern of lovely swatches of the best fabrics and the loveliest melodies of human courtship to be found in the Bible and indeed in written literature to this day.

· V ·

In our discussion of the Song of Songs a number of assumptions are necessarily made. The woman and man are likely ideal types of female and male. The man and the woman in the Song have no proper names, and the identification of the man with King Solomon is without convincing evidential support. They are both peasant couple and royal couple, because they are humanity generalized and personified. Despite the imperfect unity of the Song of Songs, the text supports the assumption that the woman and man retain a consistent character throughout the text.

In any construal of the Song of Songs it is well to note from the beginning an array of difficulties. Erotic sensuality and sexuality, even if contained by laudable human behavior, has seemed to generations of readers a peculiar biblical theme. Thus allegorical or spiritual readings of the Song of Songs abound. These interpretations are edifying and consistent with overall biblical themes, and yet quite subjective and impossible to establish from the text, especially in their contradictory variety. As in the Hebrew book of Esther, there is no mention of God in the Song of Songs, except perhaps in one verse of the last chapter (8:6). If there is Hebrew history in the Song, it also remains vague and hard to substantiate. If there are borrowings from the literature and myths of the surrounding cultures of the east, those literary influences are tantalizing but also inconclusive. Every text is influenced by the context within which it was composed, and yet original literature transcends and transforms all its antecedents.

· VI ·

All texts are not merely deposits of information but also obligations of interpretation. Everything is seen and is read from a point of view, and that is the beginning of some kind of interpretation. If the Song is not in some way a unified composition, whether the structure stems from one original author or one final editor, there can be no configuration that encourages an overall interpretation. The Song of Songs should first and foremost be read for itself as one book of the Bible with its own integrity. At the same time the surrounding ancient and pagan near east culture adds a literary background to the poetry, and the spiritual and liturgical readings, both Jewish and Christian, add a religious foreground to the Song. The poetic background is well employed to illumine the literal reading. The mystical foreground is perhaps best regarded as a further level of meaning to be contemplated simultaneously with the literal.

A straightforward and literal reading of the Song of Songs should be the place to begin. It is impossible to ignore these songs as examples of erotic poetry of a gentle and delightful tone, celebrating human sexual love between a woman and a man. Although the religious commentators of the Song have been almost exclusively allegorists seeking the spiritual reading, the literal reading as love-lyric was defended in the patristic period by Theodore of Mopsuestia (392–428) and a few others. In the late eighteenth century it was the literary figure Johann Von Herder who argued most persuasively that the predominant allegorical school of interpretation should not prevail over a literal reading of the Song of Songs as a collection of love poetry. In the nineteenth century the outstanding commentator Christian Ginsburg also furthered the literal reading of the Song. In twentieth-century criticism the reading of the Song of Songs as secular love poetry is widely accepted by biblical scholars as the primary place to begin, even though further levels of meaning can be added to a literal reading of the biblical text. No one in the contemporary Catholic world has done more to foster a careful and open reading of the Song as wholesome love poetry with religious overtones than the biblical scholar Roland Murphy. Reversing the allegorical interpretation of the *Jerusalem Bible,* the *New Jerusalem Bible* concludes: "Nothing indicates that a key is needed for decoding the Song or that anything should be read into it other than the natural meaning of the text: it is a collection of songs celebrating the loyal and mutual love that leads to marriage" (1028).

Love lends heightened senses. The Song presents very erotic poetry, although it is never lascivious. The erotic quality of the love depicted is always reverent and respectful of the dignity of the beloved. It never descends to the objectification of the body characteristic of pornography. Though the Song is sensual, it is never prurient. The imagery never depicts sexual intimacy without the veil of indirection, circumlocution, or allusion. Although it is straightforward and unabashed in its celebration of the human body, the Song remains modest and persistent in its awareness that to reveal less is to reveal more. Sexuality thrives not only on open disclosure but also on further hidden mysteries.

The sexual ambiance in the Song is exuberant. Even though in the Song itself there are no explicit moral parameters, there is no promiscuity. Wholehearted love itself provides its own integrity. Love's innocence protects it from a fall, and the idealistic and Edenic quality of these love poems has prompted commentators to think of the Song as a poetic restoration of paradise lost, or as an imaginative vision of paradise found in a future still to be achieved. "In its own way, it teaches the excellence and dignity of the love that draws man and woman together, it exorcises the myths attached to love in those remote times and presents a love as free of puritanical restraint as it is of licentious excess" (*New Jerusalem Bible,* 1029).

In reading the Song of Songs as secular love poetry of a most wholesome and poignant quality, one is not leaving out the spiritual concerns of the allegorical interpretations of church communities. The literal reading presents the Song as spiritually erotic, which is not altogether different from the allegorical reading that presents the song as erotically spiritual. The conflict in human sexuality is not so much between the body and the soul, or the flesh and the spirit. Both the body and the soul when selfish are opposed to the body and soul when generous. Thus the conflict is not between profane love and sacred love; it is between sin and grace. All sexuality in the last analysis is a matter of spirituality.

Let us try to summarize. Cultural and theological assumptions or presuppositions prevail in all interpretation of any text. The stoics from the time of Philo of Alexandria sought a further meaning hidden in the gross behavior of the Homeric gods. The Platonic tradition found the material world an emblem of a more perfect spiritual reality. The monastic commentators like Bernard of Clairvaux sought a further meaning in the Song beyond its apparent erotic interest. "That *veritas* [truth] is found hidden *sub umbra et figura* [in half-light and in symbol] is an essential concept of medieval hermeneutics in general" (Matter, 7). Without the literal sense, however, the spiritual sense is untethered. And, converesely, without the spiritual sense the literal sense is unfulfilled.

The future will judge us just as we now judge the past. "Our cultural presuppositions, like theirs, and the extent of our exegetical progress, if any, will be scrutinized by the next generation of faithful interpreters" (Murphy, 41). Human love has its own independence given by the creator, but it is not a sovereign love. Sexual love has its own goodness, but it is not an absolute love. The literal reading of the Song should not overwhelm the spiritual, nor vice versa. We need to affirm both the beauty of creation and the glory of God. Interpretations should be both/and rather than either/or. "And we have no right to set a limit to God's inspiration" (*New Jerusalem Bible,* 1028). The question always remains this: Does a particular reading of the Song of Songs give life?

· VII ·

In the biblical text of the Song of Songs the reader will note considerable repetition of words and images, and even whole lines. In the verse commentary there is also some repetition. Because the reader may consult the commentary only for one part of the Song, it seemed acceptable to repeat in some instances central ideas, much as the Song itself does.

All quotations from the Bible are taken from the *New Revised Standard Version* (copyright by the National Council of Churches of Christ in the U.S.A.). The translations of Augustine, Lucretius, and Dante are mine. The translation of Theocritus is by Gretchen Reydams-Schils. Some brief quotations in the commentary are not attributed. They belong either to Gretchen Reydams-Schils or Sharon Toffey Shepela, both collaborating readers of the text. In some instances a line was quoted by memory and the source remains unremembered.

· VIII ·

The bibliography of the Song of Songs is enormous. In this book I have borrowed from innumerable commentators, who themselves borrowed from the best studies of the Song that preceded them. Some of the ideas I have read about were also discovered spontaneously in my own reading of the Song. Some of my own ideas may prove wrong; others are of no great moment. In sum, my own commentary is a melange, a bouquet of flowers of interpretation. To give credit with a specific reference for every thing I learned from somewhere else would make the book a tissue of footnotes. I hope I have not taken material unfairly, and I do acknowledge in the bibliography the books to which I am most indebted. My comments would be informed by a love for the biblical text, and I hope a prayerful devotion of soul toward the mystery of the God who is author of the Song of Songs and of whom St. John says: "God is love" (1 Jn 4:8).

A New English Version
of the Song of Songs

THERE ARE SEVERAL dozen English translations of the Song of Songs. Not
only does every Bible have a translation of its own, but there are many
monographs which include an original translation. There are scholarly team
efforts, like the revered King James version of 1611, or the New Revised
Standard Version of 1989. There are individual poetic efforts such as those by
the well known twentieth-century poet Robert Graves and more recently by
Marcia Falk. Before trying my hand at my own version of the Song I have
read many translations of the Hebrew, pored over annotations to the construal
of each Hebrew word, and weighed arguments and evidence for this or that
interpretation based on the ambiguities of the original Hebrew. I tried to be
a fair referee in sorting out an enormous amount of scholarly opinion. I have
consulted every English Bible I could discover, and every translation where
so ever found. I have widely roamed through lexicons, interlinear versions,
commentaries with endless footnotes, and various biblical sources and references. Jerome's masterful translation of the Song, which for a thousand years
was the Vulgate Bible of the Western world, I have read in the Latin. I have
tried to be especially sensitive to the poetic possibilities that a translator in
fidelity to the original Hebrew should not overlook. I do not myself, however,
read Hebrew.

Reynolds Price writes that the King James Bible is a "lyric original" and "a
continuous poetry rooted in and blossoming from our only means of knowledge: the human body and its fragile organs." The King James version remains
both a translation and great literature. Many versions since have been either

He speaks:

My heart you have ravished, my sister, my bride!
You have melted my heart with one flash of your eyes. (4:9)

Let me look upon you and listen to your voice,
For your face is fair, and your voice is melody. (2:14)

the one or the other. I try not to depart more than necessary from this most respected English translation of the Bible; I try equally to be contemporary and accurate. In attempting to make the Song sing, I have done a poetic version and not a new translation. I hope, however, that my composition presents a careful yet literary English rendition, one not unworthy of the original Hebrew of the Song of Songs.

Although I have borrowed a phrasing from this or that previous translation, I have also tried to avoid copying the work of others in English. If the wording is sometimes similar, there is often no good alternative. Goats are goats; sheep are sheep. It is hard to find synonyms that are not ridiculous. When I write "your hair is like a wave of goats flowing down the hill slopes of Gilead"[4:1], my line is not identical to anyone else's. No one writes "hill slopes" and I do so to capture the interior rhyme of goats and slopes. A wave flowing down not only suggests the woman's full wavy hair, but the interior rhyme of flow and down enhances the melody of the whole line. Overall the line has the sounds of many liquids. My version of this line is thus original and borrowed at one and the same time. Finally, I offer my rendition of the Song of Songs as my labor of love, something I desired to do for myself as well as for the reader, something I had to do to steep myself in the text in preparation for speaking of its deeper meanings.

In the verse by verse commentary my own text of the Song of Songs is presented underneath that of the King James. It must stand on its own worth, however, as a supplement and a complement to that ancient and beautiful translation, and in comparison with the many other translations of the Song that vie for poetic quality in the English language.

Poem One

1:1   The Song of Songs, which is Solomon's.

1:2   May he kiss me with kisses of his lips.
       Sweeter than wine your love.
1:3   Delightful your fragrance;
       A perfume unsealed your name.
       No wonder maidens love you.

1:4   Sweep me along with you.
       Let us dash away.
       The king has drawn me to his chambers.
       We shall glory and delight in you;
       Surpassing wine is your love.
       Surely they should love you.

1:5   Darkened I am, still lovely,
       Daughters of Jerusalem,
       Just as the tents of Kedar, or the pavilioned draperies of Solomon.

1:6   Do not gaze long at me because I am swarthy
       And the sun has burnt me.
       My mother's sons were incensed with me.
       They tethered me as watch keep of the vineyard;
       On my own vine I spent no care.

Poem Two

1:7   Love of my soul, tell me where's your pasture land,
       Your noonday resting place.
       Tell me lest I roam as a tramp amid the flocks of your fellows.

1:8   Should you not know, most beautiful among women,
       Track the flock and graze your kid goats
       Close by the tent site of the shepherds.

1:9   To a mare among Pharaoh's chariots
       Would I compare you, O my soul.

1:10   Lovely your cheeks laced with jewels,
       Your throat with necklaces.

1:11   We will craft for you golden circlets
       Enjoined with fine silverwork

1:12   While the king was couched within,
       My nard spread out its fragrance.

1:13   A sachet of myrrh is my true love
       All night between my breasts.

1:14   A bouquet of henna blossoms is my love
       From the gardens of Engedi.

1:15   How beautiful you are, my love,
       So beautiful!
       Your eyes are doves.

1:16   So beautiful you are, my love,
       How delightful!
       Our repose in green foliage.

1:17   The beams of our abode are cedar,
       The cross-beams of cypress.

2:1   I am a flower of the field,
       A lily of the valley.

2:2   Like a lily amid the brambles,
       So the love of my soul among women.

2:3   As an apple tree in a dense woodland,
       So is my loved one among men.
       In his shadow I love to linger,
       And his fruit is sugar in my mouth.

2:4   To his wine rooms he transports me,
       And his cover over me is love.

2:5   Nourish me with raisin cakes; restore me with apples,
       For I am so lovesick I faint.

2:6   His left hand cradles my head
       And his right hand stays me.

2:7   Give me your word, daughters of Jerusalem,
       By the gazelles and wild deer of the fields,
       Do not rouse nor raise up love until its time is ripe.

Poem Three

2:8   The voice I love!
       Here he comes bounding down the mountain sides, springing over
           the hills.
2:9   My beloved is like a gazelle, a young hart.
       There he stands beside our wall,
       Peering in the windows, looking through the latticework.
2:10   My love speaks and says to me:
       Rise up, love of my soul, my beauty, come away!
2:11   Lo, winter is over, the rains are done and gone.
2:12   Flowers spring from the earth; pruning-time is here,
       And the murmur of the mourning dove is heard throughout our
           land.
2:13   On the fig tree green fruit is ripening,
       And the blossoms of the vine perfume the air.
       Rise up, love of my soul, my beauty, come away!

2:14   My dove, in the clefts of the rock,
       In the crannies of the cliff,
       Let me look upon you and listen to your voice,
       For your face is fair, and your voice is melody.
2:15   Corral the foxes, the small foxes that ravage the vineyards,
       For now our vineyard is all blossom.

2:16   My beloved is mine and I am his.
       He feeds among these lilies.
2:17   Until the evening breeze rises and shadows dissolve,
       Turn back to me, my heart's love;
       Be like a gazelle or a young hart on the mountains of Bether.

Poem Four

3:1   On my bed in the night I sought my soul's sole love.
       I sought for him but found him not.
3:2   I will rise up and comb the city,
       In the roads and crossroads I will seek out the love of my soul.
       I sought for him but found him not.

3:3   The night-watchmen discovered me in their rounds of the city.
Have you seen my sole love?

3:4   Hardly had I passed them by when I found my soul's sole love.
I clung to him and would not let him loose till I led him to my
    mother's house,
To the room where she gave me birth.

3:5   Give me your word, daughters of Jerusalem,
By the gazelles and wild deer of the fields,
Do not rouse nor raise up love until its time is ripe.

Poem Five

3:6   What is this coming up from the desert like a cloud of smoke
Suffused with myrrh and frankincense, a blend of every bouquet?

3:7   Lo, the carriage-bed of Solomon; sixty bodyguards surround it,
The valiant ones of Israel.

3:8   Every one of them a fine swordsman, veteran soldiers,
Each with sword at hand on guard against the terrors of the night.

3:9   King Solomon built himself a carriage-bed of wood from Lebanon,

3:10   Its posts overlaid with silver and its canopy with gold,
Its couch of purple weave, its woodwork inlaid with loving care.

3:11   Come out, daughters of Jerusalem,
And look upon King Solomon, daughters of Zion,
Wearing the crown his mother gave him on his wedding day,
On the day of his heart's desire.

Poem Six

4:1   How beautiful you are, love of my soul, you are beautiful!
Your eyes behind your veil are doves.
Your hair is like a wave of goats flowing down the hill slopes of
    Gilead.

4:2   Your teeth are like a flock of ewes at shearing time,

Come up from their wash,
All paired with twins,
No one of them uncounted.

4:3 Your lips are like a scarlet ribbon; your mouth gently bowed.
Your cheeks behind your veil rosy as cloven halves of pomegranate.

4:4 Your neck is like the tower of David roped with bucklers;
A thousand shields dangle from it, all the armor of the valiant.

4:5 Your breasts are like a pair of fawns, the twins of a gazelle,
That nibble amid the lilies.

4:6 When the evening breeze rises and shadows dissolve,
I will draw near the mountains of myrrh, the hills of incense.

4:7 You are altogether beautiful, love of my soul, and nowise marred
are you.

4:8 Come down from Lebanon, my bride, come along with me from
Lebanon.
From the height of Amana, from the peaks of Senir and Hermon,
From the lairs of lions and the haunts of leopards.

4:9 My heart you have ravished, my sister, my bride!
You have melted my heart with one flash of your eyes,
With but a sparkle of your necklace.

4:10 How exquisite your love, my sister, my bride!
Your love sweeter than wine, the fragrance of your perfume
surpassing all spice!

4:11 Your lips distill wild honey, my bride; honey and milk under your
tongue,
And the breath of your clothing like the harvest airs of Lebanon.

4:12 A garden enclosed is my sister, my bride; a garden closed off, a
fountain sealed,

4:13 A paradise of pomegranates, with all the choicest fruit: henna with
nard,

4:14 Nard and saffron, sweet cane and cinnamon, with every scented
wood,
Myrrh and aloes, with all aromatic spices.

4:15 You are a garden fount, a well of living water falling from Lebanon.

4:16 Rise up north wind; come up south wind!
Blow through my garden that its sweet airs may commingle.

Let my true love come into his garden and eat of its hand-picked
    fruits.

5:1   I come into my garden, my sister, my bride;
    I gather up my myrrh and my spices,
    I eat my honey dripping from its comb,
    I drink my wine with my milk.
    Eat, friends, drink! Drink deep of love!

Poem Seven

5:2   I was asleep, but my heart still waked;
    Lo, the love of my heart is knocking:
    Open up to me, my sister, love of my soul, my dove, my perfection!
    For my head is damp-wet with the dewfall,
    My hair with the nighttime mist.

5:3   I have taken off my clothes, am I to dress again?
    I have bathed my feet, am I to soil them?

5:4   My lover slipped his hand into the door slot.
    My body trembled to its depth for him.

5:5   I rose to open to the love of my heart,
    My hands suffused with myrrh slipping over the latch of the lock,
    My fingers wetted with liquid myrrh.

5:6   I opened out to my lover, but my beloved had turned aside and
      gone away.
    My heart went slack when he left me.
    I looked for him but I did not recover him;
    I called out for him but he did not respond to me.

5:7   The night watchmen came upon me as they went about the city.
    They beat me and they hurt me.
    They uncovered my cloak, those guards around the walls.

5:8   Give me your word, daughters of Jerusalem,
    Should you find my heart's love—speak of this to him;
    Speak of my heartache for him.

5:9   Why does your love differ from anyone else, O most beautiful
among women?

Why does your love differ from anyone else that you so entreat us?

5:10   My lover is fresh-shining and flesh-fair;
Eye-catching amid thousands.

5:11   His head is gold, fine gold;
His curls are fronds of palm, raven black.

5:12   His eyes are as doves beside white running waters,
His teeth laved in milk, and set like gem stones.

5:13   His bearded cheeks are like spice beddings, rife with pungent
blossoms.

His lips crimson lilies, gilded with glistening myrrh.

5:14   His rounded arms are as gold adorned with precious stones.
His midriff is of ivory, smooth and veined with sapphire.

5:15   His legs are alabaster columns set down upon golden pedestals.
His stature is like Mount Lebanon, arresting as its cedars.

5:16   His mouth is honey sweet; he is altogether delight.
Behold the love of my heart, the love of my soul, O daughters of
Jerusalem!

6:1   Where has your beloved gone, O most beautiful among women?
Where has your love brought himself?
We would seek him with you.

6:2   My heart's love came down to his garden, to the beddings of spice,
To meander in this garden and to browse among the lilies.

6:3   I am my beloved's and he is mine.
He feeds among these lilies.

Poem Eight

6:4   You are as lovely as Tirzah, my sole beloved, lovely as Jerusalem,
Awesome as an army on parade.

6:5   Take your eyes away from me, for they make me wild.
Your hair is like a wave of goats flowing down the hill slopes of
Gilead.

6:6   Your teeth are like a flock of ewes at shearing time,
Come up from their wash,
All paired with twins,
No one of them uncounted.

6:7   Your cheeks behind your veil rosy as cloven halves of pomegranate.

6:8   Sixty the queens, eighty the concubines,
Nubile maidens without count.

6:9   One, only one is my dove,
So perfect, the treasure of her mother, the dearest of her who
    birthed her.
When women look on her they rave about her;
Queens and concubines sing her praises.

6:10   Who is this who appears like the dawn,
Resplendent as the moon, irradiant as the sun,
Awesome as an army on parade?

6:11   To the nut grove I came down to look over the valley greening,
To see were the vines in blossom, were the pomegranates in bloom.

6:12   Before I was aware, my reverie carried me in a chariot beside him.

Poem Nine

7:1   Spin around, spin, O Shulammite!
Spin, spin around, so that we may look upon you!
Why would you look on a dancing Shulammite twisting betwixt two
    sides?

7:2   How lovely your feet in sandals, O prince's daughter!
Your thighs are so curvaceous,
Like contours sculpted by an artisan.

7:3   Your netherlands are a valley bowl,
Festal wine in sure supply.
Your belly a mound of wheat rimmed with lilies.

7:4   Your breasts are like a pair of fawns, the twins of a gazelle.

7:5   Your neck a tower of ivory.
Your eyes are pools in Heshbon by the gates of Bath-rabbim.

Your nose a tower of Lebanon facing Damascus.

7:6   Your head held high like Carmel,

And your hair deep lustrous like purple;

A king is tangled in its tresses.

7:7   How beautiful and how exquisite you are,

How dear, my beloved, my maiden of ecstasy!

7:8   Your standing is like a palm tree,

Your breasts as date clusters.

7:9   Yes, yes, I will climb the palm tree and put my hands on its limbs.

May your breasts be like grape clusters

And your breathing as the aroma of apples.

7:10   Your mouth is like a fine wine

Smoothly running over [lips and teeth].

7:11   I am my beloved's and his desire is for me.

7:12   Come, my heart's love, come into the fields,

Let us pass the night amid the villages.

7:13   Let us be off early into the vineyards; let us see if the vines are

sprouting,

If the grape blossoms have opened, and the pomegranates are in

flower.

There will I give you my love.

7:14   The mandrakes perfume the air, and on our lintel's every delicacy;

A fresh and ripened harvest, O my heart's love,

I've held in keep for you.

8:1   Would that you were my brother, given milk at my mother's breast!

Were I familiar with you in public, no one would think less of me.

8:2   I would take you to my mother's house.

There you would enlighten me.

I would have you drink of spiced wine,

The liquid blend of my own pomegranate.

8:3   His left hand cradles my head,

And his right hand stays me.

8:4   Give me your word, daughters of Jerusalem,

Do not rouse nor raise up love until its time is ripe.

Poem Ten

8:5   Who is this coming up from the desert, leaning against her lover?
Under the apple tree I roused you, where your mother conceived
    you,
There you were quickened within her.

8:6   Fasten me as a seal on your heart, as a seal on your arm;
Strong as death is love, perduring as the grave its bond.
Its flashings are flarings of fire,
A flaming forth of God (Yah).

8:7   Bottomless waters cannot extinguish love, nor floodwaters
    overcome it.
Were anyone to barter all they owned for love, how it would be
    ridiculed.

8:8   Our little sister, she yet has no breasts.
What shall we conclude on the day she is pledged to marry?

8:9   If she be a wall, we shall armor her with silver;
If she be a door, we shall close her up with cedar board.

8:10   I am a wall and my breasts are like towers;
And in his eyes I was a vessel of peace.

8:11   Solomon kept a vineyard in Baal-hamon.
He turned the vineyard over to caretakers;
A thousand silver coins the cost of its fruit.

8:12   My own vineyard is mine alone to give;
The thousand for you, O Solomon,
And two hundred for the caretakers of the fruit.

8:13   Garden mate, my companions are all ears;
Let me hear your voice!

8:14   Leap up and away, my own love,
Like a gazelle or a young stag upon the mountains of spices!

Preliminary Perspectives

A LITERARY PURVIEW

Human Mutuality as Point of View

· I ·

THE SONG OF SONGS celebrates the human body. Throughout its one hundred seventeen lines the Song cherishes the flesh of a woman and of a man. God created them male and female: "God saw everything that he had made, and indeed, it was very good" (Gen 1:31). The garden imagery of the Song reclaims Eden, and the woman and man in this love poetry give a glimpse of Adam and Eve without the shame and the blame of sinfulness. The submission of the female and the domination of the male after the fall is altogether missing in the Song, where equality of voice and sheer delight in the embodied being of the beloved suffuses the entire ambiance.

The Song of Songs seems to reverse in a quite remarkable way the human world in the garden of paradise according to the account in Genesis. If Eve was helpmate to Adam and if that order of creation connotes any inferiority in the mind of the biblical reader, the Song upholds the woman, who is valued as much as the man. If Eve's origin from the rib of Adam seems to the biblical reader a subordinate derivation, the woman of the Song sings another tune: "My beloved is mine and I am his" (2:16) and "I am my beloved's and he is mine" (6:3). Her body is indeed a garden for his enjoyment, but his body is a garden for her delight as well. Indeed the Song does nothing but magnify the happy condition of man and woman without the fall into sin. Mutual love is created in the Song without embarrassment. Both the woman and the man give equally passionate invitations to lovemaking (see 1:2–4, 7–8; 2:13–14; 4:8,16; 7:12; 8:14). In the Song of Songs one sees without immodesty just how "two become one flesh" (Gen 2:24).

If Eve seems to be blamed in the biblical account of eating the forbidden fruit, which she gives to Adam "who was with her" (Gen 3:6), the woman in the Song in all innocence invites the man to "come into the fields" (7:12), where she will give to him choice fruits "held in keep" just for him (7:14). After the fall Adam and Eve are described in a now sinful world, where domination and alienation reveal the human condition. If the biblical account of woman and man after the fall seems to emphasize the regrettable and sinful domination of woman who is told "in pain you shall bring forth children, yet your *desire* shall be for your husband, and he shall rule over you" (Gen 3:16), the Song of Songs seems to replace that world order by an appeal to a love altogether reciprocal and unspoiled: "I am my beloved's and his *desire* is for me" (7:11).[1] Accordingly, in the Song of Songs there is a dissolution of the banishment and the "curse" laid upon Eve in the garden. Her desire for her husband becomes in the Song's paradise regained a restoration of the original God-given mutuality, for now she claims his desire is equally for her. The issue is not a new advantage of women at the expense of men, nor the old advantage of men at the expense of women, but rather a loving dance together, where either may lead and either may follow, where none is pushed nor anyone dragged.

The fall in Genesis is more story than history. The condition of innocence and love intended by God may not have been so much lost as never achieved. In that sense the Eden story is as much about a future to bring about as it is about a past to recover. Above all, it is a story of human hope rather than lament.

After the fall great sorrow came into Paradise. Between woman and man there arose mutual recrimination and blame. Mutual attraction degenerated into exploitation. The Song of Songs redeems that world in a vision of love without lust, two in "one flesh" as the creator intended, one in heart and soul, united in equal self-giving. In the Song mutual desire leads to consummate delight in each other. The woman in the Song seeks sharing and intimacy,

---

[1]The same Hebrew word for *desire* is used in both biblical passages. The earliest mention that I note of this remarkable reversal of the Eden story was found in Christian Ginsburg, who wrote in the nineteenth century (*The Song of Songs*, 12–20). I find the same insight repeated in Morris Jastrow, Jr., writing in the early part of the twentieth century (*The Song of Songs*, 222–23). Further elaboration of the contrast between Eden after the fall and the Song of Songs can be found in Phyllis Trible, "Love's Lyrics Redeemed" in *God and the Rhetoric of Sexuality* (Philadelphia: Fortress Press, 1978), 144–65.

and yet she does not fear the loss of who she is. Nor in any way does the man. In paradise lost man and woman become antagonists; in paradise regained woman and man become partners in a duet. Indeed it is possible to read the Song of Songs not only as a return to paradise but also as a celebration of the human erotic relationship at its best, a truce in reality, an enclosure of suspension, an alternative to asceticism. Surely this is the love song God intended for humankind in the beginning. Only in the trinitarian life of the one God is there complete interpersonal relationship, while each person remains an integral identity. But, human beings were made in the image of God.

· II ·

Woman and man in the Song of Songs share a blameless sexual freedom reminiscent of the imagined reciprocity of emotion and love of Adam and Eve in Paradise before the fall. Both male and female can be assertive and each sex can be receptive. Both the woman and the man invite the other to come away (2:13 and 7:12). Each searches in the night to find the beloved (3:1–5 and 5:2–7). Both the man and the woman delight in the body of the other. They seem equally able to tease each other and to be desolate at the thought of losing the other.

A woman needs to know why she is attractive, why she should yield, and why she carries such life power. Many men might approach; she needs *one* who will abide with her. A man needs to know why he among many is chosen. Many women might yield; he needs one who wants him. Communion is thus a world they together pursue throughout their courtship, now one leading, now the other. "The sexual egalitarianism of the Song thus reflects a metaphysics of love rather than a social reality or even a social ideal" (Fox, 330).

About a third of the Song of Songs is dialog, and of the ten monologs, five are female and five are male. The verbal dialog is equally uninhibited. Their spoken delight in each other is expressed in similar terms—wine, artifacts, doves, trees, lips, blossoms. More so than in the love poetry of Israel's neighbors, the Song shows a sustained dialog between woman and man that characterizes their communion. "The poet chooses to show us how lovers behave— with each other and with others—thereby revealing their thoughts entirely through their dialogue" (Fox, 264).

Implicit throughout the Song is the value given to human emotion. Both the woman and the man take seriously what the other feels. The goal is not calculation and the power of dominance. Conversation in their courtship explores the respected individuality of each of them. Here is no reluctant mistress, no pleading man. Here is no timid woman, no insistent man. Here is no inaccessible woman, no rapacious man. Here is no submissive woman, no aggressive man. Because they share their emotions openly and reciprocally they come to know each other and to know themselves. "My beloved is mine and I am his" and "and for me is his desire" (2:16, 6:3, 7:11). "This wisdom book teaches that human passion is both noble and ennobling. Furthermore its attraction and vitality are natural to both women and men" (Bergant, 276).

In the Song of Songs to one's surprise there is no hint of a gender divided world, no suspicion that women are essentially any different in courting and in love than men. There are no stereotypical male/female roles the lovers must play. Neither sex lords it over the other. No lovers' quarrels, no battle of the sexes. The power of woman is respected, but it is not feared. There is harmony between man and woman, and sympathy between nature and human beings. The world of the Song of Songs is the world as it was meant to be, the world without sin's miasma, the world without oppression of any kind, a world of spontaneous exchange of love and of human respect, without hint of unfaithfulness, no one subjugated and no one elevated.

The woman in the Song stands in her own right. Her value is not determined by her use to a husband or her fecundity for the ongoing life of society. Woman is a sexual person. She is contemplated as a human subject rather than looked upon as a sexual object. She is not defined as the practical and prudent household woman of Proverbs (31:10–31). Nor is the woman in the Song a stereotype of all women, though she may be offered as a model, just as the relationship may be. The Song presents a young woman, who is chaste, independent, and able to feel, to appreciate, and to investigate the wealth of her sexuality. She exists in a world that assumes a freedom that a patriarchal world did not extend to women, whose liberty was bound up in a father's or a husband's will. In the Song of Songs, on the contrary, her body is her own body. There is no stereotype of either sex. She is presented as a human being, who happens to be a woman. She is not represented as a daughter, wife, or mother. She thinks and feels like a human being whose anatomy demands no determined destiny. There is no mention of marriage or of children. A family is neither presumed nor excluded. That question, however, is not the first question in the courtship life of this woman. She first claims an intrinsic human value, and she displays a generous human amplitude. She is rapt in the astonishing unfolding of her own physical being as a woman. To own her own sexuality is a simple birthright that she claims without apology. She is never merely a sexual attraction and she is hardly ever passive. The Song is always her song.

Throughout the Song of Songs the initiative is the woman's most of all. She pursues him, because she is allowed to know her own desires and to act upon them. She is not what a man might imagine a woman to be, nor is she a woman who becomes a female impersonator behaving as she thinks a man might expect. She simply wants him, and she has some idea how to go about wooing a lover. She seeks intimate pleasure, yet the Song remains innocent of any moralizing. Phyllis Trible writes: "Love for the sake of love is its message, and the portrayal of the female delineates this message best." An inherent goodness prior to further concerns of human responsibility is here celebrated, although responsibility is there in the obvious mutual respect, based solidly on respect for themselves. They love themselves, and therefore they can love the other freely and with great trust.

All the events in the Song are narrated from her point of view. We see through her eyes, "whereas from the boy's angle of vision we know little besides how he sees her" (Fox, 309). More than half of the lines are hers, and many of the remaining ones are addressed to her. In her imagination he speaks but not vice versa. The first and last line of the Song are hers, and they are delivered to him in an imperative voice, though innocent of any harsh tone. Her emotions, thoughts, words, imagination, yearning, and erotic fantasies are revealed in her own unashamed and outspoken words. She says it like it is. She commands attention by her intensity. There is no scene in the Song from which she is absent.

In the struggle with her family over her courtship she jeopardizes her reputation. She risks herself for the man she loves. No obstacle daunts her and she appears even more sturdy and more determined to initiate love than the man. The Song is her blossoming as a human being—capable, honest, sexual, resourceful—a human being who happens to be a woman. One commentator claims she is "the only unmediated female voice in Scripture." Her descriptive litany of her lover's bodily appearance is about the only such male description in the Bible (compare Sir 50:5–12). She stands out as a woman seemingly out of place, an Eve without the fall. She is the embodiment of the human love story as it might be without the oppressive consequences of sin depicted in the expulsion from the garden of Eden. She sings of a human love that should have been fully mutual, and of woman and man who would have walked with God in the cool of the evening.

· III ·

Although we cannot determine who wrote the Song of Songs, or who composed the original poetry, it has been suggested that there is internal evidence that the Song might have been written by a woman rather than by a man. The Song does seem to be the meditation of woman's heart. The entire Song might well appear to be a woman's romantic fantasy. The love life of the Song speaks insistently through a female sensibility. A father figure never appears. Reference to a mother figure, for example, her "mother's sons" or her "mother's house" occurs more than a half-dozen times. There are multiple references to female figures: woman, bride, sister, female friend, and "the daughters of Jerusalem." The thrice-repeated formula of love's declaration (2:16, 6:3, 7:11) is never once made by the man. Overall the Song discloses a woman's world.

Although the Song of Songs shows a clear portrait of a woman, the sex of the author may never be determined with certainty. Shakespeare's women in their authenticity have been applauded by women as well as by men. Juliet, Viola, and Cordelia live in literature as quintessential women. A most outrageous novel, *L'Histoire d'O*, published anonymously and thought to embody male sexual fantasy at its most intense, turns out incredibly to have been written by a woman. Most popular romance literature is written from a male point of view and filled with impostor images of women, whether or not these stories are written by women or by men. While the Song does indeed deeply reflect a woman's world, it will never be determined by intrinsic evidence alone that only a woman could have written it. The Song of Songs, however, surely raises the suspicion of a gifted female authorship or at the least a woman's inspiration. Who touches this book touches a woman. The author of the book of Proverbs says "Four things I do not understand: the way of an eagle in the sky, the way of a snake on a rock, the way of a ship on the high seas, and the way of a man with a girl" (30:18–19). In fact, the Song of Songs is more like the too wonderful way of a woman with a man.

Of Litanies and Gardens as Symbols

· I ·

"A lover's eyes will gaze an eagle blind" wrote Shakespeare ("Love's Labor's Lost," 4:3:334). "Had we but world enough and time, / An hundred years should go to praise / Thine eyes and on thy forehead gaze, / Two hundred to adore each breast, / But thirty thousand to the rest, / An age at least to every part, / And the last age should show your heart" (Andrew Marvell, "To His Coy Mistress").

An erotic litany of the visual beauty of the body of the beloved was also employed in the poetry of the ancient eastern Mediterranean where it was a well-known poetic device. Such an appreciative catalog of the parts of the human body is there called a *wasf,* a word which means in Arabic a description. During Arab wedding festivities to this day folk songs are composed with impromptu verses repeated by the assembly in chorus in praise of the bride and groom. Toasts at weddings are often a listing of the virtues and charms of the bride and the groom. Such unabashed metaphorical descriptions revel in the beautiful features of the body of the beloved, even though attention might also be given by admirers to the clothing of the bride or the groom. In oriental poetry, however, the human body remains its own principal adornment. The attractive parts of the body are nature's own dress, enfleshed jewels of especial beauty, crystallized around the beloved in the eyes of the loving beholder who draws into the light all the beauty no one else looked for enough to find.

In the Song of Songs there are four Arabic *wasf*s of the human body. Three of these four litanies describe the female body, and one the male (4:1–5 is a partial female *wasf*; 5:11–16 is a complete male *wasf*; 6:5–7 is a repeat of the partial female; 7:2–10 is a complete female *wasf*). Of the three female *wasf*s, one is complete from the bottom of the feet to the top of the head, and the other two are incomplete, concerned mostly with the head and face. The one male *wasf* is complete from the head to the feet. Many parts of the human body are mentioned in these *wasf*s: arms, legs, thighs, feet, pelvis, trunk, belly, breasts, neck, lips, teeth, mouth, nose, cheeks, eyes, head, and hair.

In the *Arabian Nights* we find a typical example in secular poetry of an erotic description or *wasf* depicting a woman:

> She was all charm, beauty, and perfect grace, with a forehead like the new moon, eyes like those of a deer or wild heifer, eyebrows like the crescent in the month of Sha'ban, cheeks like red anemones, mouth like the seal of Solomon, lips like red carnelian, teeth like a row of pearls set in coral, neck like a cake for a king, bosom like a fountain, breasts like a pair of big pomegranates resembling a rabbit with uplifted ears,

She speaks:

May he kiss me with kisses of his lips.

Sweeter than wine your love. (1:2)

Delightful your fragrance;

A perfume unsealed your name. (1:3)

While the king was couched within,

My nard spread out its fragrance. (1:12)

A sachet of myrrh is my true love

All night between my breasts. (1:13)

and belly with a navel like a cup that holds a pound of benzoin ointment. (trans. Husain Haddawy [New York: Norton, 1990], 68)

In the story of Abraham and Sarah in the Bible we read of the pharaoh's desire to take Sarah as one of his wives because of her great beauty. In the Genesis Apocryphon, discovered among the apocryphal writings in the Qumran caves, we find a quasi-religious prose *wasf* devoted to Sarah. The text greatly expands the brief biblical description of the wife of Abraham:

> How splendid and beautiful the form of her face, and how soft the hair of her head; how lovely are her eyes and how pleasant is her nose and all the radiance of her face; how lovely is her breast and how beautiful is all her whiteness! Her arms, how beautiful! And her hands, how perfect! And how attractive all the appearance of her hands! How lovely her palms, and how long and dainty all the fingers of her hands. Her feet, how beautiful! How perfect are her legs! There are no virgins or brides who enter a bridal chamber more beautiful than she. Indeed, her beauty surpasses that of all women; her beauty is high above all of them. Yet with all this beauty there is much wisdom in her; and whatever she has is lovely. (Joseph Fitzmyer, *The Genesis Apocryphon of Qumran Cave I: A Commentary* [Rome: Biblical Institute Press, 1971], 63)

The biblical *wasf* is a way of seeing as much as a way of being seen, and the body is a veil that suggests more than itself rather than a curtain that conceals. The litanies in the Song represent the whole person and not just anatomical parts of the body. The speaker reveals a lover's respect and desire, and not just the aesthetic appearance of the beloved. The human body belongs to the person as someone truly unique in this world. Sight of the human body always presumes a surrounding world picture. Sight of the human body always includes a fantasy. In the Song a litany of the beloved is always evocative. One might note that more than half of the beautiful parts of the human body in the Song refer to the head and face. The litanies in the Song of Songs celebrate more the person in the body, the beloved who is enfleshed as a whole human being.

Various litanies to the Blessed Virgin Mary might be cited as tangential examples of a catalog (or *wasf*) of the beloved, but devoted to an even more soulful praise. The ancient Eastern *Akathistos* refers to Mary as "fragrant lily," "unfailing fountain of living water," "fertile mountain raised aloft by the Spirit," "living paradise holding in thy midst the Tree of Life," "radiant dawn," and "source of the milk and the honey of love." *The Gaelic Litany to Our Lady* speaks of her as "golden casket," "graceful like the dove," "serene like the moon," "resplendent like the sun," "beauty of women," "enclosed garden," "cedar of Mount Lebanon," "Cypress of Mount Sion," "blooming like the palm tree," and "crimson rose of the land of Jacob." And the familiar *Litany of Loreto* entitles Mary "morning star," "tower of David," "tower of ivory," "house of gold," and "mystical rose." A number of these Marian images are taken from the Song of Songs.

Beautiful to sight is the human body. The proportions of the human body amaze us because of the extreme pleasure we take in the human figure. The whole body well posed suggests the transcendent human spirit. In such disclosure one senses the soul-life that animates the body. The joy of beholding the human form is amplified by the religious awareness that the human body is also temple of the Holy Spirit, an earthen vessel destined for everlasting life with God seen face to face. Artistic depiction of the nude body has thus been an inexplicable source of wonder, confusion, and joy. Women are not unappreciative of the female body and men are not unappreciative of the male body, but each sex is perhaps less fascinated by its own form. No doubt the romance of the opposite sex adds to the joy of such contemplation. Women were more often described in love poetry than men, and the male *wasf* in the Song of Songs is quite extraordinary in the Bible.

There is a considerable difference between erotic poetry and pornographic literature, or between a sensuous ballet and a nude revue. Erotic imagination depends on sexual attraction, but it appreciates the body rather than demeans it. Pornography, however, objectifies the human body and dulls the sensibilities of the viewer. If not portrayed in a way that reveals the spirit, self-disclosure always reduces the body to matter. The flesh becomes obscene. A lustful imagination mistakenly reduces the body to the alluring sum of so many parts. Respect for the body and the person who is identified with her or his body becomes eclipsed. The whole person is not valued and the body becomes an instrument for someone else's lascivious enjoyment. Lustful literature is a form of verbal battering. Looking with lust becomes a visual rape (Mt 5:28).

While the Song does detail the anatomy of the woman and of the man and speaks of various erotic charms of the body, the whole context never invites a salacious or disrespectful appraisal. On the contrary, the descriptive litanies of the body in the Song are pure celebration of the beauty of the beloved made all the more beautiful because all the more loved. The Song makes love to the heart and to the emotions with words. The Song presents a wealth of metaphorical imagery, poetic playfulness, suggested voluptuousness, and rich vitality. The bodily litanies in the Song of Songs are nevertheless a reverent litany, a verbal anointing of the beloved, and a sung praise revealing a deep regard.

· II ·

The Song of Songs as a whole seems to be an elaborate litany, not only of the human body, but also a catalog of praise of the whole body of creation. The body of this earth is lovingly named part by part. The whole Song presents a *wasf* of "mother earth" in all her material splendor. This comprehensive review of the senses—what can be seen, heard, smelled, tasted, and touched— is intensified by the concentrated emotion aroused in courtship love. The Song of Songs is thus a fascinating and lingering litany of fragrances, perfumes, spices, flowers, trees, and fruits. Flora and fauna are used in abundance in simile and metaphor. Places specific and general are evocative of a world beyond. The seasons and the times of day beautifully frame this hymn to creation. Images in the Song are affectively charged and indeed a whole world is charged with the grandeur of God.

The poets and artists of the world remind us how much we miss of sensuous delight in everyday life. Even if we take time to stop and smell the flowers, the human senses are overwhelmed with a rich, lavish, prodigal avalanche of delights beyond our capacity to absorb and to appreciate. We can be in only one place at a time, and the infinite variety of possible sensuous experience is ever known only in part. "We would have been satisfied with so much less," writes Annie Dillard. "Glory be to God for dappled things," writes Gerard Manley Hopkins. We know there is boundless delight, and we exhaust ourselves in trying to fathom it. The body itself in its ripe materiality sings of the plenitude of creation. God made us a body, and it was good. Sensuous delight remains the musical accompaniment to the love song in the human heart.

Beauty may indeed be in the eye of the beholder, and in the Song the beholder is wildly in love. The created world is the love of God embodied in material. Sexuality with all its creativity is the love of man and woman embodied in the beauty of human flesh. Love makes all things beautiful. We ascribe the beauties of nature to our own sweethearts. The garden is but the world writ small, and the Song of Songs remains a loving and lovely body of words sung as a tribute to all of creation.

The variety of sensual notes in the Song of Songs is astonishing. The courtship turns out to be not only lovers entranced with the beauty of the body of the beloved, but also lovers devoted to the body of this world. The world of the Song is thus eroticized into a world of desire that intensifies the overall attractions of the beloved. The senses are schooled in this world of delight for their encounter with human beauty. In making love to the world one makes love to the beloved, and in making love to the beloved one makes love to the world. The Song is thus a cornucopia of nouns, of beautiful things, when to be beautiful is to be beautiful in the eyes of the beloved. "There lives the dearest freshness deep down things. . . . Because the Holy Ghost over the bent / World broods with warm breast and with ah! bright wings" (Gerard Manley Hopkins, "God's Grandeur").

The senses are the doors to the body. The whole world enters into our soul through our senses in some way. We are constituted by what we ingest. The Song of Songs is a hymn in celebration of mother earth. In the Song both his mother and her mother, along with Solomon's mother, seem mysterious presences. The Latin word for material, *materia*, derived from the word for mother (*mater*). A catalog of the plenitude of mother earth found in the Song of Songs follows:

Human body: feet, thighs, pelvis, belly, breasts, neck, eyes, nose, head, hair, mouth, lips, arms, trunk, legs, teeth, cheeks

Adornments: bangles, garments, necklaces, earrings, sandals

Flowers: lily, henna, mandrake

Fruits: grape, palm date, fig, pomegranate

Trees: apple, pomegranate, cedar, cypress, palm, walnut, fig

Animals: fox, gazelle, fawn, deer, filly, goat, lamb and ewe, dove, lion, leopard, raven

Materials: gold, silver, alabaster, sapphire, ivory, rock, iron or bronze

Liquids: water (fountain, spring, flood, rain, pool, dew), wine, milk, myrrh, pomegranate juice

Smell: see spices and perfumes; see also flowers

Taste: honey, milk, wine, raisin, apple, sugar, pomegranate; see
 also spices and perfumes

Spices and perfumes: frankincense, henna, nard, myrrh,
 cinnamon, aloes, sweet cane, saffron, calamon, apple,
 mandrake

Colors: purple, green, crimson, black, ivory, blue, red

Hearing: name, voice, word, murmur of doves, melody

Touch: browse, nibble, eat, kiss, embrace, fondle, love-making

Towers: David, ivory, Lebanon

Times: winter (rains), spring, day, night, dusk (or dawn), pruning
 time, harvest time

General places: sun, moon, woods, mountains, valley, hills,
 village, rocks, road, clefts, land, pasture, tentsite, field,
 desert, yard, garden, orchard, fountain, stream, grove,
 vineyard

Specific places: Tirzah and Lebanon (north), Damascus and
 Heshbon (east), Kedar and Jerusalem (south), Carmel and
 Sharon (west)

The Song is sensuous because it speaks so often of the bodily senses. The
poetry remains deeply human, however, because it delights in the body as
the expression of the whole person, body and soul, and the whole world as
the extension of a transcendent beauty and the expression of a yet deeper
love. St. Anselm in his *Proslogion* writes of that further human yearning to
achieve a vision of the divine in the experiences of the sensual world:

> Still You hide away, Lord, from my soul in Your light and blessedness,
> and so it still dwells in its darkness and misery. For it looks all about,
> and does not see Your beauty. It listens, and does not hear Your harmony.
> It smells, and does not sense Your fragrance. It tastes, and does not
> recognize Your savour. It feels, and does not sense Your softness. For
> You have in Yourself, Lord, in Your own ineffable manner, those [qualities]
> You have given to the things created by You according to their own
> sensible manner. But the senses of my soul, because of the ancient
> weakness of sin, have become hardened and dulled and obstructed.
> (trans. M. J. Charlesworth [Oxford University Press, 1965], chapter xvii)

God created out of nothing the matter of this world. In theoretical physics one speculates that some enormous density of a boundless amount of matter compressed and concentrated to a point sparked and exploded into the vast spaces of the universe, creating edges of time and space as it yet expands beyond imagination. Human beings are of tiny size on this planet and but a speck on a burnt-out cinder in this vast billion-star cosmos. Woman and man, nonetheless, are embodied spirits. The human body, therefore, has a rare beauty made even more intense by reverence for the whole person. The human senses are a kaleidoscope of innumerable material impressions, a cornucopia of sights, smells, sounds, visions, and touches. Moreover, the human spirit can expand in its consciousness even to the uncharted limits of what can be known. "In the image of God he created them; male and female He created them" (Genesis 1:27).

· III ·

To those who know the inner garden of love, the whole world in its goodness takes on a beauty reminiscent of the original garden of paradise. Adam and Eve stand forth again. Male and female, man and woman, delight in a new creation in consummate harmony and love. In the Song of Songs the Bible re-creates an Eden of delights, an oasis in the desert, full of flowers of every color and fragrance, fruits of every shape and taste, and spices of every bouquet. God set woman and man in the beginning in a garden of such joys. Much of the courtship in the Song takes place in the countryside and outdoors—in a grove (2:1–3), in a land with flower and fruit (2:8–13), in a garden (4:12–5:1), in a valley (6:11), in a vineyard (7:13–14), under an apple tree (8:5), and at the end once again in a garden (8:13–14).

The hand of the creator put woman and man in a garden of paradise. Upon seeing Eve, Adam spontaneously and innocently rejoices in her beauty and human companionship: "And the man and his wife were both naked, and were not ashamed" (Gen 2:25). Throughout the Song the woman is compared to a garden. The vineyard garden in the Song thus emerges as the quintessential symbol of courtship love (2:15) and an image of the body of the beloved (8:11–12). Her body is an "enclosed garden," a vineyard well tended and protected, where so much of the Song's delightful playfulness is situated. She likewise cherishes the extravagant body of the man. In the Song, however, it is woman who is flower and whose body is fruitful. "Virgin forest" and "mother earth" recall how universal is the feminization of the fecundity of the divine creation.

Human sexuality in biological fact stems from the need to vary the genetic pool in the hope of enhancing the survival and welfare of the human species. Sexuality became the remedy for the mortality of human flesh. If no one died, no one need be born. Yet one can also readily imagine the physical attraction of female and male in the garden of paradise before there was death or before there was need of birth to expand the human community. Thus sexual bonding in the Song of Songs is enjoyed for its own sake and not immediately for the sake of procreation. For just such a loving communion the body and soul of woman and man were made complementary. Together they were destined to enjoy friendship with the living God and that without fear. In the beginning it was a sacred marriage.

In God's providence so much of human importance and consequence takes place in a garden. God is the first and master gardener, and Adam and Eve are seen as steward gardeners. Imagine in the garden of gardens the song of songs. Woman whose body is imagined as flower and fruit becomes the garden within the garden. Eve is conformed from a rib in Adam's side, just as the bridal church is taken from the wounded side of Jesus on the cross in a flow of blood and water (Jn 19:34). Together woman and man walk in the body of this world, that garden of abundance that is God's wonderful creation. Their lasting bond is a sacred marriage; their devotion is the wisdom of the Song of Songs.

The cultivated gardenscape is thus metaphor for the making of a world. The garden is a symbol for the creation of lovemaking. Similarly, the garden is a metaphor for wordmaking. The lovely poetry of the human language and the glory abiding in the Song of Songs stems from this cultivation of lush and potent words. Creation is an imaginative garden become real in the mind of God; lovemaking is a bodily garden; poetic song is a verbal garden. The biblical Song of Songs remains reminiscent of all the gardens of all the world.

"The Word was made flesh and dwelt among us" (Jn 1:14). It is in a garden where no body was yet laid that Jesus is entombed. From that garden the tree of life, which is the cross, bloomed with the fruit of life everlasting, which is the resurrection of the flesh. No creation-act, no lovemaking, no word-smithing can compare with the life in the garden of Mary Magdalene's searching desire. And she, "supposing him to be the gardener. . . . And Jesus said 'Mary'" (Jn 20:15–16). And she recognized the one she ever loved. No love story can be written without this garden of resurrection life as foreground and the Eden garden of the Genesis story as background. Human love that finds its fulfillment in divine love has always been celebrated in a garden.

A THEOLOGICAL PURVIEW

· I ·

Words and Sentences: Celebration of the Body

HUMAN SEXUALITY PROVIDES some of the best and some of the worst aspects of human nature. It can speak tenderly with care, and it can abuse another with disregard when most vulnerable. In its physical details sex can seem ridiculous, and in its overall impact on body and soul quite awesome. Sex is silly and sex is sublime. Sex may be trivial and it may be profound. Sex is a fountain of comedy and a pool of tragedy. Should we laugh at the befuddled spectacle we make of ourselves, or should we cry because nothing else moves us so deeply with joyfulness? The human body is playfully coy and yet intensely purposeful in engendering life. Sex may be embarrassing and sex may be a welcomed revelation of the body. Lovemaking is laughable as an adventure in plumbing, and yet poignant beyond words as an inkling of the ecstasy of divine communion. Sexuality creates both the pursuit of happiness and the happiness of pursuit. In sum, human sexuality is a puzzling mystery and a lovely gift of God who found it "in the beginning" to be good.

The Song of Songs explores the love of a woman and a man, the strange bewilderment which overtakes one person on account of another person. These songs are foremost love songs, and they sing of courtship love. The social context for the relationship of this woman and this man is not elaborated. The basic goodness of the attraction of male and female is celebrated, and the dance of their affections is a prototype of all human sexual attraction. The Song remains an innocent courtship, a love that is young, erotic, and as yet unmarried. It is a love that is embodied, because the human condition is affirmed, not disregarded. The Song sings of a love that is unique, because the beloved is unique, which is surely a belief of young lovers from time immemorial. The Song claims an ever-fervent hope in human life as God created it to be. Such a love might perdure forever.

The Song of Songs is primarily a courtship poem, but it also describes the sexual delight that a woman and a man consummate together. Physical intimacy is treated with restraint, with delicate and tender indirection. Lovemaking is presented without embarrassment, however, or apology. The Song's imagery favors a rich evocation. It sings with poetic incantation and creates its own enchantment. Much is suggested by way of allusion and much spoken by way of circumlocution. Nonetheless, the Song of Songs may arouse the reader, and precisely because it suggests to the imagination so much of the human body in its sensual mystery. As artists well know, the beautifully veiled human body can be more erotic than the nude, for the play of imagination is heightened.

Eros is everywhere felt in the Song. Sexual desire pervades each scene. Every part of the body of the beloved, both female and male, is lovingly massaged with words charged with erotic energy. The poetry displays a lush sensuality in its imagery. The lovers make love with words. Here is an unabashed celebration of creation and the human condition. Here is God's created plenty, the wonder and the mystery of human sexuality in all its youthful surprise.

The Bible contains elsewhere moral wisdom about sexuality conjoined to marriage. The Song of Songs, however, is purple-passage poetry devoted to the lovely experience of courtship love. Here are words gift-wrapped in beauty, romantic emotions that can be recited as a bouquet of verbal flowers on the occasion of a woman and a man betrothed to marry. They revel in love's sweet dreams. The Song is poignant, passionate, delightful, charming, and sexy. It celebrates the simple, innocent, Edenic mutuality of woman and man. It is a premarital courtship, without hint of mortality or future descendants, ever-surprising the reader because of the "exuberant, thoroughly erotic, and non-judgmental manner in which it depicts love between a man and woman" (Murphy, 97). The Song is beneficent rather than moralistic; it is naive rather than obscene. The Song of Songs sings of eros before it sings of agape; it celebrates the many of creation before the one of the creator. The Song sings serenely of this world, but a world that "God so loved" (Jn 3:16).

The surrender in the Song of Songs is not only that of man to woman and of woman to man, but it also remains a surrender of the person to the body. Sex is a word related to a Hebrew word for vessel or bowl. The body is warm water contained in a fragile envelope of skin. The body is, nonetheless, our human dwelling, our tent, our tabernacle, the residence of the sacred, the temple of the Holy Spirit. The assent given to human passion at its best should be a consent and a surrender of one's self through one's body to another who is the beloved. Sexuality provides the ardor to warm human relationships.

Delight is a word which comes readily to mind with the *Song of Songs*. The woman and man have not overcome a puritanical viewpoint, rather they delight in themselves and each other as one would delight in any gift of God—a sunset, a raindrop, life itself.

The Song of Songs celebrates the physical and spiritual joy that woman and man find in each other as a gift they did not earn. Marriage is mentioned in the Song of Songs only as an aside at the end of the brief poem describing the transportation of a bride to a wedding ceremony (3:6–11). Marriage is spoken of as a family expectation toward the close of the Song (8:8). There is, however, little mention in the Song of children, social obligations, or public responsibilities. The Song is innocent of the labors of the world and the cautions of society. It speaks in premoral terms of an earth in Eden time, a garden of creation as God intended it. Here is the human condition of female and male with the sheer ecstasy in one another spoken aloud when Adam first saw Eve: "This as last is bone of my bones and flesh of my flesh" (Gen 2:23). Without this basic bond of appreciation of the beloved and indeed of creation itself for its own sake, all other moral obligations, family ramifications, and implied societal outcomes remain without a rootedness in the body of the human person.

The sexuality in the Song may appear to be amoral. At the same time it is a naive and pure love because it is set in such open trust. Here is love between woman and man as it might have been in a state of innocence or as it should become in human maturity. The sexual familiarity is almost casual, and yet there is no sense of dalliance or exploitation. Both the woman and the man are on equal footing, and the quality of their love from its description is superlative. Continence is not prized, but fidelity, loyalty, and devotion to the beloved are constantly valued. Sexuality is assumed to be good, without extrinsic justification or argument. Their love is so ecstatic and so beautiful it must be good. There is no hint of bodily desire as lascivious (Prov 7) or as a burden of duty (Prov 31). Quite simply, what God made is good. To begin with a celebration of the deep goodness of courtship-love in and of itself is to lay a foundation for any and all further shaping of human purposes according to God's law. Morality must prevail, of course, but all the more keenly if the original gift is recognized.

The Song of Songs offers an unself-conscious depiction of human love as doing what comes naturally. Love is its own reward and sexuality provides its own recompense. Sexual intercourse does not consummate the marriage ceremony as much as the marriage ceremony consummates the heartfelt personal bond that already lends matrimony in its fullness its most genuine validation. Sexual communion does not need a prior social purpose to give it worth. Sexual love has its own value; it is the Lord God's gift, and "it was good." Joy never needs a moral warrant to exist. Thus the Song is an unapologetic depiction of the rapturous reciprocal love between a woman and a man. Their courtship is exuberant, thoroughly erotic, nonjudgmental, and imaginatively set apart from the social world of biblical Israel. Their love is not an argument for free love, nor for eroticism only for its own sake, and surely not for promiscuity. The invitation in the Song is "to appreciate the qualities of tenderness, joy of sensual intimacy, reciprocal longing and mutual esteem, all of which are socially desirable and beautifully mysterious dimensions of human sexual love" (Murphy, 98).

Bernini's sculpture of Teresa of Avila in ecstasy has been viewed by some as spiritual rapture and by others as disguised orgasm. The bodies of the lovers in the Song of Songs have been seen as ecstatic because their souls touch the realm of the mystical, and as nude because the Song might be read as a "hot carnal pamphlet." Indeed, we hold human love in earthen vessels and the embrace of the body is always ambiguous. One ought not, however, at first blush to think the worst. Suspicion about the Song of Songs may say more about the reader than its says about the biblical author.

Love in the Song is a love accepted in the Hebrew Bible, but it is not a typically biblical love, for it is nowise ethnic, nor explicitly religious, nor consciously ethical, nor even verbally theistic. God is not mentioned in word, with the possible exception of one verse (8:6) at the close of the text. The Song is a courtship love suffused with imagined freedom and erotic fantasy. In the poems the young woman and young man make love outside any society but their own. And yet their love is a social love, for the communion of heart that bonds them remains the fundamental cement that all subsequent social solidarity requires (I must own that I am much indebted to Roland Murphy for this understanding of the Song).

· II ·

Paragraphs and Chapters:
Celebration of the Soul

In the whole Song there are some sixty instances of a word referring to love, in sum once in every other verse. There also are forty adjectives with an affective meaning, such as beautiful, lovely, or pleasing. "Definitions" of love are more commonly catalog descriptions, each having some merit in emphasizing a quality of love, such as free, gratuitous, unconditional, benevolent, self-giving, creative, enabling, ennobling, and procreative. In Paul the hymn "Love is patient; love is kind. . . . It bears all things, believes all things, hopes all things, endures all things" is one of the best of such descriptive litanies (1 Cor 13:4–7). Elizabeth Barrett Browning's poem, "How do I love thee? Let me count the ways. / I love thee to the depth and breadth and height / My soul can reach" provides another heartfelt example. Because love is an irreducible experience, however, it may best be defined in terms of itself. A simple Italian expression for loving someone has always impressed me as going to the heart of the matter: *ti voglio bene* (I wish you well). To love someone is to seek generously the good of the beloved in every way possible. Love wishes to meet the beloved's genuine needs, including the need to return love given, should such a reciprocal love be truly appropriate.

Human love when depicted in the Bible is not without its own interpretive viewpoint that comes from the context of the whole Bible. The Song of Songs is part of the wisdom literature, whose affirmation of creation is most prominent. There is the assumption that God alone answers the desires of human life. Human sexuality, however, is seen as good; it is part of God's creation from the beginning. Male and female God made them and in the image of God. Together woman and man are given sovereignty over all of creation in order to make of this world a cultivated garden. Human sexual love is divinely instituted and divinely sanctioned in the Bible. Human love always and everywhere is precious. Courtship love is priceless. Bodily love mirrors "in a glass darkly" a spiritual love touching on the divine. Sexual differentiation is a human glory and it may also reflect in an analogous and imperfect way the relationship of love in the inner trinitarian life of God. "No one has ever seen God. Yet if we love one another God dwells in us" (1 Jn 4:12). Human love between woman and man therefore always deserves a magnanimous setting, and such is the Song of Songs.

Human language describes the sexual experience of woman and man as lovemaking. One makes love as one makes an artifact. Love is a work of art made with imagination. Love is a poem made of words spoken to the beloved in a song. Love is body language made into a dance. Human lovemaking makes new life and creates a new human beginning. Making love makes love. If sexuality is not only a function of mating but also a human language for personal expression, then making love speaks of heart-bonding with the vocabulary of a most profound bodily joy and spiritual giving. Love is intricate like so many beautiful things. In human love one weaves a web of words and deeds that wrap the beloved in metaphor. That final surrender in lovemaking is also a rehearsal for that final surrender of our body in death, whose last embrace cannot be avoided. Yet, in faith, even death's embrace makes for new life. We are born into eternal life and into God's promise of endless ecstasy before the face of God in the resurrection of the body and life everlasting.

Sexuality is thus a means of communication and intimacy, a language used by lovers from the beginning of human time. Its goodness depends on what is being said, the truthfulness of what is intended, the values expressed in this natural speech of the whole human body. Sexuality can make very profound conversation as well as trivial recreation. Human sexuality is malleable, and those who bring soul to it give soul to it. While most people would agree that at times sexuality can be just sensuous, and at other times only procreative, most of the time sexuality remains a unique blend of playfulness and human responsibility, a mix of simplicity and mystery, of the child and the adult, of right now and of forever. The marriage ceremony but celebrates a prior love and a heart given long before. That marriage covenant is confirmed in the body language of human sexuality.

In giving a beloved person access to our body as a total gift of our self we cannot gather up all that we are and can do into our hands in any one moment. Our nakedness is a blank check, a draft on the future generosity that our body may give in this passing life. We pledge the energy and service of our minds and hearts made visible in the revelation of our body, the source of all we do for each other. This is our body in its bones and flesh, but we live in time, and we cannot give ourself away all at once. Access to our body is only for the moment. Lovers thus offer a pledge to their beloved to give themselves all ways and always. The body thus becomes a token of intent and in its embrace the dissolving of any future barrier between lover and beloved.

Sexual intercourse remains the sign and sacrament of access pure and simple to oneself as bodily gift. Nakedness is a pledge and a rehearsal of the disclosure of our heart and the work of our hands over a lifetime. Hence lovers cherish the anticipation of access and the privilege to be allowed to unveil another. In the undressing of the body there is always promise of a further revelation. That epiphany is the bestowal of the gifts of the body without trespass and without cease, nothing concealed and nothing reserved, the pledge of the fullness of the future. No access is truly given when access to sex is not also access to all of one's future and one's capacities for giving and supporting a life and all its relationships. Such loving intimacy can only be given for enjoyment in a context of total care and sharing, and with the acceptance of future responsibilities that frame and magnify the sexual experience. Sex thus is open-ended and unpredictable access. Sex remains full of risk and incalculable responsibility. Bodily love is access ultimately to one's lifetime. Therefore, this temporal gift is us—our life, what we can do, where we can go, what we can accomplish. In short, given its own logic, sexual intimacy becomes marriage that is irrevocable. Women and men move toward bonding for a lifetime and not for a brief encounter. Sexual relations that are given in love and commitment are just such a unique and privileged access, and such are the clear overtones of the Song of Songs.

Sexual intercourse not only celebrates the outercourses of the past but it pledges an acceptance of the future dying that is our final death. The body is part of the person. The organs of the body are part of the total and indivisible body-person. One cannot enjoy only sexuality. That exclusion is to reduce the body to a play thing. All human bones connect to one another, including the oval bone pelvic bowl that holds the cornucopia of life. The care, health, and cherishing of the whole human body remains the culmination of the efforts and decisions of a lifetime. Maintaining the health of an attractive body involves the whole person, spirit and mind, and the whole network of life and health support systems—family, society, work, church, and overall happiness. To allow another to enter our body and to be allowed to enter the body of another demands that one become responsible for the future health and welfare of that human being whose intimacy we have known. The immense risk of life and death in sexual intercourse also stems in large part from the ever-present possibility of conceiving a child. Indeed we are responsible for the life that we embrace, and human beings shall need a creative fidelity to remain loyal to the love they have but begun in courtship.

The question that sexual intercourse puts to each person is then this. If you will die this little death with me, if you will bear being naked and vulnerable, if you will give up your control with me in such an ecstasy of an overwhelming power, will you also be with me as I die from poverty, or from sadness, or from underdevelopment, old age, illness, or accident? Do you pledge with your body to be with my body in the fear and trembling of death, who will be this body's last lover? When the whole body is overwhelmed by that final embrace, will you "die" with me as you have lived with me? In a difficult moment Jesus says to the disciples: "Do you also wish to go away?" (Jn 6:67). Every lover asks a similar question. Are you given to helping me sustain my body, its health and its beauty, its sexuality and its personality, now and in the future when I will need help? Having taken the fruits of a past care and love that brings my body to you today, can I count on you to uphold my body with a future support that I surely must have? To enjoy the harvest, one must love the field. Will you commit yourself, your physical and psychic resources, to befriend me when I shall come to count on you? Will the beloved always say and mean "with my body I thee wed." In short, does one promise "for better or for worse, for richer or for poorer, in sickness or in health, until death do us part?"

In Shakespeare's "Romeo and Juliet" the young lovers in the springtime of their lives live and die for love at first sight. Despite the social barrier of a family feud that precludes their courtship, they find in their own heart's love a validation that needs no external warrant. It would be easy to imagine the woman and man in the Song of Songs cut from the same cloth, loyal to the beloved despite all family opposition and bonded forever despite the dangers of the night, whether in Jerusalem or in Verona. One thinks of the world's great innocent love stories, those "comedies" of the human heart that have happy endings in the consummation of human courtship, such as the prototypical yearning of Adam and Eve, the biblical love of Rachel and Jacob, and the fantastical love of Miranda and Ferdinand in Shakespeare's "Tempest." In all these love stories one finds the heart's yearning, the seeking and the finding, obstacles and a final wedding or a banquet consummation. In all these love stories, as in the Song of Songs, the beloved is unique, irreplaceable, worth the sacrifice of anything and everything. Accordingly the marriage of lovers is made not of the sensuality of the earth, but from the destiny of their heavenly stars. In such sacred marriage there can be no other witness but God, in whose boundless sight they must be wedded forever.

The Song of Songs does not argue for the exaltation of romantic love or courtship love at the expense of the social and religious dimensions of human love. It is assumed in the very imagery of the Song that love is expansive. Good is diffusive. The fruit follows upon the flower. Children are indeed the fruit of the womb and lovers know no greater joy than to have pro-created with the help of God another human being made in the image of the beloved. Only human beings shall live forever, and they shall see the face of God. If you have ever seen a loving father and mother who care wisely and peacefully over a large family of children, you know you have seen a rare goodness and a wonder that validates human life without any apology.

Love spills over into a harvest from its own abundance, and the Song's only implication is that the further fruitfulness of love and its social dimensions are best guaranteed when there is a solid foundation of an initial and perduring loving friendship between the woman and the man, who bond together spontaneously in joyful appreciation of the surrounding rich world and of each other as sparkling treasures within it. The Marriage Encounter literature argues that the best way for parents to love their children is to love one another. That love will wash over their children in due time and inevitably.

· III ·

Stories and the Story:
Celebration of the Spirit

How much body is needed to foster the spirit? How much is the body the person? We are our bodies; we also have bodies. And yet we are much more than body. We speak of our immortal souls and of our spirit within the body. The mystery of the union of spirit and matter in the human being, which union is the human person, remains mysterious. That we are made for infinite life, for the sight of God, and that our body must also be food for worms and return to the dust of the earth paralyzes our imagination, confounds our judgment, and baffles our heart.

All behavior is meaningful. And sexuality in depth is an issue of spirituality. The human body remains a transaction with the holy. The sensual and the spiritual are two sides of the same coin. Sexuality in its broad manifestations is a revelation of who and what we are, and how in loving relationship and communion human beings are made in the image of God. Hence there is no merely natural or merely erotic. Love is never just physical. The Song of Songs is not unworthy of the Bible, because the body is ever with the soul, and both are for God's grace. In the irrevocable bond of the flesh of Jesus Christ there is a new creation. The body is now a graced body; the bread is now a graced bread; the dying is now a graced dying. All human life is incarnadined by the enfleshment of God.

The face of beauty, whether female or male, has ever lured the human heart from the transient earth to the revelation of the transcendent heaven.

Sacred love emerges from profane love; eternal love rises from secular love; heavenly love stems from mundane love. Plato writes: "When the real lover beholds a godlike face, the form and very image as it were of beauty, he shudders first and is surprised by some of his old awe; then gazing fixedly, pays it reverence as though it were a god" (*Phaedrus*). Even the pagan fertility cults knew in whatever distorted way that sexuality and divinity were somehow related. The Jewish Cabala links sexuality and the spiritual life. The Christian mystical tradition enjoins sexual imagery and spirituality. "In the final analysis then, what links the literal sense of the Song to the expository visions of synagogue and church is an exquisite insight; the love that forms human partnership and community, and that sustains the whole of creation is a gift of God's own self" (Murphy, 105).

It has been said that human sexuality is mostly in the head, suggesting that bodily touch takes all its resonance from personal relationship. Sex without love is an impoverished communication. It has been said, furthermore, that for the human person sex is sacred. A woman knows in some profound way she is Sarah/Eve, mother of all the living; a man knows in some profound way he is Abraham/Adam, whose life-giving seed numbers as the sands of the seashore. There is little doubt that sexual experience engenders incomprehensible desires, nostalgia for childhood joy, a foretaste of heaven on earth, an enduring hope for eternal life. The human body is a yearning for ever more intercourse with spirit, and the spirit a yearning for ever more communion with the infinite spirit who is God. Creation yearns for infinity; the body yearns for immortality.

Sexuality is thus a great mystery; it teems with symbolic meaning that is inexhaustible. The biblical authors could find no more profound imagery to speak of God's love for his people than the language of human sexuality. Paul writes: "In the same way, husbands should love their wives as they do their own bodies. He who loves his wife loves himself. For no one ever hates his own body, but he nourishes and tenderly cares for it, just as Christ does for the church, because we are members of his body. 'For this reason a man will leave his father and mother and be joined to his wife, and the two will become one flesh'" (Eph 5: 28–31).

Is the biblical Song of Songs then finally to be construed as sacred love or as profane love? Let us claim both. All profane love reveals a dimension of the sacred, because the creation is ever from the creator. God who is everything created something that is not God, but that profane something can never escape the sacred everything that continues to hold it in existence. And all sacred love reveals a dimension of the profane ever since the Son of God took flesh of the virgin Mary and was born in a stable. Jesus, whose body is our flesh and whose human love is our love, yet remains the one and only God—human and divine, eros and agape, creature and creator, the many and the one. Thus the distinction between profane and sacred may be a real one, but it is never an exclusive one.

The French proverb *qui fait l'ange, fait la bête* (who pretends to be an angel acts like a beast) suggests that the claims of the body are constitutive of the human condition. Of the equally real claims of the spirit Teilhard de Chardin writes:

> The true union that you ought to seek with creatures that attract you is to be found not by going directly to them, but by converging with them on God, sought in and through them. It is not by making themselves more material, relying solely on physical contacts, but by making themselves more spiritual in the embrace of God, that things draw closer to one another. . . . The true union is the union that simplifies . . . the true fertility is the fertility that brings being together in the engendering of spirit.

The resurrection of the body is an outrageous hope that claims the flesh and the spirit of humankind are made for God, and that the body in its life of love is a temple of the Holy Spirit. Every beloved woman and every beloved man is a promise that cannot be held in possession, a promise that points to the infinite love that made woman and man in the image of God. One should love more not less. One should desire with infinite boldness. Every human love affair hopes to convince the beloved that he or she is the beloved of God.

Of married love it is written: "When we first met, we took off our clothes and knew such pleasure. Later we took off our bodies and knew communion. Now we take off our souls and know God" (a quotation composed by the Marriage Encounter program). In lovemaking human beings want communion with the person of the beloved. The body is an entrance to the person, but we seek the person embodied and not the body impersonalized. We undress face to face, but what lovers want to see is the heart of the beloved. In the movie *Cocoon,* the woman visitor from outer space who is gamboling in the swimming pool refuses the caress of a gentleman. She explains that where she comes from lovers exchange their hearts in order to make love. At its most profound sexuality is always spirituality, and human spirituality always seeks an embodied love. Sensuality, ingestion of food, erotic arousal, all these intimacies raise the soul question, which question always implicates the God question. We are created for ecstasy of body and soul in boundless joy and for the resurrection of the body.

For Christians, Jesus who is Lord remains the ultimate spouse of every human being whose heart is wounded by love in this world. "My Lord Jesus Christ has espoused me with his ring; he has crowned me like a bride" (Antiphon in the *Roman Breviary* for the feast of St. Agnes). Augustine proclaims that the soul is espoused to God and that the world is a golden betrothal ring, but a created ring that we should not love more than the uncreated God who is our intended spouse. Dante sees in this life the unveiled face of Beatrice; in her death he sees beyond her earthly body to her heavenly body. In heaven he sees the face of Christ reflected in the eyes of Beatrice upon whom he gazes. In eternity we shall know each other in God. We shall exchange hearts with the beloved by cleaving to the heart of God. "In his light we shall see light" (Ps 36:9), and in God's love we shall know love. "As a bridegroom rejoices over the bride, so shall your God rejoice over you" (Is 62:4–5).

As the Marriage Encounter slogan promises, husband and wife at the close of life shall take off their souls and find God. Sexual love in all its ecstasy will be seen for what it is, the rehearsal and dim mirror image of the infinite joy of total communion in body and in soul with God. Then it will be clear why human beings are given such yearning for love and for union with one another. Then it will be seen that our heart's desire truly was for an eternal and infinite love.

Beethoven's "Ode to Joy" sings of an ineffable happiness. Indeed, we were made for joy, and all the loves of this created world are but the foretaste of that overwhelming cascade of God's love ever coursing in the inner life giving of the blessed Trinity. Thus human beings need never fear limitless desire in this life. Its surcease is not found in restraint, but in desire ever more elevated and daring until our yearnings are forever enfolded in the loving embrace of God. Augustine writes:

> Late have I loved you, beauty so ancient and so new. Of late have I loved you. Behold you were within me and I was beside myself. I was seeking you outside, and with no loveliness in me I grasped at those

most lovely things that you had made. You were with me, but I was not with you. Those things of beauty held me afar from you, even though had they not been in you they would not have been at all. You called to me, and you cried out for me, and you pierced my deafness. You were radiant and you were resplendent, and you drove away my blindness. You gave forth a fragrance. I took in my breath, and now I pant for you. I tasted you, and now I hunger and thirst for you. You touched me, and I am enkindled by want of your peace. (*Confessions,* x:xxvii)

Our human life is a love song, a song of songs, a love of loves. Dante speaks of "the love that moves the sun and stars," and the ancient world thought of the divine harmony of the universe as the music of spheres. Thus even the stars sing and dance their own love song. In the encircling courtship of woman and man, so poignantly rendered in the Song of Songs, we hear that melody of God's love song played out in the human body, which has been well imagined by Caryll Houselander as the "reed of God." We are God's flute, and the breath of the Holy Spirit resounds in all our love songs. Woman and man are the twin reeds that vibrate together, the exquisite oboe d'amore that the creator made to play the loveliest eternal love song of all time, to which all the stars in heaven may dance. God plays God's love though the loves of our body in this world, until we are able to hear God's own voice, God's own song, our ears finally attuned to the perfect pitch of divine love. "Hark! how the heavenly anthem drowns all music but its own." We are the beloved even now and our love song is God's song, and God's song will become our love song in that day, "the day the Lord has made." Indeed:

> They will, no doubt, rejoice as much as they love, and they will love as much as they know. How much will they know You, then Lord, and how much will they love You? In very truth, neither eye has seen, nor ear heard, nor has it entered into the heart of man in this life how much they will know You and love You in that life. (Anselm, *Proslogion,* xxvi, trans. M. J. Charlesworth)

On earth human love is thus a mirror in which we may see divine love. We know the love of God in the love of neighbor. The beloved is searching for the lover in the full confidence that the lover, whose voice has already been heard, is awaiting. Only the one who created our heart can fulfill its deepest yearnings. In the beatific vision of God face to face, in that most intimate embrace of divinity, our flesh in its transfiguration will altogether know that we are the beloved of the Song of Songs. In the vows of marriage the Christian woman or man is again reminded that they are the beloved in whom God is well pleased, the beloved of their baptismal vows espousing them to the God who is love. Human love between a woman and a man finds its fulfillment in the mystical marriage. Then one will know what it means to be the beloved of an infinite love. In the seeing of God we shall see all, know all, enter all, and be all. There will be pure divine access and an everlasting divine bond. Our beloveds shall be ours, and we all shall be the beloved who is God's own. The prophecy of the Song of Songs will be then be fulfilled. "I am my beloved's and he is mine" (6:3).

If our theological understanding of the relationship of human love and divine love is defensible, then there can be no erotic interpretation of the Song of Songs without a spiritual meaning, and no human soulful meaning in the poem without a sexual embodiment. Paul speaks of the flesh at odds with the spirit, but he is not talking of a necessary conflict of the body and the soul, or of physical love and spiritual love. Paul speaks of the flesh as that ego-centered lovelessness that can afflict equally the body of a human being as well as the soul. Thus freedom from the lovelessness of sin is freedom not only for the body but also equally for the soul. Indeed, in body and soul human beings are made for love and all its making.

Human love is thus a sacramental love that takes the things of the body as signs of the spirit. Bodily love is a symbol or sign of divine love. The human song contains a hint of a divine melody. The body is made in the image of the spirit. The human being is created in the image of God. The world of the senses is not merely carnal but at its best speaks of the spiritual hunger and fulfillment for which the physical is destined. The body is not to be jettisoned on the way to spiritual fulfillment in the love of God. The body is to be resurrected and transfigured. Jesus, who in his flesh is the great sacrament, appears to his disciples with his physical wounds, but wounds now glorified. The mystical rose blooms from its roots in the dark earth. In incarnate love the flesh is given spirit and the spirit is enfleshed.

The sacrament of the Eucharist is spiritual yet embodied. The Eucharist is sacred body and yet profane bread. The Eucharist remains physical yet not irrational. In the sacred Eucharist Jesus allows us to enter his life by consuming his body given for us. We allow Jesus to enter our lives by entering our body and soul, also given for him. It is anything but a sexual encounter; it is intimate access nonetheless. "This is my body given for you" (Lk 22:19). "All that is mine is yours" (Lk 15:31). For most people, however, the knowledge of what the incarnate love of God in the Eucharist really means takes on an immeasurably greater depth when they have known a tender, human, and embodied love.

Much of the literature of Christianity prizes virginity, not only as a preparation for marriage, but as a witness to the resurrection of the body. The advent of Jesus Christ begins a new creation, a new heaven and earth, a new human being. All is grace now, and the world becomes transfigured and renewed from top to bottom. No longer are the powers of nature supreme; no longer is evil or death the lord of the earth. Redeemed humanity receives the very life of God in order to live the life of God, now knowing and loving with the very knowledge and love of God through the Holy Spirit given in our hearts. Procreation, which was a quasi remedy to the human problem of death's persistent victory, becomes unnecessary, since death is overcome in the resurrection of the body. Married love remains a bonding of woman and man, but even such a love is not indispensable when the love of God is poured out in our hearts. In heaven we would all be united in the vision and joy of God. There would be no more tears and dying. Heaven begins even on earth in faith in Jesus Christ and the indwelling of the Holy Spirit, and thus virginity becomes a pledge, an anticipation, an expression of an impatient love for the God of love and a witness to the power of Christ and the fullness of the redemption. Augustine writes:

> What do I love when I love you? Not the beauty of the body, nor the attractiveness of the times, nor the brilliance of light so cherished by our eyes, nor the sweet melodies of all kinds of songs, nor the subtle fragrance of flowers and perfumes, nor manna or honey, nor limbs yielding in the embraces of the flesh. Not these I love when I love my God. Nonetheless, I do love a certain light, a certain voice, fragrance, food, and embrace when I love my God. It is a light, a voice, a fragrance, a food, and an embrace of my inner self, where my soul is flooded with a light that no place contains, with a sound that no time possesses, with a perfume that no airs dissolve, and with a taste that no fulfillment lessens, and in my desire to linger no satiety surfeits me. This is what I love when I love my God. (*Confessions,* x:viii)

The goal of our human life in this world is to learn how to love, how to become human. We live just as long as we need to learn to love, and then in God's providence we die. To live forever in this life shows no purpose. We yearn for fulfillment in a divine love. As a consequence death is a quasi-erotic experience. Death is the yielding of one's body to a divine lover. Death is an encounter with God where our body is not taken from us but bestowed by us. Death invites a complete self-gift given to God. Since one must die eventually, like it or not, the saints wanted to give their life in advance as a token of their sincerity. Often living as virgin lovers in this world, these women and these men were already united with the divine lover, for whom all human love is a dress rehearsal, an image held in a mirror, seen "in a glass darkly."

Sexuality is connected by its nature to procreation. When there is in heaven no more death, neither will there be a need for any more birth. Hence the gospel talks of heaven as a life without sexuality, a life like the angels who are without a body. Although heaven may not have birth and death, Christians proclaim the resurrection of the body. Could it be that the Song of Songs is also an eschatological text, that lends itself to an imaginative intimation of the resurrection of the flesh? Friendship and bonding will perdure in eternal life. The transfiguration of the body will make for inconceivable beauty. The world of time and space, however transfigured in eternity, might be imagined as the garden of supersensual delights depicted over and over again in the Song. But not just a heaven of earthly delights writ large, but a superior joy of heaven before the face of God, the face of the ultimate beloved, in whom we shall see the beloved of this world not only in the body but in fullest reality, more tangible than ever known in the flesh that walks this earth howsoever beautiful.

"You are the beloved," God says that to every human being. God is well pleased with every human being. "Can a woman forget her nursing child . . . ? Even these may forget, yet I will not forget you. See, I have inscribed you on the palms of my hands" (Is 49:15–16). God loves us more than we can love ourselves or anyone else can love us. God is more part of us than we are ourselves, for the creator never ceases to hold the creation in existence from the deepest insides of its being: "You did not choose me but I chose you" (Jn 15:16). "How beautiful you are, love of my soul, you are beautiful!" (4:1). "I exist and the whole world should dance," says Sebastian Moore.

Nicholas Lash writes:

> Hence, to *hear* God's utterance in Christ, God's "Amen," or "Yes," of friendship and forgiveness, is to *see* some celebration, marriage feast,

or banquet, even in our present circumstance. "You shall no more be termed "Forsaken," and your land shall no more be termed "Desolate;" but you shall be called "My delight is in her." and your land "Married"; for the Lord delights in you, and your land shall be married." What God's word says is what it does. And what it does is bring all things fruitfully to life, in God, transforming desert into garden, incomprehension into understanding, "foreignness" into friendship, water into wine. (*Believing Three Ways in One God* [University of Notre Dame Press, 1993], 76)

We are truly the beloved of God, even though our human life is cast among the innumerable vicissitudes of this vale of tears, this mortal life where even our next breath is not ours alone to guarantee. We see now in the Song of Songs no longer just a woman's experience or a man's; we hear the voice of God courting the human heart, the sacred marriage of everyone who has ever loved and ever shall love world without end. Amen.

A Verse by Verse Commentary

1:1

The Song of songs, which is Solomon's.

The Song of Songs, which is Solomon's.

𝒯he ancient superscription, Song of Songs, gives a title and initially suggests one song composed of songs. The Hebrew also indicates a superlative comparison. The Holy of Holies, the king of kings, the song of songs, each claim is to the superlative. We are thus told by the final editor of this biblical text that we are here given Israel's surpassing poem of finest songlike quality.

The biblical title also reveals that these superior songs belong in some way to King Solomon (circa 961–922 b.c.). This son of David and Bathsheba became a legend of fabulous wealth surrounded by an entourage of beautiful women (see a brief biography in Sir 47:12–22). King Solomon built the lavish Jerusalem temple, that magnificent dwelling place on earth of the presence of God. Solomon was hailed as the quintessential wise man who asked God for only one thing, the gift of wisdom. "The Lord kept his promise and gave Solomon wisdom" (1 Kg 5:12). The name *Solomon* is derived from the Hebrew, *shalom*, which means peace and which to this day is used as a greeting. The name of Solomon alludes to all this physical and spiritual largesse.

In the Song of Songs there are references to the rich pavilions of Solomon (1:5), to a bridal procession, apparently in conjunction with a wedding of Solomon (3:6–11), and to the vineyards of Solomon (8:11–12). It is not likely, however, that the Song of Songs was written by Solomon himself or was dedicated to Solomon during his lifetime. Nor is it clear that the Song gives an account of a particular love affair of Solomon. The Song does reflect the opulence, sensuality, and the wisdom of the literary tradition of Solomon, "who composed three thousand proverbs and more than a thousand songs" (1 Kg 4:32). Like many of the psalms attributed to David, the songs of Solomon manifest the ambiance and character of their purported author.

Solomon's name points to both a secular and sacred tradition. From the secular point of view, he is the king of kings, the master of wealthy empire and the great lover of a bountiful harem of women. From the sacred point of view he is the eminent spiritual writer of the wisdom literature of Israel, and the Song of Songs is grouped in the Bible with the book of Proverbs and the book of Ecclesiastes. The invocation of his name thus lends a framework within which these songs may be construed. In our reading of the Song we can expect to find an appeal both to the goodness of the flesh and the wisdom of the mind. Most of all we will see the bounty of the creator of the human body and soul, who is the true King of kings and Lord of lords.

Of the "lilies of the field" Jesus says "not even Solomon in all his glory was clothed like one of these" (Mt 6:29). The Song of Songs, which is Solomon's, is a song of glory, a song of love that dances, and a dance that sings of love. In the Song of Songs wisdom sings. "Let me sing for my beloved my love-song concerning his vineyard: / My beloved had a vineyard on a very fertile hill" (Is 5:1). If God is love and creation is God's love song, the Song of Songs puts pure poetry to the divine melody. This love song of love songs celebrates the love of loves.

1:2

Let him kiss me with the kisses of his mouth:
For thy love is better than wine.

May he kiss me with kisses of his lips.
Sweeter than wine your love.

The Song of Songs begins with lyrical drama. The woman's first words are a soliloquy, a voice crying out in desire for his love. The Song opens with a

She speaks:

I am a flower of the field,
A lily of the valley. (2:1)

Like a lily amid the brambles (2:2)

To his wine rooms he transports me,
And his cover over me is love. (2:2)

His left hand cradles my head
And his right hand stays me. (2:6)

lover's kiss, and one kiss upon a kiss. Shakespeare calls kisses "seals of love." In the Song there is much lovemaking, and his love "sweeter than wine" suggests a joyful welcome. His love is also described later as "sweeter than wine" (4:10). The Song indeed is a toast to love, a love pressed upon the lips and sealed upon the heart, a love "strong as death" (8:6).

For ages the kiss has been the tactile language of love, whether the brush of cousins or the crush of lovers. The labile tissues of the human body are delicate and sensual. Hence human kisses are sensitive touches. A kiss on the lips may be slight but always endearing. A lover's kiss is more intimate, for the mouth implicates access to the body. The bloodstream of lovers is separated by only a thin membrane. In the Song her lips are a "scarlet ribbon" (4:3) that "distill wild honey" (4:11), and his lips are "crimson lilies, gilded with glistening myrrh" (5:13). With the mouth and lips we not only kiss, but we also fashion the loving words that are verbal kisses and the touch of our soul.

Kisses sweeter than wine speak of taste and bouquet as well as the soft touch of the lips. In the Song the woman is the vineyard garden, which flowers in beauty, fructifies in the fruit of the vine, and whose love is consumed in the drinking of the ripened grape juice. Here is the image of an ecstatic love, a love "sweeter than wine," for love is the soul's deepest inebriation. It was at the Cana wedding feast that Jesus served the best wine, the sweetest wine, the wine of God's great love that was kept for the last.

The voice is the woman's and the initiative as well. She speaks of his willingness. Of his desire she already knows. Whether he is there in his body or only in her imagination, his presence suffuses her consciousness. Immediately we are swept up into the sung celebration of the lives of this one woman and this one man who are in love. Ben Jonson's poem captures the flavor of their infatuation: "Or leave a kiss but in the cup, / And I'll not look for wine. / The thirst that from the soul doth rise / Doth ask a drink divine; / But might I of Jove's nectar sup, / I would not change for thine" ("To Celia").

In a Christian allegorization of the Song, the woman represents the covenant of Moses crying out for the embodiment of the word of God in the incarnate Son of God. The love is the Father; the lips are the Word of God embodied; the kiss is the Holy Spirit. The revealed biblical word comes from the mouth of God, and the word made flesh is the kiss of God's lips. It is with the lips red with the flow of one's own blood that the Christian first touches the sacred bread and the precious wine, sweeter than any earthly love, the body and blood of the Lord consumed in the Eucharist. Holy communion is the holy kiss of Jesus given with words of love to his beloved. Humanity, the bride of Christ, sings this song in its yearning for that kiss of kisses.

1:3

Because of the savor of thy good ointments
Thy name is as ointment poured forth,
Therefore do the virgins love thee.

Delightful your fragrance;
A perfume unsealed your name.
No wonder maidens love you.

The Song of Songs has been called the most scent-drenched poem of all time. Perfumes and unguents abound. In a hot desert climate with little water, the skin is anointed with fragrant oils. Essential oils both soothe the skin and delight the senses. After a cleansing bath the skin is dressed for festive events, such as a wedding. Scented lamp oil brings fresh light to the darkness. Herbal oils, like camphor or henna, keep clothing fresh. Warm flesh heats the surface of the anointed skin as if the human body were an incense brazier. Thus even without touching, human beings are brought into continual communion with each other through such sweet airs. Even unanointed, the body carries its own unmistakable scent, and those close at hand and close at heart recognize it.

We cannot not smell, even with eyes closed and hands tied. We must breathe in and out. In our breathing we hold a daily intercourse with the world around us, a world of continual exchange. We breathe in the atmosphere of others who have scented it with their own essence, and then exhaled it. Others breathe in the breath we have exhaled, which was once theirs but now has been inhaled by us. We receive and we give at each moment. From the first breath at birth until the last breath in death, we must exchange the spirit of life. At the death of Jesus we read: "When Jesus had received the wine, he said, 'It is finished.' Then he bowed his head and gave up his spirit" (Jn 19:30). He lost his breath and with it gave his life. At Pentecost the Holy

Spirit descends as a rushing wind whose presence is invisible yet pervasive and vivacious.

Perfumes flow over us with a pervading fragrance demanding attention, or with a nostalgic reminiscence of fading memory. We continue to know the smells of our childhood. Home-baked bread, a damp root cellar, new mown grass, wet autumn leaves, a pine log in the fireplace, the aroma of the kitchen, the sweet smell of our mother's hair remain scented memories that never leave us. A similar fragrance brings back the original experience ever after. When Odysseus, disguised as a beggar, returns home after twenty years of war and sea travels, his old and now blind dog wags his tail in recognition of his master's scent. The sweet airs we breathe carry the constant aroma of our memories. Though we cannot name the particular bouquet, we recognize the one in whom we are enveloped. The kiss of the body is "sweeter than wine"; the name of the beloved is delightful fragrance, a "perfume unsealed."

In the Song the woman's beloved has a name whose very sound delights her like a fragrant oil that has been poured from its beaker. "A good name is better than precious ointment" (Eccl 7:1). "What's in a name?" Juliet asks in Shakespeare's drama, "a rose / By any other name would smell as sweet" (2:2:43–44). Lovers frequently coin terms of endearment known only to them. In the musical, "West Side Story," the woman's name is Maria: "say it loud and there's music playing; say it soft and it's almost like praying." Wonderful in its implication, the name of the beloved is itself a love song. In the garden Jesus speaks the name of Mary (Magdalene), and she then recognizes him risen from the dead. No wonder the nubile maidens (perhaps the daughters of Jerusalem of the following line) overhearing his anointed name are drawn into the woman's love for such a man.

The hidden name of God, the sacred tetragrammaton YHWH, was unspoken by ancient Israel. No one was so intimate with God to speak God's name. The Christian hears the name of Jesus, the Christ, that is, the anointed one, the messiah. It is the name of Jesus that saves, the name given him at his conception by the angel Gabriel, the name no one can say without the Holy Spirit (1 Cor 12:3).

1:4
Draw me, we will run after thee:
The King hath brought me into his chambers:
We will be glad and rejoice in thee,
We will remember thy love more than wine:
The upright love thee.

Sweep me along with you.
Let us dash away.
The king has drawn me apart to his chambers.
We shall glory and delight in you;
Surpassing wine is your love.
Surely they should love you.

The privacy of the king's chambers delineates a threshold that the woman of the Song is eager to cross over. She is drawn apart willingly. He has invited her to come away with him. In imagination, they elope. To take somebody into one's own private space invites further intimacy. She is drawn into his chambers, brought apart into his own rooms, his inner sanctum, where a romantic atmosphere suffuses them. Later we read "While the king was couched within, / My nard spread out its fragrance" (1:12). Both woman and man here come to each other gladly. He conducts her into his house and chambers. Later she will bring him into her mother's house and bedroom (3:4 and 8:2). She here pleads to be swept along with him. Later he will claim that he is drawn to her as a king entangled in the tresses of her hair (7:6).

The king could be construed as Solomon. Royalty, however, need not be more than a literary fiction in the Song. In love's imagination he is her king, her regal lover full of majesty, her prince charming. Love lends splendor to the beloved. Later he will return the compliment. In his eyes she becomes unique, a perfection, the queen of queens "resplendent as the moon, irradiant as the sun" while "queens and concubines sing her praises" (6:9–10).

The woman in the Song wishes to be courted. She wishes to be attracted and drawn by her beloved. In a spiritual reading of the Song one thinks of the words of Jesus in John's gospel: "No one can come to me unless drawn by the Father" (6:44), and "when I am lifted up from the earth, [I] will draw all people to myself" (12:32). The temple built by King Solomon drew Israel into the chambers of God. The Christian is drawn by the Spirit into the church, the body of Christ. "Abide in me as I abide in you. . . . As the Father has loved me, so I have loved you; abide in my love" (Jn 15:4,9).

Some readings of the Song have concluded that the woman is in dialogue with the daughters of Jerusalem, who proclaim here "we shall glory and delight in you." This shift of person from "sweep *me* along" to "*we* shall glory" confuses the reader. We saw above a similar shift of person from "kisses of *his* lips" to "sweeter than wine *your* love" (1:2). Such shifts occur in poetic usage in Hebrew. Thus the woman more likely refers to herself while continuing her soliloquy: "Surely they should love you."

Some interpretations of the Song have argued that the king and the rustic lover, who appears subsequently, are rivals for the woman's love. The king has sequestered her in his chambers, and she then later makes appeal to her shepherd lover to run away with her. More likely the king is a royal fiction for her one and only lover, whom she imagines here in the regal role of the sovereign of her love.

1:5

I am black, but comely, O ye daughters of Jerusalem,
As the tents of Kedar,
As the curtains of Solomon

Darkened I am, still lovely,
Daughters of Jerusalem,
Just as the tents of Kedar, or the pavilioned draperies of
   Solomon.

*T*he woman admits that her skin is darkly colored, but she claims she is beautiful nonetheless. The issue here is not race and the natural hue of one's skin, but the darkening caused by exposure to sunshine. Fair skin belongs to the leisure class, who need not labor in the heat of the day. A contrast is drawn between the woman in the Song made to work in the family vineyard and the daughters of Jerusalem, who are spared field labor because of their city or court connection. The darker the skin's complexion, the lower the status. Only field workers and servants have weathered skin. Later in the poem ivory and alabaster-colored skin is esteemed (5:14–15). Most likely the woman is embarrassed by the suntan of her skin, yet she is insistent that her darksome mien does not spoil her overall beauty.

Beauty is in the eye of the beholder. Fair is beautiful to some people; dark is lovely to others. Black is beautiful. The woman in the Song flies in the face of human weakness, human bias, and says, I am a woman who works in the fields, and I am as beautiful as a queen. One thinks of Byron's poem: "She walks in Beauty, like the night / Of cloudless climes and starry skies; / And all that's best of dark and bright/ Meet in her aspect and her eyes: / Thus mellowed to that tender light / Which Heaven to gaudy day denies." Love thus covers the beloved with fair regard. In a spiritual vein one may recall the vulnerable love of the "suffering servant" in Isaiah: "I did not hide my face from insult and spitting. The Lord God helps me; therefore I have not been disgraced" (Is 50:6–7). Mary of Nazareth was all too poor and all too young, but she was the chosen one nonetheless.

Qedar or Kedar is a distant site in the wilds of the northern Israel desert. "Let the desert and its towns lift up their voice, the villages that Kedar inhabits" (Is 42:11). The goats of the Bedouin in the desert have long black hair, and their skins were made into tents of dark color. The pavilions of Solomon were elaborate tents made with sheets of mohair. The woman's hair is twice compared to a "wave of goats flowing down the hill slopes of Gilead" (4:1 and 6:5). Black is her hair, "deep lustrous like purple" (7:6). The tent skins are hung with the opaque black hair on the outside. From only inside the tent would the light filter through. Just as the dark tent-skins curtain off a private space, so the dark skin and dark hair of the woman in the Song veil her face. To look upon her is but to begin to know her inner bright loveliness. One might recall Yahweh's love of lowly Israel in the nomadic years of its desert sojourn on the way to the promised land.

The daughters of Jerusalem function in the Song somewhat in the manner of a chorus in ancient Greek drama. In conversation they provide a foil, a public viewpoint, and a neutral sounding board. They represent "everywoman," and they function as an inner audience. Their inclusion allows the speaker to dramatize her inner soliloquy.

References to the daughters occurs six times (1:5, 2:7, 3:5, 5:8, 5:16, and 8:4). In each instance their appearance allows the dialog to change its course smoothly. Whether or not the Song of Songs is one poem or a loosely gathered anthology, the inclusion of the daughters punctuates several sections of the Song with a marked transition (2:7, 3:5, 8:4). Such strategic shifts in the Song are neatly negotiated by this literary device. The daughters of Jerusalem thus function as quilt sashing that enable the pieces of the Song's patchwork to hang together. With their appearance in the dialog the reader comes to know that the action is completed and a new development is now to take place. The daughters of Jerusalem may also remind the Christian reader of the women witnesses of the passion of Jesus to whom he says: "Daughters of Jerusalem, do not weep for me, but weep for yourselves and for your children" (Lk 23:28). On the road to Calvary the legend of Veronica's veil, offered to Jesus as a napkin, captures as no other image the human face disfigured in suffering yet beautiful beyond words in its radiance bestowed by love itself.

1:6

Look not upon me, because I am black,
Because the sun hath looked upon me:
My mother's children were angry with me;
They made me the keeper of the vineyards;
But mine own vineyard have I not kept.

Do not long gaze at me because I am swarthy,
And the sun has burnt me.
My mother's sons were incensed with me.
They tethered me as watch keep of the vineyard;
On my own vine I spent no care.

After the woman's assertion of her dark color as nature's own cosmetic and her beauty as more than skin deep, she directs the eyes of the onlooker away from her. She explains her condition to those who surround her as possible critics (principally the daughters of Jerusalem). Her brothers made her work in the family vineyard, because she had failed to take care of her own. The implication is that she herself is the unkept vineyard, and her family was alarmed about her dalliance, entered upon without their approbation. Later in the Song her brothers discuss how they are to arrange the day of her betrothal (8:8–10). It is possible to see her as a fatherless Cinderella figure, overworked and coarsened by the ill treatment of her "mother's sons." As the psalmist says: "I am like a stranger to my mother's sons, like a foreigner to my family" (Ps 69:8).

Vineyards were typically fenced in to protect the grapes from marauders, such as the foxes (2:15), or thieves in the night. A vineyard was thus an enclosed garden of blossoms and of fruit. The lover will later describe the woman as "a garden enclosed, . . . a fountain sealed" (4:12). In the Song it is clear that the woman's body is a vineyard: "My own vineyard is mine alone to give" (8:12, and see also 2:15, 7:9, 7:13). It is her heartland she has not tended as her family might have wished. Less likely has she been lazy; more likely has she given away her affections. Unveiled she has given the sun access to her skin and the sun has long gazed on her body. Her dark skin is thus the proud emblem of her devotion. She has unveiled herself to her lover and given him access to her vineyard. She may have given her body in love, although a woman often gives her whole heart long before such physical intimacy.

In Isaiah we read of the courtship love of God for the chosen vineyard: "For the vineyard of the Lord of hosts is the house of Israel, and the people of Judah are his pleasant planting" (5:7). In the Christian reading of the Song it is Mary of Nazareth who is the daughter of Zion and emblem of the new Israel:

> [Eve] "was that vineyard whose enclosure her own hands had enabled death to violate, so that she could taste its fruit; thus the mother of all the living became the source of death for every living creature. But in her stead Mary grew up, a new vine in place of the old. Christ, the new life, dwelt within her. When death, with its customary impudence, came foraging for her mortal fruit, it encountered its own destruction in the hidden life that fruit contained. All unsuspecting, it swallowed him up, and in so doing released life itself and set free a multitude of men. (Sermon by St. Ephrem in the *Roman Breviary Office of Readings* for Friday of the third week of Easter)

In these first few lines of the Song of Songs we have already celebrated the full range of the senses of the human body: the touch of lips in a kiss

(1:2), the fragrance of perfume (1:3), the sound of the beloved's name (1:3), the taste of wine (1:4), and the color of her skin (1:5). We move later through levels of intimacy from a brush of the surface of the body to the depths of the eyes, revealing the soul. The Song is sensuous because it speaks often of the body with its senses. The poetry remains deeply human because it delights in the body as the soulful expression of the whole person. This first poem of the Song ends with an allusion to the cost of loving. Even in their exuberance, human beings need answer only this: How intensely in their bodily lifetime have they loved?

1:7
Tell me, O thou whom my soul loveth,
Where thou feedest, where thou makest thy flock to rest at
   noon:
For why should I be as one that turneth aside
By the flocks of thy companions?

Love of my soul, tell me where's your pasture land,
Your noonday resting place,
Tell me lest I roam as a tramp amid the flocks of your fellows.

This initial dialog between the woman and the man marks the beginning of another poem, or division (1:7–2:7) within the Song. The lovers' duet will continue in the following poem as well (2:8–2:17). In this courtship conversation there is flirtatious banter, coquettish teasing, and striking praise. Persistent is the pursuit of happiness as well as the happiness of pursuit. The woman entreats the man to tell her where he will pasture his flock during the noontime heat of the day. Seeking shade and repose in the desert, the shepherds take their midday rest. Noon marks the transition from morning to afternoon. It is a static time of bright light and fiery heat, and it suggests a moment of critical decision.

The crucifixion of Jesus takes place at noon. It is a cosmic love story gone awry, the rape of God, and even though divine love is unrequited, a poignant fidelity endures. The woman in the Song speaks of loving him with her whole being, as she later claims several times (3:1–4); he is "her soul's sole love." One is mindful of the hope of Israel to love God "with all your heart, and with all your soul, and with all your might" (Dt 6:5). Like the lovers in the Song we are creatures always in dialog with our God, who pursues our friendship even to "pitching his tent" in our midst (Jn 1:14).

She searches for him in the shepherd fields; later he will search for her in her house (2:9, 14). She fears, wandering camp to camp in search of him. Must she disguise herself? She may be taken for a camp follower, a vagabond at best, a prostitute at worst. Does she in fact seek an uncertain rendezvous with him? Does she know quite well where they meet and that they will soon meet there again? Feigning ignorance, is she teasing him with playful banter? Is her veiled threat more designed to disguise her affection for him? All the above may apply.

The poem is suggestive of many readings. What remains certain is her initiative in the courtship and her persistent invitation to the beloved. She begins the dialog. Women may have courted men in their own indirect ways for ages, but the woman in the Song shows a candor and a direct leading not often attested in courtship literature. Hers is a remarkably free and uninhibited expression of female desire. She is not the stereotypical woman of her time and place for whom marriage was arranged by the men in her family. And the man responds to her. One finds an exhilarating gender equality in the Song of Songs.

This verse is both light-hearted and soul-seeking. It reveals the simple hide and seek of young lovers, when anticipation is half the delight. It suggests the search for the meaning of life in the land of true love. She would feed in his pasture land; he would "feed among" her lilies (6:3). In the gospel two disciples ask Jesus where he lives. "Come and see!" (Jn 1:39) When Jesus asks Mary of Bethany where they have buried her brother Lazarus, "whom Jesus loved," she says: "Come and see" (Jn 11:34). God dwells in the noontime light of love; but mortal human beings come to dwell in the midnight of the grave. Hence the search for the soul's eternal beloved charts the course of human courtship.

A spiritual reading of this verse might also see the divine shepherd of Israel. "The Lord is my shepherd, I shall not want" (Ps 23:1). Jesus declares: "I am the good shepherd" (Jn 10:11). At the close of the Bible we read of the victorious lamb of God who becomes the shepherd guiding the blessed to "springs of the water of life, and God will wipe away every tear from their eyes" (Rev 7:17). In the Song of Songs we have seen the man described as king, and now as shepherd. We know he is also the beloved. For Christians these three titles, king, shepherd, and bridegroom, were the cherished names of Jesus the Christ.

1:8

If thou know not, O thou fairest among women,
Go thy way forth by the footsteps of the flock,
And feed thy kids beside the shepherds' tents.

Should you not know, most beautiful among women,
Track the flock and graze your kid goats
Close by the tent site of the shepherds.

The shepherd gives vague direction to the woman seeking his whereabouts. Her tease is returned, for the implication remains that she very well knows their trysting place. In his eyes she is the most beautiful among women. She also is portrayed as a shepherd. Women were often given charge of the young goats after their weaning.

His exchange with her here may recall the tender encounter and wooing between Jacob and Rachel. She comes to the well to water her flock, and he uncovers the well for her. Jacob then pledges his love to Rachel at first sight (Gen 29:1–12). For twice seven years he labors to win her father's consent to marry, "and they seemed to him but a few days because of the love he had for her" (Gen 29:20).

In the Song the woman is described as beautiful a dozen times, and in this verse in the superlative (also 5:9 and 6:1). The Marian reading of the Song sees the woman as the Blessed Virgin Mary, symbol of the church and spouse of God. "Most beautiful among women" is reminiscent of Gabriel's words to Mary: "full of grace" or "favored one" (Lk 1:28) and "blessed among women" (Lk 1:42). The tent of the shepherd in the Song may recall the tabernacle tent of the covenant during the exodus wandering of Israel in the desert. The Lord

God as shepherd of Israel and caretaker of vineyard Israel round out the images of divine embodiment we see in the Song (see Ps 80).

Goats have long been associated with lusty sexuality, as the satyr figure of mythology shows. A "kid goat from the flock" was the gift that Tamar, disguised as a prostitute, was to be given by Judah that he might come in to her (Gen 38:16–17). One might also recall the ritual scapegoat burdened with the sins of the people and then driven out into the desert. Sexuality in the Song is always delicate. Emotional overtones wash over the feelings like the many fragrances that suffuse the poetry. The imagery invites but does not insist upon unveiling the sexuality that nestles in its innocent shadows.

In a more thoughtful reading of the text, the verse might suggest that the body is not the enemy of the soul. To follow the trail of the flesh is not to miss the spirit. The pursuit of bodily fulfillment is in the end the pursuit of spiritual fulfillment, for human beings are body and soul. The love of woman and man is a sign of the love of God for humankind. The flesh is not bad, though sometimes it is sinful. Its leadings are worthy of trust. We blush when we tell lies, because our body is embarrassed. The promptings of human love always have a bodily component, and the body remains a friend whose inner eros pastures our pursuit of an infinite beauty.

1:9
I have compared thee, O my love,
To a company of horses in Pharaoh's chariots.

To a mare among Pharaoh's chariots
Would I compare you, O my soul.

The man compares the woman to a spirited female horse in the rich stables of Egypt. The compliment may not be readily appreciated. The primitive animal energy of the horse was considered a power beyond the human. The speed and grace of such a vital creature astonished those who tamed it. To harness a horse was to display animal spirits bent to human purpose. One may recall the line in Shakespeare's "Richard III" when the king now unseated from his slain horse is desperate to save himself in battle: "A horse! a horse! my kingdom for a horse!" (5:4:7). In the Bible horses were used mostly for warfare, and the horse-drawn chariot was the ancient version of the military tank. The war-horses lauded in the book of Job were fearless, feisty, bellicose animals serving their masters (39:19–25). Egypt bred the best horses, and the pharaoh would have enjoyed an ample supply. The chariots of the pharaoh also carry overtones of the pursuit of the Jewish people in the passover exodus from Egypt, when horse and chariot were overwhelmed in the sea. Pharaohs took enormous pride in their war machine, but the psalmist decries trust in violence rather than trust in the care of God: "Some take pride in chariots, and some in horses, but our pride is in the name of the Lord our God" (Ps 20:7). In the Song the man takes pride in the beauty of his beloved and in all her female power to move another human being.

Some readers of the Song have thought that the comparison suggests a mare let loose among the stallions. War-horses were always stallions. A single estrous filly or mare will excite stallions and render them intractable. The stallion's sexual urge is irresistible. Thus the woman in the Song would be praised for her compelling sex appeal. In short, the man acknowledges she is overwhelming. The excitation of stallions is not likely the focus of this text, but the wonder and power of the woman surely is.

In the verse that follows, the woman is complimented because of the ornaments that adorn her body. Thus the comparison to a horse may suggest the decorated tackle of a royal horse. The bridle harness, in particular, would be studded with silver and jewel work. The metaphor comparing her beauty to a filly or mare seems best understood as a combination of the beauty of the raiment and of the body of the horse. Later in the Song there are poems in praise of several parts of her body considered as nature's own adornment of her appearance. Arabian fillies move with such agility and fluid vivaciousness. A young woman carries the flesh on her bones with a similar astonishing grace and poise, and she moves with an equal delight for all who behold her. In this magical locomotion a beautiful quality of the female is displayed and indeed appears awesome. In Theocritus there is a similar description of Helen of Troy: "As the cypress towers an ornament to its garden, / Or like Thessalian steed to its chariot, / So too rosy hued Helen is an ornament to Sparta" (*Idyl* xviii, 30–32).

The man addresses her, "O my soul." These are words of endearment suggesting friendship and not just romance. Friendship between a man and

woman courting was not presumed. Marriages were arranged. Many times in
the Song, however, she is called soul friend. In the feminine this particular
word is otherwise unattested in biblical Hebrew. The soul informs the whole
human body just as the love of the woman and the man animates their whole
life. As Romeo says of Juliet: "It is my soul that calls upon my name: / How
silver-sweet sound lovers' tongues by night" (2:2).

1:10
Thy cheeks are comely with rows of jewels,
Thy neck with chains of gold.

Lovely your cheeks laced with jewels,
Your throat with necklaces.

*O*ur human acquaintance begins when we face each other. Dante never
forgot the first time he saw Beatrice. What our eyes fasten on and what
draws us to the mystery of the human person is the unique configuration and
animation of the face. The beauty of Helen of Troy perturbed kingdoms: "Was
this the face that launched a thousand ships?" ("Doctor Faustus," Scene 14).
With these words the playwright, Christopher Marlowe, celebrates the striking
power of a beautiful woman's face to stir men's souls. The Song here praises
the man's encounter with his beloved face to face.

Her cheeks are laced with jewelry forming a veil that half reveals and half
conceals her face. It is this knowing her and not knowing her that draws him
further into her mysterious presence. One may imagine she wore earrings,
and likely a headband over forehead and temples supporting a curtain of
jeweled pendants. Her throat was probably circled in tiers with necklaces.

The woman is a picture of the quintessential bride of the East. "As a bride
adorns herself with her jewels" (Is 61:10), the woman in the Song is adorned.
In the ancient East wealth was passed down in precious stones and metals,
which were easily secured and moved. The family jewels were given to the
bride of the eldest son, and she wore them in splendor on their wedding day.
A rich family may have gathered over the years many necklaces inlaid with

jewels, and with all this wealth the bride's head, neck, and bosom were comparisoned. A poetic comparison with the harness trappings of a royal mare may well be plausible.

In Ezekiel we read of the Lord's everlasting mercy toward Israel, a people born like an infant helpless, poor, and naked. As Israel comes into nubile womanhood, the Lord lavishly dresses her for the divine wedding: "I clothed you with embroidered cloth and with sandals of fine leather; I bound you in fine linen and covered you with rich fabric. I adorned you with ornaments: I put bracelets on your arms, a chain on your neck, a ring on your nose, earrings in your ears, and a beautiful crown upon your head. You were adorned with gold and silver, while your clothing was of fine linen, rich fabric, and embroidered cloth" (16:10–13). And the Bible ends with the vision of the "new Jerusalem, coming down out of heaven from God, prepared as a bride adorned for her husband" (Rev 21:2).

In a spiritual reading of the Song the virtues of the soul become more beautiful than the care of the body: "Do not adorn yourselves outwardly by braiding your hair, and by wearing gold ornaments or fine clothing; rather, let your adornment be the inner self with the lasting beauty of a gentle and quiet spirit, which is very precious in God's sight" (1 Pet 3:3–4). A Christian reading might be mindful even of the crown of thorns that lends a terrible bleeding beauty to the "holy face" of Jesus in his passion, a passion prompted by a compassionate love for each human being in their agony.

1:11
We will make thee borders of gold
With studs of silver.

We will craft for you golden circlets
Enjoined with fine silverwork.

Gold and fine silverwork here describe precious jewelry. Most likely spangled bracelets, anklets, and armlets are intended. Possibly anonymous admirers or the daughters of Jerusalem are imagined as the speakers. The lover here may assume the voice of majesty, the royal we. He would give her jewelry of gold and silver to set off her loveliness. The silverwork settings attract light and add luster to the precious gold. All the metal craft bestows a magnificence intended to draw attention to the rare value of the woman herself. She is the precious jewel, the sole pearl without price, for whom "he went and sold all that he had and bought it" (Mt 13:46). The gold and silver make only an encircling setting, like the mounting for a rare diamond in a finger ring.

Gold has suited lovers because the metal is rare, highly valued, and brilliant to behold. So is the beloved in the eyes of her lover. Later she will describe his head as made of pure gold (5:11). Gold does not change; it does not rust, tarnish, or corrupt. Such love is like treasure in heaven, "where neither moth nor rust consumes and where thieves do not break in and steal. For where your treasure is, there your heart will be also" (Mt 6:20–21). The icons of the Eastern Church paint the heavenly sky golden because God's life is unending life. Beyond time, God is eternal. Human love hopes for that same everlasting communion, whose rehearsal is sought out within the lifelong promises of this world. Golden wedding bands speak a message of a love deeply cherished, a love faithfully promised, a love perduring for all times and all places, a love unto eternal life. Such a bond shares in the divine love of God for humanity.

In ancient Greek mythology Aphrodite, goddess of love, is married to Hephaestus, the god of craftmanship. She is young and beautiful; he is older and his body misshapen. From elaborate war shields to intricate jewelry, the work of the skilled metal smith seems a divine creativity. The union of feminine beauty and male creativity becomes intriguing. With divine power women create new life with the fruit of their womb; men must contrive to make something living with their hands. The love between woman and man, however, must be equally created by both of them, and the golden circlet that their lives do form is a work of mutual persevering artistry. Human bonding is the most beautiful artifact of all. In its golden setting of eternal life, such love is the work of human hands and the very creation of God.

One thinks readily also of the gifts of gold, frankincense, and myrrh brought by the kings from the East to Jesus at his birth (Mt 2:11). These gifts are metaphors that celebrate the communion of the bridegroom and the bride, Israel and its Lord God, the church and its Christ Jesus. When Peter was implored for mercy by a lame beggar at the gate of the temple he said: "I have no silver or gold, but what I have I give you; in the name of Jesus Christ of Nazareth, stand up and walk" (Acts 3:6). At heart it is always God's love that enables human love to dance.

1:12
While the King sitteth at his table,
My spikenard sendeth forth the smell thereof.

While the king was couched within,
My nard spread out its fragrance.

𝒯he Song returns to the subtle world of fragrances with their nostalgic and pervasive presence. Nard, myrrh, and henna blossom are each given a voice in this conversation of perfumes (1:12–14). Our airy breath is our life stream. The breathing out of the whole body is its especial scent. Some combination of perfumery and individual bodily character creates the allure and mystery of this intimate communication of the lovers here in the Song. Such is the ambiance of sensual romance.

"While the king was couched within" echoes an earlier line, "the king has drawn me apart to his chambers" (1:4). Royalty reclines on couches while banqueting, and this posture supported leisure and dalliance. A chaise longue or a morning bed might present the equivalent. Some sort of enclosure, probably rounded, is implied. In this privacy and seclusion with the king, her love for him expands as precious perfume pervading the whole space. One may recall Plato's "Symposium," where a discussion of the nature of love sparks the conversation. The spiritual reading of the Song has understood the king's rooms to be the temple where the Lord dwells, or the womb of Mary where the word was made flesh, or the inner soul where the Holy Spirit dwells.

Nard is a perfume derived from a plant native to the Himalayan mountains. Spikenard is pure nard, which was expensive and highly prized in the Mediterranean world. In Mark's Gospel we read: "a woman came with an alabaster jar of very costly ointment of nard, and she broke open the jar and poured the ointment on his head" (14:3). Thus the fragrance of her nard suffuses the one she loves. As Jesus tells the guests at the dining table: "she has done what she could; she has anointed my body beforehand for its burial" (Mk 14:8). Without counting the cost, she bestows her self upon the beloved. That is why Jesus promised her that "wherever the good news is proclaimed in the whole world, what she has done will be told in remembrance of her" (Mk 14:9). In the parallel version in John we read: "Mary [of Bethany] took a pound of costly perfume made of pure nard, anointed Jesus' feet, and wiped them with her hair" (12:3). The woman in the Song compares herself to the penetrating fragrance of nard in the intimacy of the king's room (see also 4:13–14). In the next line she will compare him to the lingering fragrance of myrrh in the intimacy between her breasts. Our body is our first place, the space that embodies us, and more our own than any inner room.

An adage in scholastic philosophy holds that "good is diffusive of itself" (*bonum diffusivum sui*). Love and goodness spread out to all things and to all people. Good health is shared by every cell of the body. Good political life is enjoyed by every citizen. Good family life shares its home with others. A mature love between man and woman blesses everyone they encounter. Love pervades life as a good perfume that spreads itself out. Of a king about to be espoused the psalmist says: "Therefore God, your God, has anointed you with the oil of gladness beyond your companions; your robes are fragrant with myrrh and aloes and cassia" (45:7–8). When the sister of Martha and Lazarus poured out the pure nard upon the body of Jesus, and "the house was filled with the fragrance of the perfume" (Jn 12:3), she embodied her unspeakable love for Jesus. Love spends all of herself, pours out her life, and gives of her own secret sweet essence.

1:13
A bundle of myrrh is my well-beloved unto me;
He shall lie all night betwixt my breasts.

A sachet of myrrh is my true love,
All night between my breasts.

Sachets of sweet-smelling herbs have long been used to freshen clothing. Boutonnieres worn in the lapel or corsages on the shoulder not only please the eye but persistently delight the memory with a fragrant reminder. A few central words taken from the monk's morning meditation were arranged as a spiritual nosegay to keep the soul mindful of God's love throughout the day. Lockets worn on a necklace carry an image of the beloved and warm the heart. A cross or a medal on a chain worn on the breast above the heart brings the spiritual to mind.

Myrrh is an aromatic gum or resin secreted from the stems of a shrub found abundantly in southern Arabia. In the myth of Myrrha she prays the gods to deliver her from her overwhelming illicit passion. Myrrha is turned into a tree: "She weeps, and the warm tear-drops trickle down, / Not without honor, for that distillation / Still keeps her name; men call it myrrh, no age / Will ever forget the word" (Ovid, *Metamorphoses* [10:501–04]). Myrrh was known as the fragrance of passion and the sweet perfume of love. In the description of an erotic dalliance in the book of Proverbs we read: "I have perfumed my bed with myrrh, aloes, and cinnamon. Come, let us take our fill of love until morning; let us delight ourselves with love" (7:17–18). When Joseph was sold into slavery by his brothers, the caravan of traders that bought him carried "spices and resins" into Egypt (Gen 37:25). In the book of Esther the harem maidens to be brought to the king's bed were anointed for "six months with oil of myrrh" (2:12). To the Christ child the kings from the East offered gifts of gold, frankincense, and myrrh (Mt 2:11). Myrrh was also used as a narcotic medicine for pain, and as a pungent preservative to delay the odor of death and the body's rapid decay. On Calvary the soldiers who crucified Jesus "offered him wine mixed with myrrh; but he did not take it" (Mk 15:23). With "a mixture of myrrh and aloes" (Jn 19:39) Nicodemus anoints the dead body of Jesus for burial. Above all, myrrh was expensive.

In the Song her beloved is likened to a sachet of myrrh lying between her breasts, its fragrance warmed by her own flesh. He lies next to her heart. Later in the Song his lips are described as "crimson lilies, gilded with glistening myrrh" (5:13). "Myrrh and aloes" are included in the catalog of ointments and fragrances found in the enclosed garden that is the body of the beloved (4:13–14 and 5:1), and into this garden he is invited to come. Her "fingers [are] wetted with liquid myrrh" (5:5). She is the mountain of myrrh upon which he loves to gambol (4:6). In sum, the man lying in the woman's bosom all the night is so fragrant that she needs no other perfume in the day.

Every child has known a mother's breast. The Song speaks of her mother's milk (8:1), and the Song speaks of a sister's budding breasts (8:8). The origins of life center on the feminine. She is the comfort of love and the necessity of food, and both freely given when one is hardly distinguished from the other. All this childhood delight lingers in the image of a woman's breast. Later in the Song he describes her breasts as beautiful twin fawns of a gazelle that nibble amid the lilies (4:5 and 7:4). Now she holds him tenderly as a sachet of myrrh that rests between her breasts. In the excitement of young love a woman's breast gives an indescribable comfort—not only for him, but for her. Night and day his fragrance is thus kept at heart. He abides with her both in body and in spirit. Of the divine love indwelling in us Paul writes: "Or do you not know that your body is a temple of the Holy Spirit within you, which you have from God, and that you are not your own? For you were bought with a price; therefore glorify God in your body" (1 Cor 6:19–20).

1:14

My beloved is unto me as a cluster of camphire
In the vineyards of En-gedi.

A bouquet of henna blossoms is my love
From the gardens of Engedi.

Half-way along the southwestern shore of the Dead Sea, Engedi is a wilderness oasis in a rocky ravine. The name means fountain or spring of the kids (wild goats). It is mentioned in the catalog of the cities of Judah listed in the book of Joshua (15:62). The semitropical climate and fresh water made Engedi a garden source of the best grapes, spices, and perfumes. Personified "wisdom" in her flourishing is described in Sirach: "I grew tall like a palm tree in Engedi, and like rosebushes in Jericho" (24:14).

Parallel lines in Hebrew poetry are a standard artistic device. The repetition of a similar statement provides unity, and the variation in the imagery provides diversity. She calls him a sachet of myrrh and then in parallel a bouquet of henna. Both are sweet-scented; both include intimations of intimacy. The sachet lodging between her breasts and the oasis in the wilderness suggest romance. Her body is the vineyard (1:6); she is the garden (4:12). He rests on her heart; he is rooted in her ground. Her embodied love is the oasis in the desert where his life blossoms. She is the life-giving paradise in an otherwise barren and dead landscape.

Many of the spices, perfumes, flowers, and fruits of the Song of Songs will be recognized by the reader as exotic flora. Henna is an aromatic shrub of Palestine. Al-henna is also known as camphire and as cypress. During the spring a common variety of henna blossoms with abundant clusters of creamy-white flowers. Their fragrance is penetrating and sweet. From the henna leaves and root a dusky reddish dye is extracted. To this day henna is used by women as a cosmetic to color fingernails, skin, and hair. The oil from the henna berries also provides a perfume.

Our imagination might capture the role that henna plays in the Song by considering how particular flowers bring their own rich connotation. Think of magnolias and southern hospitality, honeysuckle and summer country, orchids and prom dances, sweet-william and forget-me-nots, and my love "like a red, red rose." Perhaps clusters of lilac blossoms in early springtime best suggest the appearance and fragrance of Oriental henna. In some Palestinian wedding traditions the bridegroom brings a large bouquet of henna blossoms to the home of the bride. Hence in the Song her beloved is readily compared to a bouquet of henna blossoms. In another wedding custom both bride and groom are immersed in a perfumed bath of henna water. In his baptism the body of Jesus sanctified the waters of the Jordan river, so the beloved who lies as myrrh in her bosom or as henna in her garden perfumes her body and spreads out its combined bouquet in the king's chambers (1:12).

More than two dozen times in the Song the woman will refer to the man as the *love* of her life (Hebrew, *dodi*). She is ever mindful of him. His presence in her heart remains a sweet fragrance. In biblical history Israel had lusted after false gods. Her many idols became adulterous lovers. To keep ever in mind the commandment to love the one God alone and above all else, choice words of the Bible (Dt 6:5) were sown into a piece of cloth worn around the forehead. Gerard Manley Hopkins wrote a poem entitled "The Blessed Virgin Mary Compared to the Air We Breathe." Spiritual presence is like the breath of life we must take in day and night. Love is the spiritual breath of our soul's life, the indwelling of the God who is love in our hearts and whom we touch in one another when we love as human beings.

1:15
Behold, thou art fair, my love; behold thou art fair;
Thou hast doves' eyes.

How beautiful you are, my love,
So beautiful!
Your eyes are doves.

*T*he lover declares that his soul-love is beautiful and her eyes are all doves (see also 4:1). Later the woman speaks of his eyes as doves (5:12). Tennyson writes: "In the spring a livelier iris changes on the burnish'd dove; / In the spring a young man's fancy lightly turns to thoughts of love" ("Locksley Hall"). Doves are vivacious birds that are shy, skittish yet calm. Their flight is surprisingly agile. Doves radiate a gentle and simple peacefulness. Mauves and soft grays color the dove, and its feathers are a marvelous blend of subtle rainbow shadings. Eyes that are doves are pure, dark, innocent, large and wide-open. Unlike the hawk whose eyes are focused sharply on an elusive prey, the dove gazes all around with a timid vigilance. The iridescent iris of the dove may readily suggest a comparison with the glistening eyes of the beloved.

Addison writes: "A beautiful eye makes silence eloquent." In the story of Jacob's courtship we read: "Leah's eyes were lovely, and Rachel was graceful and beautiful" (Gen 29:17). Beautiful eyes and a beautiful body remain sisters. In the Song the woman is both Leah and Rachel. Her eyes are doves and she is beautiful: "So beautiful!" In the icons of the East the eyes are enlarged, but the ears are not prominent. It is the whole person who listens to the word of God, which is more than sound. In the Song there is no mention of ears, no music other than the poignant opera of the human voice in loving conversation. It is our eyes that are miniature globes scanning the horizon of planet earth. We can contain the whole world in our transcendent vision. The human eye is small but sees so far, even to the stars. Life emerged long ago from the oceans. In our mother's womb we floated as in a primordial sea. We see through a tiny lake within our eyeball itself. As rain washes the globe of the earth, tears bathe the ball of the eye with saltwater. God first created the light by which we see. Indeed, God is light, and with the psalmist we can say: "in your light we see light" (Ps 36:9).

To his "how beautiful you are" (1:15) she repeats "so beautiful you are" (1:16). His "so beautiful" is echoed by her "how delightful." Contrastingly he focuses on her eyes and she looks upon the space they share together. She surveys the floor and ceiling of their verdant bower (1:17). Women often focus on the general and men upon the particular. Women readily see the pattern and men the detail. He sees her eyes and she sees their home. He gazes at the beauty of the present, and she contemplates the present blending into the future. For men courtship can be now and brief. Union comes swiftly and sometimes without commitment. For women courtship includes future stability. Union ripens slowly and most often with heartfelt attachment.

For the male in the subhuman animal kingdom impregnation is the purpose behind the courtship. For the female the nest is the task and the longer-term needs of offspring. Human beings, however, are self-conscious creatures and their behavior spiritual as well as physical. Men desire willing access and women desire an enduring bond. He looks into her eyes; she looks into their surroundings. He sees her; she sees them. It is said that men give love for sex, and women give sex for love. The mature man, however, wants sex ensouled in love, and the mature woman wants love embodied in sex. Human sexuality is always more than the physical. Courtship is an introduction to the spiritual. His and her fantasies may differ, but nobody holds a mere body in their arms. Women and men draw around the bare bones of the beloved the robes of their profound dreams. Sexual union is a response not only to the beloved but also to the heart's courtship of an unknown and boundless love, for God's love implicates all loves.

1:16
Behold, thou art fair, my beloved, yea, pleasant:
Also our bed is green.

So beautiful you are, my love,
How delightful!
Our repose in green foliage.

$\mathcal{T}$he woman describes their sylvan trysting place. In the outdoors they have found their seclusion. Down to earth is their bower. The green land is their rest. Shakespeare writes: "One turf shall serve as pillow for us both; / One heart, one bed, two bosoms, and one troth" ("Midsummer Night's Dream," 2:2:41–42). Mother earth is an ancient wedding bed, fresh and ever-renewed with life, the ground of our being. In their mutual love woman and man share humbly (*humus* means soil) in the creation story. In the garden of Paradise "the Lord God formed man from the dust of the ground" (Gen 2:7). Isaiah writes: "We are the clay, and you [God] are our potter" (64:8). In the Song the man and woman create their own arbor paradise as God intended "in the beginning."

Women perhaps more easily than men find that their sexuality and their personhood cannot be separated. Within their body their sexuality is centered and wholly part of them. Women seem inclined to integrity. They experience the parts of the human body as organic, and the body itself as coherent with the whole person whom they love. Women's sexuality tends to be more physically diffused, and not as focused on genital sex as a man's. She dances with her whole body; he probably is more conscious of his feet. Where men might need integration of body and person, women might need discrimination to bring a global awareness to a particular resolution. Where men at times yearn for sight of a woman's body and the delight of female charms even anonymous, women at times may yearn for romantic and vague dreams, a prodigality of emotional attachment given without clear purpose. In the Song she does indeed delight in his beauty, but she also keeps her eye on the overall setting of their courtship. The woman finds her beloved beautiful, but she also delights in the whole circumstantial space in which they remain surrounded.

1:17
The beams of our house are cedar,
And our rafters of fir.

The beams of our abode are cedar,
The cross-beams of cypress.

$\mathcal{A}$fter describing the greenery floor of their bower the woman looks up toward the sky and the interlaced branches of the trees, which provide a shaded roof over them. One visualizes a framework of tree trunks and overarching branches, a cathedral ceiling that lifts a high canopy. Because cedar and cypress are out of place in the fields where shepherds tend their flocks, these words enjoy a poetic largesse. As Roland Murphy says succinctly, the arbor scene may be "more evocative than locative." What is suggested in this fantasy is a trysting place of forest splendor, personal secrecy, and romantic intimacy.

Cedar, cypress, juniper, pine, and fir are evergreen trees not always distinguished in the Bible with precision. The mountains of the north country were the source of the famed cedars of Lebanon. In the Song the woman describes the man's overall bearing "like Mount Lebanon, arresting as its cedars" (5:15). A long-lived and slow-growing tree, cedar is prized for all manner of wood work. Cypress is also a most durable wood. In the Bible we read that Noah was instructed to build the ark of cypress (Gen 6:14). Cypress wood hardens with age and becomes almost indestructible. Cemeteries often plant cypress trees because the enduring wood and the evergreen leaves are apt symbols of undying life.

"Cedar, cypress, and algum timber from Lebanon" (2 Chr 2:8) were valued woods, royal timbers, hauled from forests of Lebanon and floated down the coast (1 Kg 5–7). The wood of these particular trees was thought fit for the house of God in Jerusalem, the temple of God of which David dreamed and which his son Solomon constructed. The beams and ceilings of the Jerusalem temple were mostly of cedar. Cedar wood is particularly fragrant when cut into boards. Wisdom personified speaks of her dwelling place with Israel: "I grew tall like a cedar in Lebanon, and like a cypress on the heights of Hermon" (Sir 24:13). Isaiah writes: "The glory of Lebanon shall come to you, the cypress, the plane, and the pine, to beautify the place of my sanctuary; and I will glorify where my feet rest" (60:13). The forest dwelling of the man and woman in the Song is thus reminiscent of the temple indwelling of the Lord God. In the wild they know their own sanctuary in the house that beauty built: "Annihilating all that's made / To a green thought in a green shade" (Andrew Marvell, "The Garden").

The trees overhead are entwined and make a baldachino of braided branches. The Song alternates the voice of a man and woman, a warp and a woof, woven into a courtship pattern. The love life of this woman and this man are knit together with the verbal intercourse of the Song of Songs. We see entangling glances; commingled fragrances, reciprocal intimacy, and over all a web of romance gently laid like tender spring leaves on the limbs that will screen the heavens from the land. Their feet are placed on the good earth greening and their eyes look up and beyond. Their bodies are rooted in the soil but their love flowers in the fresh air. No wonder in the next verse she calls herself "a lily of the field" and her beloved "an apple tree in a dense woodland." Between the greensward and the deep blue sky their human love is suspended as the choice fruit of a garden world.

2:1
I am the rose of Sharon.
And the lily of the valleys.

I am a flower of the field.
A lily of the valley.

*T*he woman compares herself to a flower of the field. She holds herself to be but a nameless flower that blooms in springtime when the rains have past and the sun grows brighter. Isaiah writes: "The wilderness and the dry land shall be glad, the desert shall rejoice and blossom; like the crocus it shall blossom abundantly, and rejoice with joy and singing. The glory of Lebanon shall be given to it, the majesty of Carmel and Sharon. They shall see the glory of the LORD, the majesty of our God" (35:1–2). She may be teasing him with her modest claim to be just a common wildflower easily overlooked. Yet she knows she is truly beautiful in his eyes. She may be testing him in her understatement of her beauty, for even a single common wildflower remains a miracle of astonishing glory embodied in a fragile creation of a divine artistry unduplicated by any human endeavor. To be one of many spring flowers is her claim. She is common yet she is spectacular. Attractive as a flower with bright color, delicate form, soft texture, and sweet fragrance, she is a nubile young woman in her fresh bloom. The attractive robes of a woman bear a resemblance to the petals of a flower, which channel life-giving seed that will bear ripe fruit in due season.

"A lily of the valley" provides a parallel description. The first springtime flowers of the field are bulbs, which already enjoy a root system mature enough to sprout stem and blossom by the warmth of a spring sunlight. Crocus, hyacinth, tulip, narcissus, iris, cyclamen, asphodel, daffodil, scarlet martagon, and the white Easter lily have all been nominated as the "lily of the valley." The King James Bible speaks of the "rose of Sharon," which may be the wild red anemone that carpets in brilliant crimson the fields of Israel in the spring. The fertile Sharon plain runs along the coast of the Mediterranean sea between Haifa and Caesarea in Palestine. The red anemone, popularly called pasque-flower, or windflower, would fit the later simile in the Song of lips like "crimson lilies" (5:13). Shakespeare writes: "Of Nature's gifts thou mayst with lilies boast" ("King John," 3:1:53). The lily in the West and the lotus or water lily in the East are both flowers with a cup. The calyx [cup] or chalice of the lily, the Holy Grail, the womb of life, round out the life-giving associations of this flower. Whatever the specific plant, the lily in the Song surely suggests a lovely flower with delicate liliaceous petals. In the Song "lily" is best taken as a generic term for any early spring bulbous wild flower of the fields, just as the "apple," which is her metaphor for him (2:3), is a generic term for any pome both beautiful and succulent.

In artistic depiction of the annunciation, the angel Gabriel typically appears with a lily stalk in his hand. Mary, the mother of Jesus, is praised in litany as the mystical rose, the pure white lily, the fairest flower of all creation, "our tainted nature's solitary boast." In the gospel we read: "Consider the lilies [of the field], how they grow: they neither toil nor spin; yet I tell you, even Solomon in all his glory was not clothed like one of these. But if God so clothes the grass of the field, which is alive today and tomorrow is thrown into the oven, how much more will he clothe you—you of little faith!" (Lk 12: 27–28). In sum, all human beings, howsoever humble, are each and every one God's beloved and beautiful creation.

2:2

As the lily among thorns,
So is my love among the daughters.

Like a lily amid the brambles,
So the love of my soul among women.

𝒯o the woman's shy boast that she is but a "flower of the field" and a common "lily of the valley," the man counters that she stands out like a single lily in a tangle of brambles. In comparison with other women, he holds her to be a flower discovered among thorns. "No good tree bears bad fruit, nor again does a bad tree bear good fruit; for each tree is know by its own fruit. Figs are not gathered from thorns, nor are grapes picked from a bramble bush" (Lk 6:43–44). In his eyes she remains the most glorious of flowers, a lily amid brambles, all the more beautiful because the more loved.

In the flower kingdom the fruitful agenda of springtime blossoming is facilitated by rainbow colors, the fragrance of the flower, the approachability of its blossom. Flowers are attractive and their allure promotes their fruitfulness. A young maiden in the springtime flowering of her life must seem to those around her as desirable and fruitful, a woman ready for marriage and childbearing. The Bible speaks of the "fruit of the womb," and there is no fruit without the flower. There is no family life without the courtship of love. Weddings are lavishly decorated with flowers, which are beautiful in their abundant bouquet of color, shape, and scent.

From the tiny shy violet to the big brash sunflower the world of bloom is fantastic. Nature remains the supreme imagination that defines the beautiful. Who can estimate this vast glory displayed in the flora of the earth where wildflowers bloom in profusion, mostly unnoticed and hidden, yet each a triumph of creation? Tennyson speaks of how the world is somehow distilled in a single flower for those who have eyes to see and heart to embrace such mystery: "Little flower—but if I could understand / What you are, root and all, and all in all, / I should know what God and man is" ("Flower in a Crannied Wall"). No wonder that enfolded in the many petals of the rosebud a more consummate beauty is seen than meets the eye. Earthly beauty is a preview of heavenly beauty, human love a ladder to divine love, and the garden rose a prelude to the mystical rose.

In the story of the innocent Susanna [her name means lily] amid the wicked elders, this attractive and decent woman is falsely accused of adultery (Dn 13). She is altogether vulnerable with apparently no one to defend her. When she is freed by the wisdom of Daniel from the threat of her accusers, she appears all the more good because of the evil of her detractors. Against the dark background, her light shines. In the end the wheat will emerge from its entanglement with the weeds (Mt 13:24–30). And the lily is all the more transfigured in our eyes when surrounded by brambles. "Where sin increased, grace abounded all the more" (Rom 5:21).

2:3

As the apple tree among the trees of the wood,
So is my beloved among the sons.
I sat down under his shadow with great delight,
And his fruit was sweet to my taste.

As an apple tree in a dense woodland,
So is my loved one among men.
In his shadow I love to linger,
And his fruit is sugar in my mouth.

*H*aving just compared her to a lily shining among the brambles, she in turn compares him to an apple tree flourishing in a wildwood. He flowers and bears fruit in the woods where other trees are less noticed and desirable. Metaphors among lovers depend upon the ambiance. Pilots speak of their sweetheart as the air under their wings. To her this man is a tree of life, rooted in the earth and lifted to the sky, outstanding among all other forest trees.

The shade of this tree comforts her and protects her from the sun in the heat of the day (compare 1:6). Beneath his limbs she would rest. The psalmist prays for protection: "Guard me as the apple of the eye; hide me in the shadow of your wings" (17:8). Buddha came to his great enlightenment while sitting under the Bodhi tree. While sitting under a fig tree, Nathaniel is revealed to Jesus (Jn 1:48). Augustine was converted while sitting underneath a fig tree and reading a letter of St. Paul. The poet was wise who said only God can make a tree.

The edible apple is not native to biblical lands where apple trees remain rare and do not thrive in the hot dry climate. Some commentators have thought that the native quince provides the proper reference in the Song. The apricot, which was introduced into the near east from China, and which is the first fruit tree to flower in spring, has also been suggested. Any succulent fruit fleshy on the outside, such as pomegranate or plum, would also fit the context. Hence one might conclude that the apple in the Song is a generic term for any pome, both delectable and delicious, just as the lily in the Song is a generic term for any early bulbous flower, both plentiful and delicate.

In Genesis the forbidden fruit in the garden of Eden is not named. European legend speaks of Adam and Eve eating an *apple*. The apple is perhaps the quintessential fruit. It has a fragrant smell, a sweet taste, a bright color, a globular palm-sized shape, a smooth touch. From a springtime snow shower of tiny white blossoms to an autumnal tree laden with luscious fruit, the apple is quite enticing—a tree apt for paradise.

Later in the Song she will ask: "restore me with apples, / For I am so lovesick I faint" (2:5). And he will pant after her: "May your breasts be like grape clusters / And your breathing as the aroma of apples" (7:9). Her beloved is the apple of her eye, "his fruit is sugar in my mouth." Her body is for him a "paradise of pomegranates, with all the choicest fruit" (4:13), and he is invited "to come into his garden and eat of its hand-picked fruits" (4:16). Lovers would eat each other up as sweet fruit whose body becomes their body. They find in each other a banquet of delight. His "mouth is honey sweet" (5:16) and her "mouth is like a fine wine" (7:10). Wedding cake is bread made sweet-bread because blended with sugar. Ordinary life is made sweet-life when blended with human love. The Christian reader will recall the Eucharist wherein the body and blood of a divine love is given as precious bread and wine, the banquet of an eternal love and the foretaste of a future life in God's paradise. "O taste and see that the Lord is good" (Ps 34:8).

2:4

He brought me to the banqueting house,
And his banner over me was love.

To his wine rooms he transports me,
And his cover over me is love.

*J*ust as the king transported the woman in the Song to his chambers (1:4), so now her beloved transports her to his wine rooms. This royal kiosk may be a lover's fantasy of an enclosed space of intoxicating joy, such as the imagination associates with plentiful wine and celebration. The wine rooms may be cellars where wine is made, vaults where stored, or a banquet hall where wine is drunk. Indeed the vineyard itself where the wine grapes are grown may be implicated. Love's imagination need not be precise, for it dwells in much exuberance and no place is too romantic.

The King James Bible gives the wording often quoted for the conclusion of this verse: "and his banner over me was love." It has been a text dear to the heart of the commentators in the mystical tradition. Exactly what is placed over the woman has been an uncertain matter. One meaning of the Hebrew word in question suggests something like an insignia, a flag, a pennant, bunting or wrapping, an emblem of some sort. Another meaning less widely argued holds that the Song speaks here of a glance, a look, a deliberate intent. Thus his intention is love. I have chosen to render the text: "his cover over me is love." Cover includes both meanings. A cover is a banner or emblem, as a book cover, for example. A cover also suggests an implicit or not immediately apparent intent, as a cover or camouflage. She knows his intent is love in transporting her to his wine rooms, but the world does not know. Hence the thrust of the conclusion of this verse is that she set the record straight: "his cover over me is love."

In the Bible when Ruth lies down beside Boaz, he puts his mantle over her as a sign of betrothal (Rt 3). He is sleeping alongside the harvested grain to guard it at night. Harvest time was festival time replete with wine and song. It was a time of dalliance as well. Love spoken of here in the Song suggests a sexual love, but it also includes a wider love. Both the literal reading of the Song as erotic love poetry and the mystical reading as spiritual communion should be allowed complementary standing in one's mind. As all great poetry, the Song moves simultaneously on several levels.

Charity is the form of all the virtues. "Above all, maintain a constant love for one another, for love covers a multitude of sins" (1 Pet 4:7). The final end of all human activity is to love somebody. We eat the food that sustains our body in order to enable us to love somebody. We work to put a roof over our head to keep the rain from our table so that we may relate to somebody. No matter what we do, our activity is a means to love's end. To enter into a personal relationship with the spirit that is embodied in another human being gives meaning to human life. We are bereft without the cover over us that is love. "Beloved, let us love one another, because love is from God; everyone who loves is born of God and knows God. Whoever does not love does not know god, for God is love (1 Jn 4:7–8).

In the mystery of the incarnation Christians believe that whatever one does in the body touches also upon the God who is with us in our human flesh. When Jesus changed the six stone jars of water into the best wine at the wedding feast in Cana (Jn 2), the banner over wedded love was a divine love. In the transformation of wine into the body and blood of Jesus received in the Eucharist, the banner of love has become the real presence of an abiding and profound divine love. In depictions of Jesus as the victorious lamb of God, who triumphs over death, one usually sees a white banner representing the victory of the resurrection from the tomb. In the Christian funeral liturgy, a white pall, reminiscent of the dead person's baptismal robes and their promise of an eternal love, covers the coffin like a mystical flag or banner of love that is protective to the end. "And his cover over me is love."

2:5

Stay me with flagons, comfort me with apples:
For I am sick of love.

Nourish me with raisin cakes; restore me with apples,
For I am so love-sick I faint.

*B*ecause the woman feels faint, she calls out for food. Love has wounded her and taken her breath away. Her physical life is overwhelmed by the intensity of her emotional life. She wishes to consume raisins and apples, sweet foods that will restore her vitality. The very aroma of ripe fruit may have worked as a smelling-spice to revive a dazed consciousness. Some commentators have thought that raisin cakes, which were shaped into erotic images associated with pagan cult, explains the rhetoric of this passage in the Song. In his lament of the adulterous people of Israel, Hosea mentions how "they turn to other gods and love raisin cakes" (3:1). Although such cultic influences in Hebrew poetry are always possible, they rarely are proven.

Lovesickness is a vague term for romantic emotional exhaustion. "Absalom had a beautiful sister whose name was Tamar; and David's son Amnon fell in love with her. Amnon was so tormented that he made himself ill" (1 Sam 13:1–2). Shakespeare writes of Cleopatra: "The barge she sat in, like a burnish'd throne, / Burn'd on the water. The poop was beaten gold; / Purple the sails, and so perfumed that / The wind were love-sick with them" ("Antony and Cleopatra," 2:2:196–99). If the woman in the Song is undone by her love, her suffering remains bittersweet. Lovers gladly bear the pangs of their fascination. Her appeal may be addressed to anyone within hearing, or more likely to the chorus of the daughters of Jerusalem (2:7). Later she will make a similar disclosure to them: "Speak of my heartache for him" (5:8).

2:6
His left hand is under my head,
And his right hand doth embrace me.

His left hand cradles my head
And his right hand stays me.

*T*he woman discovers that only love itself cures lovesickness. She describes her lying in the arms of her beloved. We do not know whether he is present in reality or if she brings him to herself in imagination as the fulfillment of her wish to be revived with the food of love. At the end of the Song she will make the same exclamation (8:3). I have rendered the text "his right hand *stays* me," for it implies a firm embrace that calms or soothes a fretful body, which dovetails with her condition both lovesick and faint.

Human hands are healing in their wondrous touch. After the voice the hands remain the most expressive resource of the human body. In touch the feelings of the heart are embodied in a language that rivals the words of the mind. One might readily assume they are lying in each other's arms. In the Song his posture does not exclude fondling and sexual arousal, but the affection portrayed here is quite broad. The line that follows gives a caveat: "Do not rouse nor raise up love until its time is ripe." In sum, the Song recognizes a gentle rhythm in the affairs of the human heart.

A woman in love gives her heart away, and her body follows as the day the dawn. A man in love gives his body away, and his heart follows in wonder and gratitude. Passion cannot be all wrong when love is right. Juliet's love for Romeo is self-validating, as is Heloise's for Abelard, and Hester's for Arthur Dimmesdale (Nathaniel Hawthorne, *The Scarlet Letter*). Such love brings a consecration of its own prior to any social blessing given or withheld. Indeed the condition I describe is premoral. A lover feels true love is beyond the law, for the integration of body and soul is its own proof. She will want to come to establish the integrity of her love in the world, and to downplay a possessive hold on the heart's devotion to just one person and the world well lost. He will want to come to know for whom he would die, and to downplay achievement in the world accomplished regardless of love lost.

2:7

I charge you, O ye daughters of Jerusalem,
By the roes, and by the hinds of the field,
That ye stir not up, nor awake my love,
Till he please.

Give me your word, daughters of Jerusalem,
By the gazelles and wild deer of the fields.
Do not rouse nor raise up love until its time is ripe.

*C*ommentators are divided whether the speaker is the man or the woman. There is more general agreement that this line urges that love itself must not be untimely excited, rather than that the man or the woman alone must not be aroused. If the words are spoken to love personified, the case for the continuation of the woman as speaker is stronger. The daughters of Jerusalem need not be present. They may serve here as an inner foil for the soliloquy of the woman.

One may wonder why anyone would take an oath "by the gazelles and wild deer of the fields." It has been proposed that "Lord God of hosts" in Hebrew sounds somewhat like the Hebrew for gazelles and wild deer. Hence this phrase is possibly a euphemism for the divine name, which ought not be vocalized, and never so in a profane way. The English phrase "jiminy cricket" is a similar euphemism for Jesus Christ.

"Ripeness is all" says Edgar in Shakespeare's "King Lear" (5:2:11). When is the fruit ripe to pluck from its bough? "There is a time for every matter under heaven: a time to be born, and a time to die; a time to love, and a time to hate" (Eccl 3:1–2, 8). Everything has its own time. Love has its own time. The body may be ready for sex before the soul is ready for commitment. The heart may be ready for love before the mind is ready for discernment. One may propose marriage too soon, and may conclude too late. Look before you leap, but the one who hesitates is lost. There are no rehearsals for living, however, and young lovers cannot postpone loving until they are wise. Nor can the aged who have achieved a wisdom delay the passage of the body's time. One can hope that love and wisdom might overlap, for love may come early and wisdom late.

The Song urges that love be not raised up untimely. First love often generates profound emotion. Dante's young love for Beatrice perdured a lifetime. Romeo and Juliet attest to the intense loyalty of the human heart. All sexual experience that involves the gift of one's self, body and soul, creates a heartfelt bond with a partner. By its very nature human sexual intimacy links human beings to each other. Initial bodily experiences particularly impress themselves permanently on the human spirit. One can give away one's self "once and for all" only once. Often a later love cannot command that wholeheartedness that love's first encounter bestowed. First love creates a lasting bond. The person with whom one was virgin before and married thereafter shares a unique experience that can never be repeated. A threshold is crossed. If the love is profound, a lifelong gratitude will prevail. If the love is superficial, a quiet despair may follow. Nothing will be quite the same. To urge that love be heartfelt and ripe before consummated remains a genuine wisdom.

The request that love be not aroused before it is ready is repeated three times in the Song (2:7, 3:5, and 8:4). In each instance it seems to mark a clear division of the text. The command to let love emerge in due season seems to allow a break so that a new subject may be introduced. The adjuration itself calls for a strategic pause in the courtship between the woman and the man, and as such it serves well to mark a break in the development of the Song.

2:8

The voice of my beloved! behold, he cometh
Leaping upon the mountains, skipping upon the hills.

The voice I love!
Here he comes bounding down the mountain sides, springing
over the hills.

*I*n this third poem (2:8–2:17) of the Song, the woman is probably engaged in reminiscence. She recounts his words to her from a memory suffused with delight. Even the sounds of his feet running toward her speak his devotion. She remembers a welcome visit from him in the springtime. Joyfully she recalls her sight of him striding down the mountains, skipping over the hills, running toward her home while calling out her name. In short, she sees him and she hears him—the man she loves!

His voice carries an invitation, and as the scene develops he will propose to come away with her. Winter's withdrawal is over; spring's pressing approach is nigh. To be swept away by the impulsion of passion is a dear fantasy in the hearts of young lovers. Love runs to the beloved. In a courtship display, described here as a dance of graceful leaps, he approaches her presence and woos her consent to run off with him.

The *word* of God opens the creation story in the Bible. God speaks a sovereign *word,* and there is light. No one sees God; we know God's presence by the impact of God's *word.* After their fall from grace, Adam and Eve "heard the sound of the LORD God walking in the garden at the time of the evening breeze" (Gen 3:8). The first man and woman hear God, but because of their sin they hide in fear. The woman in the Song is not fearful; the voice she loves comes to seek her out and to propose their union. Their love is altogether innocent. Subsequently the man will ask to see her face and to hear her voice.

Then her word becomes melody to his ear (2:14 and 8:13), and they would sing their love.

The Song of Songs is read in the Jewish synagogue during passover season. Isaiah writes: "How beautiful upon the mountains are the feet of the messenger who announces peace, who brings good news, who announces salvation, who says to Zion, 'Your God reigns'"(52:7). The Christian reading will hear the voice of John, the precursor of Jesus, the "voice of one crying out in the wilderness . . . make his paths straight. Every valley shall be filled, and every mountain and hill shall be made low" (Lk 3:4–5). The Word of God is the only Son, the beloved of God and the divine bridegroom. God spoke and love was made flesh. Henceforth earthly love is the sign of heavenly love, and human life finds its fulfillment in the divine. Through the word of God made flesh the soul enjoys a spiritual communion that celebrates the love story at the heart of all love stories, the love of God for humankind. Such love bodes no obstacles in its path. Human history is a "divine comedy," wherein the marriage of the human and the divine may be delayed by the unfolding of human history complicated by its sinfulness, but the wedding feast at the last is assured. So it is in the Song.

2:9

My beloved is like a roe or a young hart:
Behold, he standeth behind our wall,
He looketh forth at the windows,
Showing himself through the lattice.

My beloved is like a gazelle, a young hart.
There he stands beside our wall,
Peering in the windows, looking through the latticework.

*H*e bounds across the hills in eager search for her. She surveys the fields of his fellow shepherds to find him (1:7–8). She will again seek him in the city in the dead of night (3:1–4). Pursuing the beloved is bittersweet pleasure, for while the absence is bitter the yearning is sweet. "Parting is such sweet sorrow." In the Song the initiative is often hers, but regardless of who begins the courtship dance of hide and seek, the other follows with a corresponding invitation.

Gazelles are antelope native to biblical lands. Like the feral deer they are shy and small, agile and graceful, creatures of slender limbs and fragile beauty. The etymology of the Hebrew word for gazelle is related to the word for beauty. Their large wide-open liquid black eyes make them seem aware of their vulnerability. In the popular imagination the stag or young buck is particularly a symbol of sexual prowess. Later in the Song her beloved is again compared to a gazelle, that is swift and bounds over the mountains in delight of her (2:17 and 8:14).

He comes alongside her dwelling. "Our wall" suggests she is living in her family house. We hear several times later of her mother, although never of her father. Her brothers are mentioned at the beginning and ending of the Song. They act as father surrogates who discipline their younger sister (1:6 and 8:8). He comes not to peek furtively like a peeping tom. As he calls out to her, he is steadfastly gazing into her windows in hope of finding her at home. She hears his voice. He yearns to see her face. She dwells on his words sounding in her heart. He wants to see the beloved before his eyes. She listens; he looks. She is aroused by his voice, and he by her appearance. They are both rapt in anticipation.

We do not know exactly what the wall, windows, and latticework represent. All three Hebrew words are used only in the Song and not elsewhere in the Bible. There may be screens or shutters on the windows of her home. In romantic terms she is the house and he seeks entry. Later he will knock and ask her to open her bedroom door in the middle of the night and let him in (5:2).

The mystical tradition has read this verse of the Song as the divine courtship of the human soul. And divine love is everlasting. Paul writes: "For we know that if the earthly tent we live in is destroyed, we have a building from God, a house not made with hands, eternal in the heavens" (2 Cor 5:1).

She speaks:

Here he comes bounding down the mountain sides, springing
over the hills. (2:8)

My beloved is like a gazelle, a young hart.
There he stands beside our wall,
Peering in the windows, looking through the latticework. (2:9)

2:10

My beloved spake, and said unto me,
Rise up, my love, my fair one, and come away.

My love speaks and says to me:
Rise up, love of my soul, my beauty, come away!

The woman amplifies in her memory his words. He "sings" to her a spring-time lyric of a lover courting his beloved. The young human heart brims over with expectation and desire just as springtime itself swells with the buds of new growth. Flowers finally break forth and express the rising sap and new-found vigor pressing upward for new and more abundant life on earth. Shall not man and woman in their love for each other rise up with fertile bodies and dance along with all the rejuvenated creation in the miracle of spring? "Rise up, love of my soul, my beauty, come away!" is repeated verbatim at the end of this courting invitation (2:13).

He appears to speak to her, but what she reports is likely a conversation that has already taken place. This whole passage of the Song suggests a prolonged reminiscence of an earlier welcome visit from the beloved. He invites her to come away with him into the countryside. It is spring and the whole earth is coming to life from winter's sleep. Up and away! Later she will invite him to a lovers' tryst in the burgeoning planted fields: "come, my heart's love, come into the fields, / Let us pass the night amid the villages" (7:12). Throughout the Song she is the garden; her gift of self is its cherished fruit. Tenderly she welcomes her true love to "come into his garden and eat of its hand-picked fruits" (4:16). He would draw her not only to come away from her house (2:10), but also to come down from the mountain heights where in his fantasy he imagines her most inaccessible: "Come down from Lebanon, my bride, come along with me from Lebanon" (4:8). Even more poignantly he will ask her to let him come into her bedroom in the early hours of the morning: "Open up to me, my sister, love of my soul, my dove, my perfection!" (5:2). Back and forth they exchange invitations to come away. To his busy disciples Jesus says: "Come away to a deserted place all by yourselves and rest a while" (Mk 6:31). To the disciple, Nathaniel, following Jesus and asking him where is he staying, he turns and invites him: "Come and see" (Jn 1:39). And thereafter he will follow him.

His plea to her is not only to come away into the fields but to rise up. The gift of love is to be an elevation of her life. The religious sensibility will hear echoes of the resurrection theme of Eastertide. This mortal life is invited to rise up and come into the fields of eternal life by the God who is revealed as love itself. In the gospel Jesus brings to life again his friend Lazarus, the brother of Martha and Mary. Jesus cried with a loud voice, "'Lazarus come out!' The dead man came out, his hands and feet bound with strips of cloth, and his face wrapped in a cloth. Jesus said to them, 'Unbind him, and let him go'" (Jn 11:44). In the imaginative depictions of the descent of Jesus into hell, he calls out to those who died and were restrained in that land of darkness and bids them come forth. Then he leads them through the now open gates of heaven. In the mystical tradition the way to God is given even in this life when, lifting our minds and hearts to God, we come away and pray.

2:11
For, lo, the winter is past,
The rain is over and gone;

Lo, winter is over, the rains are done and gone.

Winter seems never-ending just before the approach of Spring. Weariness with the cold and cloudy season oppresses the human spirit. Life cannot endure without the warm light of sunshine that grows the food our bodies must consume. Because the atmosphere insulates the earth, even when the sun has turned and the days no longer grow shorter, the cold lingers behind the coming of the light. Winter thus dawdles; it never seems quite over. Human yearning for spring and its expectation are quite drawn out. With warmer days the heart expands and hope blossoms out. Winter is finally over. The season of night and cold is done and gone. To bend Shakespeare to our purpose: "now is the winter of our discontent / Made glorious summer" ("Richard III," 1:1:1–2).

In Palestine the cold winter air brings the rains that will give moisture for the spring harvest. While we know from the popular lyric that April showers bring May flowers, we never know for sure that the spring rains are over. Showers follow each other in waves. Our hopes of sunshine are brightened and then drowned out. The rainy season, like winter itself, can seem endless.

The Song promises the end of the dreary rains, which are also "done and gone." The sun has broken through the clouds. Light has overcome darkness. New spring life has won out over winter death.

In a religious context the death-dealing waters of the great flood in the Genesis story are contrasted with the life-giving waters of baptism. Now is the time of the rainbow in the sky, when the sun of God's day breaks out of the clouds and color returns to the earth. The dove that brings back to Noah's ark an olive branch of peace on earth suggests a comparison with springtime when "the murmuring of the mourning dove is heard throughout our land" (2:12).

2:12

The flowers appear on the earth;
The time of the singing of birds is come,
And the voice of the turtle is heard in our land;

Flowers spring from the earth; pruning-time is here,
And the murmur of the mourning dove is heard throughout
   our land.

$\mathcal{P}$oets will say that the flowers bloom in spring because the earth is full of joy. Theologians will say that the blossoming earth reveals the hidden delight of the creator shining forth in fragile petals of ravishing colors. Botanists will say that the flowers provide a courtship display designed by an insistent nature bent keenly upon fertility and fruitfulness. Whatever their reason to be, the flowers of springtime have ever cheered the hearts of human beings. The word for flowers in the Hebrew text in the Song is the diminutive form of the word for sparkle. One might imagine a field dotted with tiny gem-colored wildflowers, eye-catching blossoms radiant on the land, just as golden sparkles of sunshine that ripple on the surface of a lake. We are dazzled by their carpet display. Even the prevailing monochrome desert scene has its moment of glory when shy but brilliant spring flowers decorate an arid landscape. Indeed, we are overwhelmed with the abundant and lavish bouquet of the wildflowers of the earth. Gerard Manley Hopkins writes:

> Nothing is so beautiful as Spring—
> When weeds, in wheels, shoot long and lovely and lush;
> Thrush's eggs look little low heavens, and thrush
> Through the echoing timber does so rinse and wring
> The ear, it sounds like lightning to hear him sing; . . .
> What is all this juice and all this joy?
> A strain of earth's sweet being in the beginning
> In Eden garden.
>
> ("Spring")

If one makes allowance for the later springtime in a more northern clime, one might capture the tone of this line of the Song in the popular song—"June is bustin' out all over" (Richard Rodgers).

The cultivated vineyards are also in bloom. The grapes are beginning to form. Pruning-time comes in the early spring at the end of dormancy. Delight in this moment when the harvest is all budding promise is evident several times in the Song (2:15, 6:11, 7:13). The Hebrew text here is not easily construed, and the King James reads: "the time of the singing (of birds) is come." Whether the language points to the courtship singing of the birds before they build their nests or to the springtime cultivation of the vineyard, the fauna or the flora, the implication is the same. Spring is the time to husband the forces of the birds and the bees so that the fruits of all the earth may be set agrowing before the winter comes back again. Spring is the time of courting and nesting. Spring is the time to be fruitful and to nurture life.

The murmuring of the dove completes the scene of the spring tryst of the lovers in the Song. Smaller and more brownish than the domestic pigeon of modern cities, the mourning dove has a peculiarly soft plaintive voice. The mourning dove is a close cousin of the doves of Palestine, such as the migratory turtle dove. The soughing of nesting doves has long been symbolic of lovers whispering inarticulate endearments to each other. Lovers are imagined as two "love birds," and "lovey-dovey" is colloquial for romance.

Mother earth remains here the haunting overarching metaphor, and April the time. In a spiritual reading of the Song one might hear echoes of another love song: "'I am the true vine, and my Father is the vine grower. He removes every branch in me that bears no fruit. Every branch that bears fruit he prunes to make it bear more fruit . . . . Abide in me as I abide in you. Just as the branch cannot bear fruit by itself unless it abides in the vine, neither can you unless you abide in me. I am the vine, you are the branches" (Jn 15:1–5).

2:13

The fig tree putteth forth her green figs,
And the vines with the tender grape give a good smell.
Arise, my love, my fair one, and come away.

On the fig tree green fruit is ripening,
And the blossoms of the vine perfume the air.
Rise up, love of my soul, my beauty, come away!

*F*igs and grapes add another dimension to springtime in the Song. Their fruits are food and drink. The first fruit mentioned in the Bible is the fig, quite plausibly the forbidden fruit in the story of Adam and Eve. "So when the woman saw that the tree was good for food, and that it was a delight to the eyes, and that the tree was to be desired to make one wise, she took of its fruit and ate; and she also gave some to her husband, and he ate. Then the eyes of both were opened, and they knew that they were naked; and they sewed *fig* leaves together and made themselves aprons" (Gen 3:6–7).

Under the shade of a fig tree or vine arbor a gardener might enjoy relief from the heat of the sun. In restful tranquility one might contemplate the sweet ripening of summer fruits. To linger in their shade was a sign of peace and prosperity (1 Kg 4:25). To this Edenic world first glimpsed in the early fruit and tender blossoms of springtime, the man invites her to come away. The beginning bloom of love in Israel's youth in the desert recalls the courtship love of God: "Like grapes in the wilderness I found Israel. Like the first fruit on the fig tree, in its first season, I saw your ancestors" (Hos 9:10).

The blossoms of the fig tree are inconspicuous, and in spring the unripe green fruit appears before the leaves open out. These early figs promise a later sweetness. Jesus uses the fig tree to teach a lesson about awaiting the fullness of time. "From the fig tree learn its lesson: as soon as its branch becomes tender and puts forth its leaves, you know that summer is near" (Mt 24:32). When ripe the fig fruit splits open, the pink flesh within is suggestive of the flush of sexual attractiveness, and the many seeds of sexual fruitfulness. T. S. Eliot writes: "At the first turning of the third stair / was a slotted window bellied like the fig's fruit" (*Ash Wednesday,* III, 12–13).

The Song is frequently the account of a woman's courting a man, but here she is thinking back on his wooing of her. "Rise up, love of my soul, my beauty, come away!" He sees in her more than meets the eye. In the beauty of the body lies a hidden promise. Romance brings us a hint of heaven regained, a peek at the beauty behind all beauty, a foretaste of the goodness and delight of endless bliss, a pledge of God who is the joy of our youth. We would see God face to face. Whether nostalgia for past joy or pledge of future happiness, whether cornucopia of life here and now or hope of a new heaven and a new earth, woman remains for man, and man remains for woman a promise of a further mystery. In our love and its wild fascination we draw each other to own that secret desire to dwell with God in the embrace of an infinite ecstasy.

It is in Bethphage [which means "house of unripe figs"] that Jesus begins his Easter procession into Jerusalem. The palm branches laid down by his followers carpet the road. Not until Calvary will it be manifest that the cross is the tree of life on which hangs the eternal fruit. The life of springtime must pass through the burdening of a long hot summer before the fruit is harvested. In the Song, "rise up, love of my soul, my beauty, come away!" repeats the lover's earlier invitation (2:10). He is insistent; the journey of love begins with a first step. Now is not the time to fret about how winding the trail may become. Love blooms in spring in its rich splendor, and the memory of its extravagant prodigality must sustain lovers all along the long way. It would be hard to find in all the Bible, and indeed in all of fine literature, a more inviting lyric of spring (2:8–13).

2:14

O my dove, that art in the clefts of the rock, in the secret
   places of the stairs,
Let me see thy countenance, let me hear thy voice;
For sweet is thy voice, and thy countenance is comely.

My dove, in the clefts of the rock,
In the crannies of the cliff,
Let me look upon you and listen to your voice,
For your face is fair, and your voice is melody.

*W*hen frightened a dove will not leave its hiding place. Like swallows, the rock-doves find crevices and holes in the rocky fastness where they can nest in safety. Jeremiah writes: "Leave the towns, and live on the rock. . . . Be like the *dove* that nests on the sides of the mouth of a gorge" (48:28). Doves make up a large family of birds (Columbidae), and the rock-dove is the feral pigeon often domesticated in our cities. Pigeonholes in our desks are reminiscent of the tiny tight spaces that these shy birds require for their refuge. Rock-doves are monogamous lovebirds and tender caregivers with their nestlings. Like a dove, the woman in the Song is hidden, inaccessible to pursuit in the "clefts of the rock" and the "crannies of the cliff." The psalmist writes: "O that I had wings like a *dove!* I would fly away and be at rest; truly, I would flee far away; I would lodge in the wilderness; I would hurry to find a shelter for myself from the raging wind and tempest" (Ps 55:6–8). And Jesus sending his disciples forth "like sheep into the midst of wolves" warns them "to be wise as serpents and innocent as *doves*" (Mt 10:16).

Because she is a gentle woman with tender voice and soft dove eyes (1:15), she is called "my dove" by her beloved. Later we will hear: "Open up to me, my sister, love of my soul, my *dove,* my perfection!"(5:2), and "One, only one is my *dove,* / So perfect, the treasure of her mother, the dearest of her who birthed her" (6:9). Desirous to see her face and hear her voice, he is calling her forth from the protection of the rocks. He courts her physical presence, for her face represents her whole bodily person and her voice her soul. Even though her heart may be ready, she still delays to come away with him. Their courtship ritual remains a delightful verbal dance like the aerial display of mating doves. In reminiscence she here delights in their amorous ways, exquisitely played out and yet well assured that in the end "my beloved is mine and I am his"(2:16).

In a spiritual reading of the text, the image of the dove carries overtones of peace, love, and sacrifice. In religions that worship female deities, the dove as symbol of the realm of heaven hovers about the figure of the love goddess, such as Venus Columba. In mythology the soul separated from the body flew to the heavens in the form of a dove. Columbaria (from *Columba* or dove) are small niches like dovecotes designed to house the cinerary urns that contain the ashes of the dead. In pictorial representation of the incarnation of Jesus the overshadowing of the Virgin Mary almost always shows a descending dove. Joseph and Mary offer in the temple "a pair of *turtledoves* or two young pigeons" as the ritual redemption of the life of their first-born son (Lk 2:24). In John's baptism of Jesus in the Jordan river "the Holy Spirit descended upon him in bodily form like a *dove*. And a voice came from heaven, 'You are my Son, the Beloved; with you I am well pleased'" (Lk 3:22). The Song's portrayal of the woman as a dove hidden in the rock thus carries overtones of much more than just a human love story. Woman is also Godlike and shows forth God. Eve as well as Adam is made in the image of God.

In truth God is the face of love, and God is the voice of love, hidden in the world and yet even now manifest. The psalmist writes: "My soul thirsts for God, for the living God. When shall I come and behold the face of God?" (42:2). Jesus becomes the revelation of the Father and the word of God made flesh, "what we have heard, what we have seen with our eyes, what we have looked at and touched with our hands, concerning the word of life" (1 Jn 1:1).

2:15
Take us the foxes,
The little foxes, that spoil the vines:
For our vines have tender grapes.

Corral the foxes, the small foxes that ravage the vineyards,
For now our vineyard is all blossom.

*A*fter the grape vines blossom, the new grapes begin to form. Now they need protection from wily ravagers. Small foxes find their way through any opening in the vineyard enclosure. They burrow dens and ruin roots; they despoil the fruit. Hence the alarm to capture the foxes. One might recall Aesop's fable of the fox who could not quite reach the grapes and pretended they were worthless. Thus "sour grapes" became a proverbial expression for desire frustrated and then scorned. And Jesus says of himself: "Foxes have holes, and birds of the air have nests; but the Son of Man has nowhere to lay his head" (Lk 9:58).

It is likely the woman is the speaker. The motivation for her exclamation remains uncertain. Does she singsong to him a festival ditty well known to the vine tenders of the countryside? He asks to hear her voice; now he has heard it, but without any revelation of an inner consent to his invitation. Does she make up a bit of nonsense to keep him at bay? Or is the line a part of a courtship song? Is she teasing him, comparing him to a sly fox, the male predator of "little red riding-hood" fame and of whom all good girls are taught to be careful? Jesus calls the wicked King Herod "that fox" (Lk 13:32).

She is the vineyard in so many instances throughout the Song from beginning to end: "on my own vine I spent no care" (1:6) and "my own vineyard is mine alone to give" (8:12). The vineyard is the quintessential garden—fragrant blossoms, rest in the shade from the heat of the day, fruit to eat and wine to drink, and an inebriation foreshadowing the joy of sexual passion. However, like the dove in the rock or like the vineyard all hedged around, she seems inaccessible to his desires. Ensconced in her dwelling she teases and coyly flirts with him. Does she say here a no that means yes? Coquetry creates that delicate balance of moving away and moving toward someone at one and the same time. Half the fun can be in the chase.

This line about the wild foxes remains light-hearted. Yet, overtones of a heavier awareness may be heard. Some pursuing can be a stalking. Rapaciousness in all its manifestations remains the fundamental human sin. To take what must be given is always evil. Adam and Eve rip off the forbidden fruit. Sinful persons snatch what does not belong to them. The sinner claims a lordship over his or her own happiness. Howsoever rationalized, rapacious invasion is never love. The fox thus becomes a symbol of any deflowering disguised by guile. In contrast the lovers in the Song always give themselves to each other. In that mutual bestowal is their vineyard enclosed.

2:16
My beloved is mine, and I am his:
He feedeth among the lilies.

My beloved is mine and I am his.
He feeds among these lilies.

$\mathcal{M}$utual shared love is the height of human love. He "is mine and I am his" reflects the woman's understanding of the self-gift of love. They belong to each other. More easily said than done, but the words are here a promise as well as a present achievement. Later in the Song the same reciprocal love is proclaimed but in reverse order: "I am my beloved's and he is mine" (6:3). Body and soul she is neither more nor less his than he is hers. In a spiritual vein one might hear an echo of the reciprocal love of the Lord God for the beloved people of Israel. "Then you shall live in the land that I gave your ancestors; and you shall be my people and I will be your God" (Ezk 36:28). Or "I will put my law within them, and I will write it on their hearts; and I will be their God, and they shall be my people" (Jer 31:33).

Earlier in the Song she called herself "a lily of the valley" (2:1). "He feeds among these lilies" suggests he feeds on her. She is his pasture, his garden, his vineyard, his flower and its fruit. "My heart's love came down to his garden, to the beddings of spice, / To meander in this garden and to browse among the lilies. / I am my beloved's and he is mine. / He feeds among these lilies" (6:2–3). He delights in her body as in a bed of lilies. She delights in being his food and in sustaining his life. One might hear a spiritual echo of a provident and loving God: "The Lord is my shepherd, I shall not want. He makes me lie down in green pastures; he leads me beside still waters; he restores my soul" (Ps 23:1–2).

Like the orchid the lily is an exotic flower, which evokes an erotic ambiance. Lilies appear to be a symbol for physical intimacy. The soft, crenelated, labile tissues of the lily suggest sensitivity. They are beautiful to behold and easily bruised. Lips are compared to lilies (5:13), and feeding among the lilies suggests kissing. The Song later describes the woman's breasts as "a pair of fawns, the twins of a gazelle, that nibble amid the lilies" (4:5). Small fawns meandering in a field of scented lilies would easily be covered with their fragrance. Her breasts are scented sweet, for she says he rests between her breasts as "a sachet of myrrh" (1:13).

Quite simply the woman in the Song delights in his enjoyment of her sexuality, which surrounds herself. Still, their erotic life is not a world apart. She has a past full of feelings and memories. The several references to her mother's care are a reminder that she is connected to a history (see 3:4, 6:9, 8:1, 8:2, 8:5). She also has a future with all its uncertainties and need for faithful care. The satisfactions localized in parts of the body are given life by their connection to the whole body and by the body's life-bond to family and to the support of others.

When one has no intention of cultivating mind and heart, one asks a person to split the body from the self and its wholeness. There is no hint in the Song of such a disintegration of body feelings and personal commitment. The human body is integral. The human person ought never be a sexual object, convenient and reusable, to be taken up now and discarded later. Every part of us is part of something else and all parts are related to the whole. Our bones connect. One cannot take just the promise of joy that is the sexual experience. That promise is connected to the whole person, body and soul, and destined for God. One cannot fairly take just the moment. The moment is always a moment bound for eternity. The soul of the Song resides in its capture of the present paradisical moment without any moralism ("he feeds among these lilies") together with a lasting bonding ("my beloved is mine and I am his"). Here is a celebration of physical love between equals, which promises joy and responsible caring.

2:17
Until the day break, and the shadows flee away,
Turn, my beloved,
And be thou like a roe or a young hart
Upon the mountains of Bether.

Until the evening breeze rises and shadows dissolve,
Turn back to me, my heart's love;
Be like a gazelle or a young hart on the mountains of Bether.

*S*hadows dissolve both with the coming of daybreak that drives away darkness and the coming of nightfall that obscures the light that casts shadows. The planet Venus is sometimes the morning star and sometimes the evening star. Whether it is dawn or dusk remains unclear in this scene of the Song. If dawn, the night tryst must end, but she wishes him to stay "until the day break, and the shadows flee away" (King James version). If dusk she invites him before it becomes dark to gambol "like a gazelle" over the mountains. The psalmist writes: "I am gone like a shadow at evening" (109:23). More likely the scene is set in the early evening. In Palestine the cool breeze from the Mediterranean sea flows over the land in the evening. In the Genesis story Adam and Eve "heard the sound of the Lord God walking in the garden at the time of the evening breeze, and the man and his wife hid themselves from the presence of the Lord God among the trees of the garden" (3:8). Night is falling and he must leave her. Later in the Song we again read: "When the evening breeze rises and shadows dissolve, / I will draw near the mountains of myrrh, the hills of incense" (4:6).

No one knows for sure what mountains are here intended. Bether in its etymology may signify hills riven by valleys or deep canyons. Some readers see a veiled allusion to the female figure of the beloved. The resemblance of the female breasts to mountains has not been lost on the male imagination (for example, the Grand Tetons in the Rocky Mountains). An undulating landscape might suggest the curvaceous body of the woman. The mons veneris is an ancient icon of female sexuality as a sacred mountain of the goddess of love. One need not be so explicit, however, and the Song is never indelicate. The erratic and playful pursuit of the lover would explain the scene. Turning his attention with a direct gaze upon the beloved, he yet moves like a gazelle that changes direction so spontaneously as he romps on the mountain sides. "Turn back to me, my heart's love" need not mean he has left her, but that she wishes him never to run away. Earlier we read: "Here he comes bounding down the mountain sides" (2:8). And the last line of the Song echoes this same passionate yearning: "Leap up and away, my own love, / Like a gazelle or a young stag upon the mountains of spices!" (8:14).

The whole poem (2:8–2:17) is her sustained recollection of him. Never go away, she says. Her daydream is a woman's reveling in her welcome of romantic play that she knows in advance will come again. She is rehearsing in her heart the delight of being desired over and over again. In effect she says to him: I am all yours, my beloved. The vineyard blossoms and the field of lilies are yours and you are mine. Make the most of them. Frolic at will. Seize the day!

En*thu*siasm stems from the Greek root word for God (*Theo*). There is no human passion surpassing the mystic's love for the divinity. How astonishing the human spirit dancing in an ecstasy of delight on the holy mountain of the infinite and transcendent God. The revelation of God's love on Mount Horeb as well as the transfiguration on Mount Tabor remain intimate beyond words! That God wishes to be so approached and so known is more than anyone might have dreamed.

3:1

By night on my bed I sought him whom my soul loveth:
I sought him, but I found him not.

On my bed in the night I sought my soul's sole love.
I sought for him but found him not.

*N*ighttime in the poem follows the evening setting that concludes the previous poem (2:17). Entwined in sleep man and woman cleave to each other in the night. Their bodies conform to the curve of their other half. They are nested together in the dark. Shakespeare's Juliet cries out: "Come, gentle night, come, loving, black-brow'd night, / Give me my Romeo" (3:2:20). Later the woman in the Song will say to the man: "let us pass the night amid the villages" (7:12). Now alone she is sleepless on her bed in the night because her heart is restless. In the middle of the night the human heart is at times pierced with a feeling of desolate aloneness. Has she lost her beloved? Has she ever known him? In a spiritual reading one may think of the dark night of the soul in the experience of the mystics, or of the isolation of Jesus in the agony in the garden of Gethsemani when the disciples fell asleep: "And it was night" (Jn 13:30).

Shakespeare says: "We are such stuff / As dreams are made on" ("Tempest," 4:1:156). Perhaps she is only daydreaming, reminiscing with alarming fantasy upon an incident in the past when they were apart and she thought him lost to her. Perhaps she is dreaming. Her fear turns the dream into an anxious nightmare. And perhaps she is recounting an actual experience of looking for her beloved in the middle of the city in the middle of the night. She may have missed a rendezvous; he may not have come to her as promised. Are we awake or are we dreaming when we are deeply in love?

A similar seeking occurs later in the Song (5:2–7). Then the beloved knocks on her bedroom door. Awakened suddenly she hesitates to open her door, and when she does undo the lock, he is nowhere to be seen. Frantic with despair that she has turned him aside when she should have invited him inside, the woman dashes through the darkened city. Accosted by the night watchmen, she seeks in vain the one she loves and has lost. And who in love has not known something of the "the terrors of the night" (3:8)?

The Song of Songs remains playful yet serious courtship. The man and woman seem to enjoy an adult game of "hide and seek." They delight to tease each other. He hides amid his fellow shepherds; she hides in the hollows of the rock like a shy dove. The theme of all dramatic comedy is the concatenation of obstacles to a final happiness. The marriage is eagerly anticipated but regrettably delayed. Untimely separation and seemingly hopeless anguish are finally resolved in the end with the marriage ceremony, the banquet feast, the blissful ending. They live happily ever after.

In Shakespeare's "Tempest," Prospero would have his daughter's suitor earn by hard labor his welcome to Miranda's heart and hand in marriage. He is given a huge pile of wood to chop. She remains at his side to make his labor sweet in the deserving of her. The reception of the gift is always made more delicious by the enticement, the anticipation, and the delay of the consummation. We allow ourselves to grow hungry that we might better feast. The Song enjoys this delightful seesaw of search and find, of sadness and joy, paradise lost and paradise regained. If all of life remains ultimately a search for the hidden God whom the human heart loves, human courtship is a wonderful rehearsal. In the gospel we are promised: "'Ask, and it will be given you; search, and you will find; knock, and the door will be opened for you'" (Mt 7:7).

In his account of the mystical union with God in prayer, John of the Cross wrote love poems to speak the unspeakable:

In dark night
with longings kindled into loves
—O lucky venture!

I set out unseen,
my household now at rest.

In darkness and in safety,
by the secret ladder, in disguise,
—O lucky venture!—
in the shadows and in hiding there,
my household now at rest.

In the lucky night,
in secret so nobody saw me
and I saw no thing,
with no light no guide other
than that burning in my heart.

It guided me
more sure than noonday light
to where awaiting me
was someone I knew well,
there where no one appeared.

O guiding night!
O night more lovable than dawn!
O night uniting
love with loved one,
changing her into her love!

Against my flowering breast,
all kept for him alone,
he lay asleep
and I was fondling him,
and fanning cedars gave a breeze,

The castle air,
as I played with his hair,
and he with his serene hand

touched me on my neck,
and put all of my senses in suspense.

I lay and I forgot,
my face reclined upon my love;
all ceased and I let go,
leaving my care
among the lilies out of mind.

> Translation and copyright by John Dunne, C.S.C., in *Love's Mind: An Essay on the Contemplative Life* (Notre Dame, Indiana: University of Notre Dame Press, 1993) 100–101.

3:2

I will rise now, and go about the city
In the streets, and in the broad ways
I will seek him whom my soul loveth;
I sought him, but I found him not.

I will rise up and comb the city,
In the roads and crossroads I will seek out the love of my
    soul.
I sought for him but found him not.

*S*he leaves her bed. She bestirs herself to find the beloved. High and low, far and wide, in roads and crossroads, everywhere she seeks out her "love of my soul." The searching of the woman is reminiscent of the perennial search of the human soul for love itself. In mythology Psyche searches the night for Eros, who represents the mystery of love once glimpsed and then lost to sight. Was her visitor in the night her true love or a monster in the dark? Once having lost Eros, Psyche must then search throughout her life in the highways and byways to find the love she once knew in dark mystery. So unfolds the fall from grace, the loss of innocence, the child turned adult, the wonder become doubt.

Isaiah writes of seeking God: "My soul yearns for you in the night, my spirit within me earnestly seeks you" (26:9). Mary of Nazareth says to Jesus: "Child, why have you treated us like this? Look, your father and I have been searching for you in great anxiety" (Lk 2:48). Mary of Magdala exclaims to the one she loves, whom she mistakes for the gardener: "Sir, if you have carried him away, tell me where you have laid him, and I will take him away" (Jn 20:15). Paul writes: "For now we see in a mirror, dimly, but then we will see face to face" (1 Cor 13:12).

Advent is indeed the human season. Always we must wait to find the beloved. Our temporal life is an ongoing search for a boundless love for whom our soul ever yearns. The divine comedy is the human soul in search of its divine spouse, who all along is hidden yet eagerly waiting to be found. Human beings were created to be joined in love with their creator. Indeed, absence amplifies presence. Greater the joy when the beloved is lost and then found.

Solitude is an unavoidable aloneness, which is mindful that it is the human predicament to be a-part, alone, all-one. Solitude is well distinguished from the loneliness that the love of another can overcome. No one, however, who holds a loved one in their arms through the night escapes solitude. The other remains other, however intimate the touch. We would cleave to each other, but we can never merge. We strive to be as one, yet we must remain ourselves. We ever remain tangled lovers, who promise each other a communion whose inevitable shortcomings leave us all the more in solitude in the middle of the night. Only in God who is everything is no one of us ever alone. Only God is always with us, around us, and in us. The creator alone in all ways sustains us in our being.

And in faith we know the Holy Spirit ever dwells in each human body as in a temple. Most of our life we are asleep to this divine love. Paul writes with a sense of urgency: "you know what time it is, how it is now the moment for you to wake from sleep. For salvation is nearer to us now than when we became believers; the night is far gone, the day is near" (Rom 13:11–12).

Like the woman in the Song, we need the courage to seek the beloved with all the risks of a fully responsible human vocation to love another and to love God even in the night. Note how her search is active. She sought him and found him not, and rather than wait passively for the beloved to appear, she goes after him, even in the dark, and even in danger. She must be confident of herself, knowing herself strong, and she must want him very much.

3:3

The watchmen that go about the city found me:
To whom I said, Saw ye him whom my soul loveth?

The night-watchmen discovered me in their rounds of the city. Have you seen my sole love?

The nightwatch was a precaution against the terrors of the night, especially marauders in the dark when the city was asleep. The patrol would walk the city walls (city limits) with an eye to quell any disturbance of the peace. Police cruising city streets at night provide a contemporary illustration. A woman alone walking the streets in the dead of night was suspected of being a prostitute (a streetwalker). Lovelorn she is searching for him who is lost, but the police find her. The scene is poignant. Clad in her night dress and against all odds she asks armed guards if they have seen her sole love. How would they know him and why would they care? In her desperation she presumes the whole city ought to identify her beloved, because he is so special to her. The human heart remains relentless in its courtship pursuit. No obstacles, no passage of time, is too much for the perseverance that courtship love inspires. "Strong as death is love, perduring as the grave its bond" (8:6).

To her question the guards presumably reply in the negative. They do not stop her; they do not take her cloak. Later in the Song the nightwatchmen accost her wandering in the city in search again for her beloved: "They uncovered my cloak, those guards around the walls" (5:7). Now she passes by. Immediately thereafter she finds him whom she had sought. One is reminded of the indispensable providence of God in the psalm: "Unless the Lord guards the city, the guard keeps watch in vain. It is in vain that you rise up early and go late to rest, eating the bread of anxious toil; for he provides for his beloved during sleep" (127:1–2).

The Song of Songs is a quintessential human love story. No one else will satisfy but the one and only beloved. Human love recognizes that the beloved is unique, and that a true love is a love forever. No one else but the beloved is her "sole love," no bond less than a bond once and for all: "My beloved is mine and I am his" (2:16). There will never be another you is the lover's delight. Love is not for just some body, but for this somebody who is unique.

Romeo and Juliet will prevail in their love for each other despite every obstacle of their birth and circumstance. They cannot marry anyone else, for love is not just about the body, which is more or less the same for us all, but about the eternal person, the "sole love." Their love must be lasting; it must be bonded in the sight of God and thus forever. Though star-crossed lovers, theirs is a marriage made in heaven. They will have no compromise and their bond is forever. So too in the Song.

The Christian may well see the paradigm divine love story in the bond between the Holy Spirit and Mary of Nazareth, the mother of Jesus who is Lord. In Mary's free consent the marriage of heaven and earth takes place. No creature is equal in being with the creator, but in the word made flesh the divine love story is embodied forever in the human love story.

3:4

It was but a little that I passed from them,
But I found him whom my soul loveth:
I held him, and would not let him go,
Until I had brought him into my mother's house,
And into the chamber of her that conceived me.

Hardly had I passed them by when I found my soul's sole
   love.
I clung to him and would not let him loose till I led him to my
   mother's house,
To the room where she gave me birth.

Scarcely has the woman asked the nightwatchmen if they have seen her "soul's sole love," but she discovers him. One might imagine that the beloved was only hiding. Teasing depends on timing—too long absence becomes sorrow. Thus he wants to be found. Now she will take no chance that he go away again: "I clung to him and would not let him loose." In the Gospel Jesus says to his friends: "A little while, and you will no longer see me, and again a little while, and you will see me" (Jn 16:19). "So you have pain now; but I will see you again, and your hearts will rejoice, and no one will take your joy from you" (Jn 16:22).

In the Song her mother is mentioned several times but never her father. Her brothers appear to take the guardian role of a father (1:6 and 8:8–9). Nonetheless, she demands her own way, and her brothers remain only a complication in the accomplishment of her own design. The story focuses on her initiative. The woman courts her beloved as much as he courts her. The Song is indeed a woman's story and the house is her mother's. Here lies no fallen or postlapsarian world where woman is subject to her husband and must bear children in pain and sorrow. Unlike the description of the psalmist she is not a hesitant bride taken to her husband's house: "Hear, O daughter, consider and incline your ear; forget your people and your father's house, and the king will desire your beauty" (Ps 45:10–11). She takes her beloved to her "mother's house, to the room where she gave me birth." In the Song there is mention of his chambers (1:4), and he leads her to his wine rooms (2:4). To her mother's house he presumably comes by day to court her (2:8–13), and by night to seek a secret tryst with her (5:2–6). Her mother's house is where the romance centers. He will address her as "the treasure of her mother, the dearest of her who birthed her" (6:9). Later in the Song she wishes he were a blood brother "given milk at my mother's breast" (8:1).

The moment and place of our conception is always shrouded in mystery, unknown finally to anyone but God who eternally wills us to life. For the yet unborn the womb is our mother's house and our own garden of paradise. Birth is the beginning of a fall into individuality, that loss of innocence in the very claiming of personal responsibility. The woman in the Song takes her beloved into her mother's room, perhaps into the bed where her mother conceived her and gave her birth. At the close of the poem she will take him again to her mother's house to share the secrets of a woman's erotic love for a man: "I would take you to my mother's house. There you would show me. I would have you drink of spiced wine, the liquid blend of my own pomegranate" (8:2). Themes of courting (3:4), birthing (6:9), feeding (8:1), and mating (8:2) are thus woven together around her "mother's house."

Mater, *materia*, the matter of all life, such is the material of mother earth. Eve is mother of the living. A mother represents home and food, and so the woman in the Song is depicted as a garden of shelter and a cornucopia of fruitfulness. A mother's love is an apt archetype of human love. In human courtship lovers seek in their beloved that blissful union of two in one that every human being once knew in some way with their mother. From her we all came, because of her we were fed, and by her we grew. That nostalgic mother's love lingers in the human heart. Launched into existence because someone carried us in, we yet seek as adults to be held and in turn to hold. A courtship love is not distant from a mother's love.

There is also the intimation of a matriarchal culture, in which the critical lineage is that of the female line. By taking her lover to her mother's house and her mother's bed, she is bringing him into the legitimate line of the culture, making him legitimate, giving him a part of the heritage. Jesus says "in my father's house there are many dwelling places" (Jn 14:2). In the Song, the woman brings her beloved home. It is a foreshadowing that Jesus of the gospels would fulfill, not just in story but in reality.

3:5
I charge you, O ye daughters of Jerusalem,
By the roes, and by the hinds of the field,
That ye stir not up, nor awake my love,
Till he please.

Give me your word, daughters of Jerusalem,
By the gazelles and wild deer of the fields,
Do not rouse nor raise up love until its time is ripe.

Three times the Song concludes that love be not roused nor raised up "until its time is ripe." As in its first instance (2:7) the line is used to close a poem or a section of the whole Song. Here as there the woman is the likely speaker. The daughters of Jerusalem, who are present in reality or in imagination, facilitate her interior conversation. The last occurrence of this line (8:4) also comes after a reference to her mother's house. All three identical adjurations (2:7, 3:5, and 8:4) follow upon an embrace of her lover.

Adolescent boys and girls do not make mature lovers. They linger in their childhood, both in its bright delight and its dark rage. The beloved comes to them charged with nostalgia. Childhood paradise lost might yet be regained. The omnipotence of childhood love is situated in a timeless and effortless world where the possible is real by mere desire. No man and no woman can create that total love in their adult lives. The stage is set for immense human disappointment. That childish nostalgia for paradise can cripple their hope for a mature human love. The love of woman and man awakens that impossible dream deep in our being, but it must not be roused or raised up "until its time is ripe." It takes wisdom and concern for another to know when and where to waken love in the beloved. Therefore, the Song pleads: do not rouse nor raise up love with its boundless expectations until love's time is ripe.

Can lovers be a waiting people, an expectant people? Can one wait for another, for the right moment, for the advent of God's love? The Spirit breathes where it wills. Not in the wind and not in the earthquake, but in the "sheer silence" does Elijah hear the voice of God (1 Kg 19:12). Like the gentle breeze the Spirit rises and falls, whence one knows not, nor when nor why. To be human is to wait for love and to possess one's soul in patience. The lovers in the Song do not apparently heed their own advice. They are not caught up in any hesitation about their love for one another nor their welcome with each other. The Song sounds rather a rhetorical warning that reflects the care and reverence with which the lovers hold one another.

3:6
Who is this that cometh out of the wilderness like pillars of
  smoke,
Perfumed with myrrh and frankincense,
With all powders of the merchant?

What is this coming up from the desert like a cloud of smoke
Suffused with myrrh and frankincense, a blend of every
  bouquet?

*T*he following five verses do not seem in any continuity with the poem that precedes (3:1–5) nor with the poem that follows (4:1–5:1). These verses (3:6–11) probably form a separate poem, a fragment perhaps of a larger marriage ceremonial. Among commentators the meaning of this verse is disputed. The text displays a royal picture of a wedding entourage. Are we to imagine King Solomon in procession or his bride being brought up to him? More likely a court escort is bringing her to him. The customary description through the speech of the man or the woman in the Song is here quite absent. We see them rather than hear them. It is not clear who is the speaker. The lavish metaphorical language evokes a heightened mystery of a sacred marriage that culminates in a coronation (3:11). In a spiritual vein such solemnity may also suggest a theophany: "Then the cloud covered the tent of meeting, and the glory of the LORD filled the tabernacle. . . . For the cloud of the LORD was on the tabernacle by day, and fire was in the cloud by night, before the eyes of all the house of Israel at each stage of their journey" (Ex 40:34,38).

Camel caravans laden with spices moved along the desert trading routes of the fertile crescent in Palestine. The dust from their movement and the fragrance rising from their pungent cargo might form a cloud of incense rising all around them like a mirage. One may recollect a perfumery or a candle shop with its "blend of every bouquet." In the Song the reference seems to be to a woman coming to meet her beloved in a procession replete with smoking incense. The woman is compared elsewhere to a garden heavy laden with every sweet spice (4:14). The theme of the Cinderella country girl coming up to Jerusalem with escort in order to marry a king is high romance. One might also imagine the caravan of someone like the "queen of the south" (Mt 12:42), of whom it was said "there were no spices such as those that the queen of Sheba gave to King Solomon" (2 Chr 9:9). Later in the Song we read of similar epiphanies: "Who is this who appears like the dawn, / Resplendent as the moon, irradiant as the sun" (6:10), and "Who is this coming up from the desert, leaning against her lover?" (8:5).

Frankincense is the sweet aromatic resin of a small tree that grows in southern Arabia (Sheba), East Africa, and the Himalayas of India. Frank incense is pure incense, undiluted, the essence of incense. In Israel aromatic incense held a large place in the temple worship. "Let my prayer be counted as incense before you, and the lifting up of my hands as an evening sacrifice" (Ps 141:2). In the gospel annunciation Zachary went into the temple inner sanctum on the chosen day to offer incense at the "altar of incense" (Lk 1:11). The magi offer the child Jesus "gifts of gold, *frankincense,* and myrrh" (Mt 2:11).

Marriage is mentioned in the Song once only (3:11). These five verses (3:6–11) tend to draw the reading of the entire Song into the biblical wisdom tradition, where human marriage is sacred marriage because divinely ordained. Other readings compare the mystical marriage of Israel and its Lord, of the church and its Christ, and of the human soul and its divine spouse.

3:7

Behold his bed, which is Solomon's;
Threescore valiant men are about it,
Of the valiant of Israel.

Lo, the carriage-bed of Solomon;
Sixty bodyguards surround it, the valiant ones of Israel.

*L*et us assume, as we did in the preceding verse, that a woman is being carried up to King Solomon in marriage procession. One imagines she travels in style reclining in a carriage-bed, a palanquin or portable chaise longue supported on the shoulders of servant litter bearers. Perhaps the Song presents here no history but only a romantic fantasy, a royal fiction, a poetical evocation that heightens the courtship love of a bonny lass and her shepherd swain. There is a regal flare to the whole scene. One might even imagine a Queen Dido in procession coming to meet Aeneas, or a Cleopatra floating on her river barge en route to meet Antony:

For her own person,
It beggar'd all description: she did lie
In her pavilion—cloth-of-gold of tissue—
O'er picturing that Venus where we see
The fancy outwork nature. On each side her
Stood pretty dimpled boys, like smiling Cupids,
With divers-colour'd fans, whose wind did seem

To glow the delicate cheeks which they did cool,
And what they undid did.

(Shakespeare, "Antony and Cleopatra," 2:2:202–9)

In the Bible King Solomon is depicted with lavish wealth, many wives, and heavenly wisdom. "King Solomon excelled all the kings of the earth in riches and wisdom" (2 Chr 9:22). Opulent is the love of the man and the woman in the Song of Songs. He excels the Solomons of the world as she surpasses "nubile maidens without count" (6:8) in a seraglio. King David is protected by a special cohort of thirty bodyguards (2 Sam 23:20–39). In the Song the woman is surrounded by twice that precaution; sixty bodyguards provide safe passage for the bride, whose welfare is so cherished. She is precious and her body vulnerable. While the elaborate escort elevates the value of the woman, it may well be that the whole passage likewise exalts the man, who is powerful enough to secure such a bride.

In a spiritual reading of the Song, the Lord God is the "king of glory" (Ps 24) and Israel is the bride. "Hear, O daughter, consider and incline your ear; forget your people and your father's house, and the king will desire your beauty" (Ps 45:10–11). Paul writes of his matchmaker love for his Christian converts: "I feel a divine jealousy for you, for I promised you in marriage to one husband, to present you as a chaste virgin to Christ" (2 Cor 11:2).

3:8

They all hold swords, being expert in war:
Every man hath his sword upon his thigh
Because of fear in the night.

Every one of them a fine swordsman, veteran soldiers,
Each with sword at hand on guard against the terrors of the
    night.

Caravan protection was a necessity in the lonely stretches of desert travel. There was safety in numbers. Anything bad could happen in the dark of night, and unseen ambush was possible even by day. Of a hazardous escort for a bride we read in the Bible of "a tumultuous procession with a great amount of baggage; and the bridegroom came out with his friends and his brothers to meet them with tambourines and musicians and many weapons. Then they rushed on them from the ambush and began killing them" (1 Mac 9:39–40). (This incident recounts a reprisal of Jonathan and Simon of the Maccabee family, who were leaders in the struggle for Jewish independence, against the Nabateans, an Arabic tribe that controlled the caravan routes in Palestine.) As the ultimate protection the just man put his trust in the arm of the Lord God: "You shall not fear the terror of the night, or the arrow that flies by day" (Ps 91:5).

Nocturnal marauders worked their robbery and mayhem under the cloak of darkness. Any unidentified noise might raise alarm in the caravan because they could not see the danger. The terrors of the night were all the worse because they included the unknown. There might be perils from man or beast, from angel or devil. Tobias fears the demon in the night in his nuptials with Sarah, "whom he loved very much" and whose previous seven husbands died in the bridal chamber on their wedding night. The angel Raphael says to Tobias: "When you enter the bridal chamber, take some of the fish's liver and heart, and put them on the embers of the incense. An odor will be given off; the demon will smell it and flee, and will never be seen near her any more. Now when you are about to go to bed with her, both of you must first stand up and pray, imploring the Lord of heaven that mercy and safety may be granted to you. Do not be afraid, for she was set apart for you before the world was made" (Tob 6:17–18). As the psalmist says of his trust in the Lord: "Even though I walk through the darkest valley, I fear no evil; for you are with me" (Ps 23:4). Indeed the just remain in the hands of God: "For he [the Lord God] will command his angels concerning you to guard you in all your ways. On their hands they will bear you up, so that you will not dash your foot against a stone" (Ps 91:11–12).

The Song suggests that the bodyguards are able and veteran swordsman, ever on the alert for any peril along the way. Imagery in the Bible surrounding the sword is abundant. When Adam and Eve are driven out of the garden of Eden, the cherubim guard the way to the tree of life with a "sword flaming" (Gen 3:24). With the infant Jesus in her arms Mary of Nazareth is told by Simeon that "a sword will pierce your own soul too" (Lk 2:35). When Peter would defend Jesus in the garden of Gethsemani he says: "Put your sword back into its place; for all who take the sword will perish by the sword. Do you think that I cannot appeal to my Father, and he will at once send me more than twelve legions of angels?" (Mt 26:52–53). Indeed the word of God is "living and active, sharper than any two-edged sword, piercing until it divides soul from spirit, joints from marrow; it is able to judge the thoughts and intentions of the heart" (Heb 4:12). With the proverb and with the Song of Songs one might conclude that the pen is mightier than the sword.

3:9

King Solomon made himself a chariot
Of the wood of Lebanon.

King Solomon built himself a carriage-bed of wood from
　　Lebanon.

*O*nce again the carriage-bed of King Solomon provides the scene. Does this repetition indicate there are two litters, one for her and one for him? Perhaps the duplication is the result of editorial splicing of separate poetical texts in the final redaction. The overall action, however, continues to suggest that the woman who is to be the bride for the prospective marriage (3:11) is being brought to King Solomon, who has sent his carriage-bed and entourage to escort her in style and safety into his presence. The later reference to the witness of the daughters of Jerusalem (3:11) situates the impending wedding, whether it be imaginary or historical, in the capital city of King Solomon.

The cedar wood palace of King Solomon in Jerusalem was called the "house of the forest of Lebanon" (2 Chr 9:16). At this same time Solomon also built the temple of Jerusalem of Lebanon wood covered with silver and gold. "The glory of Lebanon shall come to you, the cypress, the plane, and the pine, to beautify the place of my sanctuary" (Is 60:13).

During Israel's wanderings in the desert, the ark of the covenant, which held the covenant of Moses (the Torah), was carried on a litter supported on the shoulders of pole bearers. The presence of the Lord God hovered over it in a pillar of cloud by day and a pillar of fire by night. The bride who is to be carried in the palanquin of King Solomon is framed as a treasure in this same precious wood of Lebanon. In effect the beloved is housed in a tabernacle. The bride is transported in a wooden ark. In the Christian scriptures it is Mary of Nazareth who carries within her the divine presence. Hence the references to her in the litany of Loreto as "ark of the covenant" and "house of gold." Just as the ark of the covenant lingers three months in the house of Obed-edom (2 Sam 6:11) before it is brought up to Jerusalem, so Mary carrying Jesus within her will linger three months with her cousin Elizabeth (Lk 1:56).

In a further Christian spiritual reading consider this contrasting image. Jesus of Nazareth, "the king of the Jews," in whom God dwells, carries his cross of wood and is nailed upon it to die. The Roman soldiers with "sword at hand" do not guard him but abuse him, and "the terrors of the night" are stark: "from noon on, darkness came over the whole land until three in the afternoon. And about three o'clock Jesus cried with a loud voice, 'Eli, Eli, lama sabach-thani?' that is, 'My God, My God, why have you forsaken me?'" (Mt 27:45–46). In the Christian revelation the wood of the cross is the hard marriage-bed prepared for the consummation of the suffering love of God for the suffering people of God. A new wooden ark is raised up to save a sinful humanity from the dark flood waters of death. In the passage through the bright spirit waters of baptism, a people of God, betrothed to God, traverse the desert and pass over into the promised land.

3:10

He made the pillars thereof of silver,
The bottom thereof of gold,
The covering of it of purple,
The midst thereof being paved with love,
For the daughters of Jerusalem.

Its posts overlaid with silver and its canopy with gold,
Its couch of purple weave, its woodwork inlaid with loving
    care.

*I*n the Song the text is somewhat obscure, and the Hebrew word translated in various versions as bottom carpet, seatback, bolster, or canopy is otherwise unattested. Exactly what the structure looks like remains uncertain, and hence the obscurity about the accouterments. Surely the Song here envisions a luxurious conveyance adorned for a bridal procession. A canopied palace bed has been argued as well, or the very throne of Solomon, for the presence of the woman in these lines is less obvious.

The posts are made of wood overlaid with silver, and the canopy with gold. The furnishings are thus encased in precious metal. The temple of Solomon in Jerusalem was built of wood overlaid with a veneer of wrought gold (1 Kg 6). The ark of the covenant was made of acacia wood covered with silver and gold. This most precious house of the Lord God was placed inside the Holy of Holies, itself an inner sanctum within the Temple.

The couchseat or cushion is dyed purple, the brilliant color of royalty. A rich reddish-blue dye was extracted from the tiny murex shellfish harvested from the sea with much labor and at great expense. The veil before the Holy of Holies was of "blue and purple and crimson fabrics" (2 Chr 3:14).

The woodwork paneling is inlaid with designs wrought "with loving care." Typically love scenes were carved. Some versions of the Song speak of the wood inlaid with ebony, with ivory, or with semiprecious stones. Again the text remains unclear and the descriptive word in Hebrew is otherwise unattested.

In a Christian spiritual reading of this text one might see the church as the new ark that brings humankind to its espousals with God. One might also recall the golden chariot carrying Beatrice, a figure of the church, in the wonderful culmination of Dante's Purgatorio (Canto 29–30). Guarded by angels from above against the "terrors of the night," this new ark of the covenant conveys to the sacred marriage in heaven everyone born of woman and loved by God in Jesus the Christ. For Christians the resurrected Jesus becomes the consummate King Solomon, whose kingdom will not end. It is within himself that Christ has brought his bride to the wedding feast, and she abides in him.

3:11

Go forth, O ye daughters of Zion, and behold King Solomon
With the crown wherewith his mother crowned him
In the day of his espousals,
And in the day of the gladness of his heart.

Come out, daughters of Jerusalem,
And look upon King Solomon, daughters of Zion,
Wearing the crown his mother gave him on his wedding day,
On the day of his heart's desire.

*T*he scene appears to be set in the capital city of Jerusalem at the wedding feast of King Solomon. In the text reference is made to the daughters of Jerusalem and the daughters of Zion. They function in the Song as the same people. Of the nuptials of the king the psalmist sings: "You are the most handsome of men; grace is poured upon your lips; therefore God has blessed you forever" (Ps 45:2). Most likely the crown "his mother gave him" is the traditional wedding garland or diadem rather than the royal crown. Wreaths or chaplets were traditionally worn for festivities, and crowns were given to both the bride and groom in some Jewish wedding ceremonies. Isaiah writes: "as a bridegroom decks himself with a garland and as a bride adorns herself with her jewels" (61:10). In the marriage liturgies of the Eastern Church bride and groom wear regal crowns, signs of the victory of their love over the anarchy of sin. Of the royal triumphal entry of Jesus into Jerusalem on his sacred wedding day John writes: "Do not be afraid, daughter of Zion. Look, your king is coming, sitting on a donkey's colt!" (12:15). And in an ironic twist, Jesus is crowned with a crown of thorns at the moment of his redemptive wedding of sinful humanity on the hard wood bed of the cross.

In history King David was the father of Solomon, and Bathsheba his mother. When David sees her bathing on the roof he takes her to himself, even though she is the wife of Uriah. Because she becomes pregnant, David conspires to have her soldier husband abandoned in the front line of battle, and then he takes Bathsheba for wife (2 Sam 11). Their first son dies at birth, but Solomon is next born. Though not the eldest son, he gains the throne of all Israel. It is Bathsheba who connives to have her son crowned successor of David. She is the power behind the throne (1 Kg 1). In the Song the mother of King Solomon gives the crown on his wedding day. The Song of Songs seems remarkably free of patriarchal assumptions.

In the Christian sacramental liturgy only the most expensive and authentic materials are crafted for use in the sacred rites. The chalice is of gold, the altar of precious wood. The vestments are of the finest linen decorated with color and texture. Incense and flowers decorate the church of God, which itself is wrought of the finest materials and with intricate architecture. Finally, God dwells not in the building with all its magnificent furnishings, but rather in the hearts and souls of the faithful who are bright tabernacles of the living God. Such is the opulent liturgy of divine love celebrated in sacrament and song. A great love such as the love of God deserves a magnanimous embodiment.

Similarly, the liturgy of human love is celebrated in the sacrament of marriage. The wedding dress is exquisite in fabric and design. There is a diamond engagement ring and a gold wedding ring. The body is bathed and specially perfumed. Cosmetics and jewelry are applied to enhance its beauty. Songs, gifts, and flowers embellish the celebration. The gathering of friends culminates in the sharing of a wedding cake, a sweet bread that is the food of ordinary life made more delicious by love itself. Such is the opulent liturgy of the love of a man and a woman celebrated in sacrament and song. A great love such as human love also deserves a magnanimous embodiment.

4:1
Behold, thou art fair, my love; behold, thou art fair;
Thou hast doves' eyes within thy locks:
Thy hair is as a flock of goats, that appear from mount
*   Gilead.*

How beautiful you are, love of my soul, you are beautiful!
Your eyes behind your veil are doves.
Your hair is like a wave of goats flowing down the hill slopes
    of Gilead.

With this verse the scene in the Song has changed from the wedding of Solomon to a descriptive litany of the woman's appearance. The beloved's eyes have earlier been seen as doves (1:15). Though a veil covers her face from the full sight of her lover, probably her large, dark eyes resemble doves' eyes and disclose to him a simple innocence and deep soulfulness. A diaphanous veil, such as a bridal veil, softens the face and eyes. No facial feature is fully seen but none is altogether hidden. An opaque veil, in contrast, hides all the face except the eyes. Veils conceal, but by the desire they arouse to lift their curtain they also reveal what is only half-hidden.

When we allow someone to see us, we give visual access to ourself. Women in some societies wear a veil in public. Strangers are not allowed to see their face. In her courtship with Isaac, Rebecca is veiled at their first encounter (Gen 24:65). No one might look upon the king's harem. Even more out of bounds, to look upon the face of God was to lose one's life. Moses veiled his face less the people be dazzled by the glory reflected on the face of the prophet, who had but seen the backside of God. Paul says: "Now we see in a mirror, dimly, but then we will see [God] face to face" (1 Cor 13:12). When Jesus dies, "at that moment the curtain of the temple was torn in two, from top to bottom" (Mt 27:51). No longer is there an impenetrable veil between God and humankind. Humanity is given access to the kingdom of God for "today you will be with me in Paradise" (Lk 23:43). And John writes "Beloved, we are God's children now; what we will be has not yet been revealed. What we do know is this: when he is revealed, we will be like him, for we will see him as he is" (1 Jn 3:2).

Sight is a special access. The poet Byron writes "heart on her lip and soul within her eye." We take someone into our self when we gaze on them face to face. Primitive people who oppose having their camera picture taken recognize that the photograph takes away from them something of themselves and puts it into the hands of whoever holds the finished picture. To see someone is somehow to know them. Disguises need only camouflage the face, for in our face lies our identity as seen by others. There is a visual intercourse we take for granted whenever we make an appearance, or as we say "grant an appearance."

Shakespeare's Olivia says to the Duke's messenger: "Have you any commission from your lord to negotiate with my face? You are now out of your text: but we will draw the curtain and show you the picture" ("Twelfth Night," 1:5:247–50). The effort to compose our appearance, to make up our face, allows us to present ourselves as we wish when we are ready for others to know us. We do not wish to be seen with our face undressed, unshaved, unwashed, or unmade, because we feel vulnerable. The painful part of losing face is that we feel unappreciated. Our social mask, our outer face or persona, is undone by humiliation. In contrast, sight that is welcome is intimacy with the beloved, whose face is not veiled to us, and in whose eyes we are well regarded.

Further discussion of "Your hair . . . hill slopes of Gilead" may be found when this verse is repeated verbatim later in the Song (6:5).

4:2

Thy teeth are like a flock of sheep that are even shorn, which
    came up from the washing;
Whereof every one bear twins, and none is barren among
    them.

Your teeth are like a flock of ewes at shearing time,
Come up from their wash,
All paired with twins,
No one of them uncounted.

*H*er teeth are white like pure white wool. In Isaiah we read: "though your sins are like scarlet, they shall be like snow; though they are red like crimson, they shall become like wool" (1:18). And in the book of Revelation: "His head and his hair were white as white wool, white as snow" (1:14). Her hair is jet black like goat mohair, but her teeth snow-white like ewes' fleece. In *Moby Dick*, Melville's chapter on "The Whiteness of the Whale" testifies to the intensity and suggestiveness ever surrounding the fullness of all color, which is the color white.

A full mouth of white teeth is held in the Song as a special compliment to the woman's beautiful appearance. Similarly "his teeth [are] laved in milk, and set like gem stones" (5:12). With normal care white teeth come with young age. Regularly shaped and spaced teeth, however, with none missing "no one of them uncounted" seems unusual enough. The beloved is thus a rare work of nature whose unmarred beauty is not often seen. Like identical twin sheep her teeth are "all paired with twins," upper and lower jaw, right and left side of the mouth.

A beautiful smile may also be implied as one of her charms, for a beautiful smile reveals the teeth of the mouth. One need not stretch a point to imagine the smile of the beloved lauded in the unexpected praise of her teeth.

The beauty and symmetry of her teeth may also suggest the overall beauty and balance of the female form. In the Song her breasts are compared to a "pair of fawns, the twins of a gazelle" (4:5 and 7:4). Indeed the whole human body is a masterpiece of twinning—two eyes, two ears, two arms, two lungs, and so forth. She embodies par excellence that balance and that harmony. One might readily imagine the man and woman as twin lovers, "in the image of God he created them; male and female he created them" (Gen 1:27).

4:3

Thy lips are like a thread of scarlet, and thy speech is comely:
Thy temples are like a piece of pomegranate within thy locks.

Your lips are like a scarlet ribbon; your mouth gently bowed.
Your cheeks behind your veil rosy as cloven halves of
    pomegranate.

*T*he lips of the human mouth are made up of thin labile tissues and the circulation of blood gives them a reddish hue. That vital color is enhanced by emotion and especially by artificial coloring. The red dye extracted from henna (see 1:14 and 4:13) was used as such a cosmetic. Later we read "his lips [are] crimson lilies" (5:13).

Scarlet is a most intense red. The dye was typically extracted from an oak tree parasite, and the color suggests sex appeal. Scarlet ladies of the night may take their origin from the story of Rahab, the loyal prostitute, who tied a "crimson cord in the window" of her house. Because she had sheltered the Jewish spies, her household would be spared in the Hebrew invasion of the promised land (Josh 2:18, 21). Despite her shady background Rabab remains one of the four women (along with Bathsheba, "the wife of Uriah" and the mother of Solomon) mentioned in the genealogy of Jesus in Matthew (1:1–18). Hester Pryne, the adulterous woman in *The Scarlet Letter,* and the passionate Scarlet O'Hara in *Gone with the Wind,* pick up the erotic symbolism associated with the color scarlet. There is no imputation that the woman in the Song is promiscuous, but surely she is exuberant. Perhaps the poet Thomas Moore could be cited appropriately: "Lips in whose rosy labyrinth, when she smiled, the soul was lost."

Her "mouth gently bowed" suggests even more than color. His mouth is "honey sweet" (5:16), and her mouth "like a fine wine" (7:10). The breath of life and our daily bread pass over our lips. With the lips of our mouth we shape our speech; we form our prayer; we extend our kiss. Shakespeare writes: "O, how ripe in show thy lips, those kissing cherries, tempting grow!" ("Midsummer Night's Dream," 3:2:139). Something much more intimate than just appearance is implied in "lips like a scarlet ribbon" and a "mouth gently bowed."

"Your cheeks behind your veil rosy as cloven halves of pomegranate" is repeated verbatim later in the Song (6:7). A full consideration of the meaning of this duplicated line will be found there. Suffice it to say at this point that the rouge color and circular shape of the sliced pomegranate well describe the young woman's healthy and blush-color cheeks.

4:4
Thy neck is like the tower of David
Builded for an armory,
Whereon there hang a thousand bucklers, all shields of mighty
  men.

Your neck is like the tower of David roped with bucklers;
A thousand shields dangle from it, all the armor of the valiant.

*P*roceeding down each feature of her head, the Song now praises the neck of the woman, which is described as a "tower of David." In the litany of Loreto, the Blessed Virgin Mary is also compared to the "tower of David." David was the great military and religious king who unified all of Palestine as one land with Jerusalem as its capital city. The psalmist says: "Walk about Zion . . . count its towers . . . that you may tell the next generation that this is God, our God forever and ever" (48:12–14). Some commentators think they have identified the tower used in the simile: "the tower projecting from the upper house of the king at the court of the guard" (Neh 3:25). Later in the song her neck is described as "a tower of ivory" (7:5), her nose "a tower of Lebanon" (7:5), and her breasts "like towers" (8:10). Clearly the Song wishes to say that her neck is a prominent and praiseworthy part of her bodily appearance, and we commonly speak of "towering strength." No doubt here is a woman unafraid to stick her neck out, for hers is an uncommon strength.

Bucklers are large body shields. Arm shields are commonly smaller defenses. In the Bible we read of "the large and small shields that had been King David's" (2 Chr 23:9). Weapons such as "the shields of gold that Solomon had made" (1 Kg 14:26), were commonly hung from the walls of fortresses, and they may bear some resemblance to the metal jewelry that hangs from a woman's neck. Her throat is described earlier in the Song as "laced . . . with necklaces" (1:10). "Men of Arvad and Helech were on your walls and all around; men of Gamad were at your towers. They hung their quivers all around your walls; they made perfect your beauty" (Ezk 27:11). Exactly how bucklers and shields were roped or hung on towers is not clear from the Hebrew text. Perhaps they made overlapping courses like steps or bands of stones on the tower inner surface. "A thousand shields" is a form of hyperbole like the "thousand silver coins the cost of its fruit" in her pricing of the vineyard of Solomon (8:11). Howsoever that may be, the point in this verse is to heighten attention to the decorous and decorated strength of the woman's long and slender neck. This flower of lovely female form is supported on a long stem.

4:5

Thy two breasts are like two young roes that are twins,
Which feed among the lilies.

Your breasts are like a pair of fawns, the twins of a gazelle,
That nibble amid the lilies.

For whatever reasons men are attracted by the shape of the female breast (8:10) and may be sensually aroused by the sight of a woman's breast (7:8–9). Until recent times, the future life of a child depended upon the milk of a woman's breast (8:1). For all these reasons the emotional connotations of the female breast are intense. Desire, love, human dreams and dark mysteries orbit the female form.

In the Song the lover see her breasts as "a pair of fawns, the twins of a gazelle." The Greek word for gazelle, *dorcas,* means beauty. Symmetrical breasts may well appear to be twins, and suckling fawns may suggest the budding breasts of a younger woman (8:8). Fawns are hidden in camouflage. They are timid and cautious, shy and vulnerable, and they appear to be in jeopardy. One may enjoy a surprising glimpse of an astonishing beauty, but the fawns are quickly hidden again. These are images not unrelated to maiden modesty and innocence.

At the same time newborn gazelles are awkward, frisky, and playful. Bambi-like fawns will ring one's heart with tenderness. The wonder of young life, the natural hesitancy of fledgling beauty, the heart-melting vulnerability of the innocent all seem well captured in the image of the fawn compared to the youthful female breast. The graceful yet unexpected motion of the breasts when the whole body moves may suggest the sudden mobility of a young gazelle. The unself-conscious appreciation of sexuality in the Song dovetails with delight in the natural beauty of a young fawn. We read in Proverbs: "Let your fountain be blessed, and rejoice in the wife of your youth, a lovely deer, a graceful doe. May her breasts satisfy you at all times; may you be intoxicated always by her love." (5:18–19).

Her breasts as twin fawns that "nibble amid the lilies," carry erotic overtones, because she later describes his lips as crimson lilies (5:13). The female breast has given nurture and satisfaction to countless young children and rare pleasure and comfort to lovers the world over. Like lying in a sunny field of new mown clover, to rest upon the female breast and breathe its human fragrance is to know a surpassing sweetness. No wonder the woman delights that "he feeds among these lilies" (2:16). Here is a joyful declaration that is repeated (6:3), and which is worth repeating.

In this litany of the body the Song presents a verbal sculpture, the bust of a woman of consummate beauty. Her head is sculpted in detail—black hair, dove eyes, white teeth (and smile), her bowed mouth and scarlet lips (both words and the nonverbal language of kisses), and rosy cheeks. Note that in the description of the woman's body the focus is upon her head and the elements distinctive of the standing human figure. Her humanity centers upon the faculties of her head, containing all the senses, which are the bodily avenues to the soul. There is a paradoxical saying that sex is primarily in the head. Obviously that is not the whole story, but communication with a human person does ensoul the joy of human sexuality. The eye is first directed to her eyes, and throughout to her face. Her neck, like a tower of David, is a royal column upholding her head. Love at first sight may be all too romantic, but no doubt human love often begins with sight. Only at the close of this descriptive litany does the text speak of the woman's breasts, for her body is altogether female and also quite beautiful to behold.

4:6

Until the day break, and the shadows flee away,
I will get me to the mountain of myrrh, and to the hill of
*   frankincense.*

When the evening breeze rises and shadows dissolve,
I will draw near the mountains of myrrh, the hills of incense.

*W*ith the coming of the evening dusk, the lover in the Song looks forward to his approach to his beloved under the cover of darkness. Earlier in the Song the woman declares: "my beloved is mine and I am his. / He feeds among these lilies. / Until the evening breeze rises and shadows dissolve, / Turn back to me, my heart's love; / Be like a gazelle or a young hart on the mountains of Bether" (2:16–17); note there the discussion of the time frame). In both instances there is no implication of undue intrigue, but rather one of seeking the beloved at the acceptable time. The lines in the Song now spoken by the man (4:5–6) echo these earlier words of the woman, and like them they provide a certain punctuation. It may, moreover, show a delicate touch of the poet to restrain any further bodily description of the woman and leave more to the reader's imagination.

"The mountains of myrrh, the hills of incense" may refer to the body of the woman in a specific way. For example, the mountains could be the scented female breasts referred to in the previous line, and earlier (1:13). The mountains may also suggest the whole woman, body entire and soul. Though the contours suggest the female breast, the perfumed mountains and hills promise abundant delight in the woman's whole bodily presence. As mountains are imposing in their grandeur, so the landscape of her whole person is pervasive in its fragrance. The same implication is also repeated in her invitation to him to gambol upon the "mountains of spices" in the closing words of the poem (8:14). The Song speaks finally not of body parts but of erotic fantasy about the whole corporeal being of the beloved. The fragrant magic of myrrh and incense conjures up whole worlds. Shakespeare writes:

> Had I no eyes but ears, my ears would love
> That inward beauty and invisible;
> Or were I deaf, thy outward parts would move
> Each part in me that were but sensible:
> Though neither eyes nor ears, to hear nor see,
> Yet should I be in love by touching thee.
>
> Say, that the sense of feeling were bereft me,
> And that I could not see, nor hear, nor touch,
> And nothing but the very smell were left me,
> Yet would my love to thee be still as much;
> For from the stillitory of thy face excelling
> Comes breath perfum'd that breedeth love by smelling.
>
> ("Venus and Adonis," 433–44)

In a spiritual reading of this line, prayers to God in loving devotion rise like incense. The holy smoke of the temple incense reminds the worshipper that sensual beauty and divine beauty are both sacred. Indeed, their airs commingle.

4:7

Thou art all fair, my love; there is no spot in thee.

You are altogether beautiful, love of my soul, and nowise
   marred are you.

$\mathcal{B}$eauty is in the eye of the beholder. From a lover beauty is lavishly
bestowed even when not indisputably claimed. The beloved is so beautiful
because so well loved. As Shakespeare's Romeo says of Juliet: "For I ne'er
saw true beauty till this night" (1:5:52). Wonderfully the person who receives
such affection will glow with an inner beauty that does transfigure the face
and the carriage of the whole body. In the Song one might imagine that the
woman has a beauty that all observers might recognize and again something
more that only her lover appreciates. "I love you not only for what you are,
but for what I am with you, drawing into the light all the beauty no one else
looked for enough to find, making me feel my goodness with your touch,
your words, yourself."

The previous litany of her bodily charms is not the checklist for a beauty
pageant. His heart has been given to her, and the whole woman from head
to toe, body and soul, is beloved. Hence she is for him "altogether beautiful."
He finds no fault in her, no flaw or blemish, no spot to mar her radiance in
his eyes. Shakespeare writes: "My mistress, when she walks, treads on the
ground: / And yet, by heaven, I think my love as rare / As any she belied
with false compare" (Sonnet 130). Of David's beloved son, Absalom, we read:
"from the sole of his foot to the crown of his head there was no blemish in
him" (2 Sam 14:25). At the opening of this particular section of the poem (4:1),
the beloved woman is extolled as "how beautiful," and now in closure she is
acknowledged "altogether beautiful."

In the human imagination perfect beauty has long been a quest for the
impossible. Hawthorne's story, "Rappacini's Daughter," dramatizes that
yearning. "Nowise marred are you" may be a lover's exaggeration, but underneath the rhetoric is the desire for the infinite perfection that is God partially
disclosed in the human being made in the image of God. In this material
world the beloved becomes the image of God for the lover. Though we carry
the tiny flame of that heavenly love in earthen vessels, yet there is a glimmer

of the divine love in every earthly love. "Beauty is God's handwriting,—a wayside sacrament" (Milton). Later in the Song the man will repeat the exaltation of his one true love: "One, only one is my dove, / So perfect, the treasure of her mother" (6:9). The whole body is finally a veil of the human person, a veil that reveals to love's eyes what is hidden. "The body charms because the soul is seen." The immaculate conception of the Blessed Virgin Mary in anticipation of the enfleshment of Jesus Christ remains the Christian understanding of the perfect love of God breaking into human history in a spotless way, "nowise marred," and drawing all humanity to the sacred marriage.

4:8

Come with me from Lebanon, my spouse, with me from Lebanon:

Look from the top of Amana, from the top of Shenir and Hermon,

From the lions' dens, from the mountains of the leopards.

Come down from Lebanon, my bride, come along with me from Lebanon.

From the height of Amana, from the peaks of Senir and Hermon,

From the lairs of lions and the haunts of leopards.

*T*he desert and the mountain wilderness were places where wild animals dwelt. Nature's laws reigned rather than civilization: "a lion from the forest shall kill them. . . . A leopard is watching against their cities" (Jer 5:6). John the Baptist, who dwelt in the desert, is usually portrayed dressed in a lion's skin. Dante's *Divine Comedy* begins with the way to heaven blocked by a leopard, a lion, and a wolf, symbols of unruly passion. Later Dante applies this very line of the Song to the church prepared for entry into heaven (Purgatorio, 30). In the Song the man invites the woman to leave her faraway, inaccessible, and lonely wilderness. He wishes her to be near-at-hand, thus receptive of his courtship, and eventually to be his very own garden of delight (4:12–5:1). He would find his happiness in her as she finds hers in him. Come be his bride, he would say; let his love shield her. She need be no longer in the wild. The present plea is reminiscent of the earlier request to leave her hiding in the "clefts of the rock" and the "crannies of the cliff" so that he might look upon her and listen to her voice (2:14). Most readers have seen here some kind of subdivision within the larger poem (4:1–5:1), because the words of the man change from a litany of the praises of her appearance to the more direct address of "my bride."

Amana refers to the mountain ranges running northeast from the northern border of Israel, and draining into the Amana river. *Senir* is the Amorite word (see Dt 3:9) referring to the very high mountain (9000 ft.) or range of mountains of that name in Lebanon. *Hermon* is the Hebrew word. It is one of the source waters of the river Jordan.

The motion here is downward from the mountain fastness. That movement repeats the head down description of the beloved (4:1–7). The head waters of the stream flowing from Lebanon become the sealed fountain in the enclosed garden (4:12), which is a figure of her whole body. As a stream gathers tributaries from along its route as it wears its way down to the sea, so the woman becomes a reservoir that waters the abundance of the garden of her love. There is to be a fulfillment of many waters coming together to make the garden "a well of living water falling from Lebanon" (4:15).

4:9

Thou hast ravished my heart, my sister, my spouse;
Thou hast ravished my heart with one of thine eyes,
With one chain of thy neck.

My heart you have ravished, my sister, my bride!
You have melted my heart with one flash of your eyes,
With but a sparkle of your necklace.

*W*hen Miranda and Ferdinand fall in love at first sight in Shakespeare's "The Tempest," Prospero exclaims with satisfaction: "At the first sight / They have changed eyes" (1:2:440–41). Love at first sight can be an overwhelming experience flying in the face of prudent calculation. Human beings do report being swept off their feet by a love that is all-enthralling. Of the overpowering love of God, John Donne writes: "Take me to You, imprison me, for I / Except You enthrall me, never shall be free, / Nor ever chaste, except you ravish me" (Holy Sonnets, XIV). In the Song the man acknowledges that one flash of her eyes melts his heart and he finds himself overcome, but delightfully so. "One of the most wonderful things in nature is a glance; it transcends speech; it is the bodily symbol of identity" (R. W. Emerson).

We have already seen the veiled eyes of the beloved (4:1). Later in the Song he pleads: "Take your eyes away from me, for they make me wild" (6:5). Here the "one flash" of her lambent eyes may be the turning of her head and the sudden reflection of the light on the liquid surface of the eye. Indeed, the eye itself may be a source of light, for a woman's soul might shine upon him whom she beholds with love. Here is the forthright glance of an equal, who both desires and is desired. She may be looking into his soul, not with shyness, but with confidence in herself and her feeling for him. She has loved him with her gaze, and she has taken his breath away with the clarity of her invitation. In Shakespeare's "Love's Labor's Lost," the pursuit of wisdom is shifted from books to the mystery of a woman's eye:

> For when would you, my lord, or you, or you,
> Have found the ground of study's excellence,
> Without the beauty of a woman's face?
> From women's eyes this doctrine I derive:
> They are the ground, the books, the academes,
> From whence doeth spring the true Promethean fire.
>
> For where is any author in the world
> Teaches such beauty as a woman's eye?
>
> (4:3:299–313).

There is some evidence that a veiled woman engaged in conversation would uncover just one eye, which was thus framed in her face like a jewel (the King James version probably assumes this reading). The well-timed batting of an eyelid or the shifting of the iris up or down or side to side is the very essence of romantic melodrama. A simple necklace of pearls diffuses the light on the surface of the face. A dazzling bright jewel held in a pendant worn around the neck catches the light in one of its many facets. "The sparkle of [her] necklace" mirrors the flash of her eyes. These moments of sudden and unexpected dazzle can be truly bewitching.

4:10

How fair is thy love, my sister, my spouse!
How much better is thy love than wine!
And the smell of thine ointments than all spices!

How exquisite your love, my sister, my bride!
Your love sweeter than wine, the fragrance of your perfume
    surpassing all spice!

$\mathcal{I}$n the beginning of this poem (4:1–7) the lover gave a litany of praises of the physical charms of the beloved. Human courtship may begin with the physical attraction of the body, but it leads to the love of man and woman that now is described as "exquisite." The woman in the Song is neither his blood sister nor his married bride. These are poetic terms of endearment. She remains his dearest one beyond all others, his intended one, and hopefully his promised bride.

Tobias survives his marriage to Sarah because he loves his bride and "sister" dearly and with sincerity and "not because of lust" (Tob 8:7). In the Bible bridal imagery often describes the love of God for the people of Israel. Hosea says: "I will take you for my wife forever . . . and you shall know the Lord" (2:19–20), and in the book of Revelation we read: "Come, I will show you the bride, the wife of the Lamb" (21:9).

Earlier in the Song the woman spoke of his love as sweeter than wine (1:2) and his fragrance as delightful (1:3). He returns the same compliment. Her love is "sweeter than wine" and "the fragrance of [her] perfume" surpasses "all spice." In the hot and dry climate of the Orient the skin was often anointed with aromatic and moisturizing oils. Olive oil permeated with a distilled essence became a perfumed balm of many purposes. Exotic spices flavored food and also scented the air. At the close of this particular poem the man will summarize his communion with the woman: "I gather up my myrrh and my spices" (5:1). Later in the Song she will say: "My heart's love came down to his garden, to the beddings of spice" (6:2). Her last words to him that end the Song of Songs invite him to leap like "a young stag upon the mountains of spices" (8:14).

The description of the woman that began with chapter four has been visual. The poet gave us a beautiful verbal sculpture. Here the Song sings that she tastes good and smells sweet. Kisses are implied, and such kisses are on the lips of the mouth as the food of love.

In a spiritual reading one will readily think of the hoped-for messianic banquet, the multiplication of the loaves in the gospel, and the Eucharistic agape in the sacrament of divine love. "O, taste and see that the Lord is good" (Ps 34:8).

4:11

Thy lips, O my spouse, drop as the honeycomb:
Honey and milk are under thy tongue,
And the smell of thy garments is like the smell of Lebanon.

Your lips distill wild honey, my bride; honey and milk under
   your tongue;
And the breath of your clothing like the harvest airs of
   Lebanon.

"*S*weeter than wine . . . the kisses of his lips" (1:2), those "crimson lilies, gilded with glistening myrrh" (5:13) mingle now in his praise of her lips sweet as honey. This line in the Song has been read as lovers' talk with wet kisses, of "honey and milk" well savored. Sweet talk, the tender words of courtship love, well up from under the tongue, and the beloved pools labile caresses and verbal kisses.

A "land flowing with milk and honey" describes the promised land in numerous passages of the Bible. In the desert the rainfall is all too scarce. In arable land, however, rain brings wildflowers whose nectar the bees turn into liquid honey from the honeycomb, and rain brings abundant grasses that the cows turn into creamy milk. With abundant water, pasture land in the wild richly supports the good life. With moisture there is life. The human body is ninety percent water. Its vital juices make the continuation of life possible. Just as mother earth yields milk and honey, the human body is a promised land flowing with milk and honey.

If there is any perfect food on the face of the earth surely it is honey—beautiful to see, sweet to smell and taste, and delicious to eat. Honey is a pure food; it does not corrupt. A sweet syrup was extracted from dates but pure honey came from bees. The nectar of innumerable flowers is distilled into honey by the work of a myriad of bees (one pound of honey represents over 500 bees, 2.5 million flowers, 20,000 bee trips, and 160,000 bee hours). There is nothing sweeter than honey. It concentrates the very essence of the garden of the world. To a man in love the woman held in his arms combines the honey from all God's creation. She is manna from heaven, the "finest of the wheat" and "honey from the rock" (Ps 81:16).

Not only are her kisses sweet and her words a land of milk and honey, but the very breath of her garments recall the good earth. The fragrance of her clothing brings the "harvest airs" of fertile Lebanon, those upper valleys where the headwaters "falling from Lebanon" (4:15) turn the desert into a pasture land flowing with milk and honey. The psalmist says: "Therefore God, your God, has anointed you with the oil of gladness beyond your companions; your robes are all fragrant with myrrh and aloes and cassia" (45:8).

In a more spiritual reading, the Lord God is sweet. When Ezekiel eats the scroll of the word of God, it became as honey in his mouth (Ezk 3:3). Isaiah writes: "Everyone who thirsts, come to the waters, and you that have no money, come, buy and eat! Come, buy wine and milk without money and without price. Why do you spend your money for that which is not bread, and your labor for that which does not satisfy? Listen carefully to me, and eat what is good, and delight yourselves in rich food. Incline your ear, and come to me; listen, so that you may live. I will make with you an everlasting covenant, my steadfast, sure love for David" (55:1–3). And of the life of the spirit Peter writes: "Like newborn infants, long for the pure, spiritual milk, so that by it you may grow into salvation—if indeed you have tasted that the Lord is good" (1 Pet 2:2–3).

He speaks:

A garden enclosed is my sister, my bride; a garden closed off,

a fountain sealed, (4:12)

A paradise of pomegranates (4:13)

A garden fount, a well of living water (4:15)

I come into my garden, my sister, my bride. (5:1)

4:12

A garden inclosed is my sister, my spouse;
A spring shut up, a fountain sealed.

A garden enclosed, is my sister, my bride;
A garden closed off, a fountain sealed,

*G*ardens and vineyards were fenced in with a hedge or barrier of some kind to keep hungry animals and greedy thieves away from the fruit. The psalmist writes: "Why have you broken down its walls, so that all who pass by the way pluck its fruit?" (80:12). Fountains and wells were covered over to protect the purity of the waters. Husbandry sought enclosure. Gardens were locked to outsiders. In the story of Suzannah the elders begin their intended seduction with an appeal to privacy: "Look, the garden doors are shut, and no one can see us. We are burning with desire for you" (Dan 13:20).

As the Song moves to its mid-point the image of the woman as the garden and her love as its fruit becomes central and dominant. The climax of the poem is quite possibly her invitation to him: "Let my true love come into his garden and eat of its hand-picked fruits" (4:16). The wild Lebanon mountains heights (4:8) have been brought down to earth and cultivated in a garden. The inaccessible dove in "the crannies of the cliff" (2:14) has made a dovecote for him alone. The beloved is the "garden enclosed"; the beloved is the "fountain sealed." She is spring earth; she is fresh water and sweet milk. "My heart's love came down to his garden . . . to browse among the lilies" (6:2). Unavailable to all others, she belongs to him because he belongs to her. "My beloved is mine and I am his" (2:16). Though the words throughout this particular poem of the Song (4:1–5:1) are his, the courtship flourishes because of her initiative. Freely bestowing herself as a gift upon her beloved strikes the dominant tone of the Song of Songs. It is only her brothers who would restrain her: "If she be a wall, we shall armor her with silver; / If she be a door, we shall close her up with cedar board" (8:9).

The virginal quality of courtship has always had a special significance. Sexuality is a tactile language that can be made untrue by misuse and trivial by promiscuity. The body is a gift, which must be well regarded in order to be well given. The "enclosed garden" and "sealed fountain" suggest someone who knows what are the boundaries. They reserve themselves in order fully to present themselves. Love is most intense when it remains a once-and-for-all gift of self. Although God can love fully each and every one of us, our body can be in only one place at a time, and our heart care fully for only one person at a time.

The Song sings of a personal partnership between a young woman and a young man, discovering themselves in a responsible way and giving themselves to each other once and for all. The entrance to the garden thus represents a privileged access, for no one else enjoys such favor. The book of Proverbs applies the image of a sealed fountain to a faithful husband devoted to his own wife: "Drink water from your own cistern, flowing water from your own well. . . . Let your fountain be blessed, and rejoice in the wife of your youth, a lovely deer, a graceful doe. May her breasts satisfy you at all times; may you be intoxicated always by her love (5:15–19). Of the unrequited love of God, Jeremiah says: "they have forsaken me, the fountain of living water, and dug out cisterns for themselves, cracked cisterns that can hold no water" (2:13). The Christian liturgy has taken the imagery of the "enclosed garden" and the "fountain sealed" and applied it to Mary of Nazareth, the woman espoused above all others to the Holy Spirit of God.

And Jesus promised the woman of Samaria at the well side: ""Everyone who drinks of this water will be thirsty again, but those who drink of the water that I will give them will never be thirsty. The water that I will give will become in them a spring of water gushing up to eternal life" (Jn 4: 13–14).

4:13

Thy plants are an orchard of pomegranates, with pleasant
   fruits;
Camphire, with spikenard,

A paradise of pomegranates, with all the choicest fruit: henna
   with nard,

The Persian word for park is the foundation of the Hebrew word in the Song translated as paradise. A garden of paradise suggests a cultivated park, a private space, an enclosed garden watered by a sealed fountain. It is reminiscent of Eden, the first artistically arranged space that humankind ever knew. "And the Lord God planted a garden in Eden. . . . Out of the ground the Lord God made to grow every tree that is pleasant to the sight and good for food, the tree of life also in the midst of the garden (Gen 2:8–9). In Ecclesiastes we read: "I made myself gardens and parks, and planted in them all kinds of fruit trees" (2:5). The woman in the Song has become a paradise of "choicest fruit," and the Song of Songs a word garden of cultivated poetic images.

Pomegranates (literally a pome with grains) are a flesh-colored globular fruit filled with innumerable corpulent red seeds. The pomegranate image was chosen for the decoration on the priestly garments (Ex 28:33–34) and to adorn the temple of Jerusalem and the king's palace (1 Kg 7:18). Popularly called a "love apple," the pomegranate is shaped like the female breast, and its abundance of seed in an oval receptacle also suggests the fertility of the womb. The juice of the pomegranate (grenadine) derived from the succulent seeds was thought to be an aphrodisiac. Later in the Song the woman with amorous intent offers him to "drink of spiced wine, the liquid blend of my own pomegranate" (8:2).

The pomegranate was a staple Palestinian fruit, and "all the choicest fruit" may refer back to the pomegranates as well as forward to the list of perfumed plants, trees, and shrubs that follow into the next line of the Song. Compare this passage describing the surpassing love of wisdom: "Like cassia and camel's thorn I gave forth perfume, and like choice myrrh I spread my fragrance, like galbanum, onycha, and stacte, and like the odor of incense in the tent. Like a terebinth I spread out my branches, and my branches are glorious and graceful. Like the vine I bud forth delight, and my blossoms become glorious and abundant fruit" (Sirach 24:15–18). Surely the woman in the Song is thought to be an idyllic garden filled with exotic fruits and fragrances from all over the earth. Indeed, her body has become the landscape of her lover's paradise. In a spiritual vein one could think of the woman of the Song as *wisdom,* abundant wisdom—enticing, enlivening, full of savor, and soul fulfilling.

Much of the history of salvation takes place in a garden. Adam and Eve "heard the sound of the Lord God walking in the garden at the time of the evening breeze" (Gen 3:8). After the fall they are locked out of the garden, which is guarded by the cherubim with "sword flaming and turning to guard the way to the tree of life" (Gen 3:24). Jesus suffers anguish, abandonment, and betrayal in the olive garden of Gethsemani. After the crucifixion he is buried in a garden "in a new tomb in which no one had ever been laid" (Jn 19:41). There Mary Magdalene encounters the risen Lord, whom she at first believes to be the gardener. Only when he speaks her own name, does she recognize him whom her soul loves (Jn 20:16).

4:14

Spikenard and saffron;
Calamus and cinnamon, with all trees of frankincense;
Myrrh and aloes, with all the chief spices.

Nard and saffron, sweet cane and cinnamon, with every
     scented wood.
Myrrh and aloes, with all aromatic spices.

To describe how exquisite is the beloved entails a litany of exotic and aromatic essences. One commentator calls it a Noah's ark of the vegetable kingdom. The Song here creates a cornucopia of fragrances in a garden of love laden with spices. As the book of Proverbs says: "perfume and incense make the heart glad" (27:9). This enchanted garden of the most costly and most delectable perfumes of the world from Africa to India was probably arranged more for its poetic and sensual impact than its utility.

The "henna with nard" from the previous line of the Song runs on into the "nard and saffron" that open this verse. Earlier in the Song we encountered henna (1:14) and nard (1:12). Saffron is taken from the stigma of the crocus flower. Because innumerable blossoms yield only a small amount of saffron, this bright yellow zesty spice remains very expensive. Sweet cane probably refers to calamus or to other aromatic canes such as ginger grass. Cinnamon, another sweet-scented wood, derives from the bark of a tree native to Sri Lanka and southeast Asia. The merchants of Babylon traded in "cinnamon, spice, incense, and myrrh" (Rev 18:13). Myrrh we have seen earlier in the Song (1:13). Aloes, popularly called eaglewood or paradise wood, refers to the scented timber wood of the aloes tree. Balaam prophesied that the tents of Israel will flourish: "like palm groves that stretch far away, like gardens beside a river, like aloes that the LORD has planted, like cedar trees beside the waters" (Num 24:6). In the New Testament aloes refers to the small aloe plant, that was commonly used as medicine and for embalming, for example, the anointing with spices of the dead body of Jesus (Jn 19:38–42). "All aromatic spices" include flavors and aromas. Possibly the reference is to balsam, one of the choicest of aromatic resins, and which is grown to this day on the terraces of Engedi (1:14). Balsam (in Hebrew meaning spice) was also a generic oil base, a kind of balm that could be combined with various rare essences.

If our body becomes what we eat, then our soul becomes what we take in through our senses. What we ingest leaves a residue for better or for worse. If we allow trash into our soul through our bodily senses, we trash our soul. Monastery communities of men and of women were built on the premise that to turn one's heart to the love of God demanded control of what impressions of the world came into the soul. The simple food, dwellings, and clothing of the monk, along with the architecture and music that surrounded the word of God, were all bent on giving good food to the soul. Hence in the Song the beloved is portrayed as a garden of every valuable planting, because she herself offers such incomparable food for love.

Moses prescribes the preparation of a fragrant, holy, anointing oil made of liquid myrrh, sweet-smelling cinnamon, aromatic cane, cassia, and olive oil, which was reserved for the consecration of sacred persons and objects (Ex 30:22–33). When even the fragrant air speaks of the beloved who is altogether welcome, we sense a pervasive presence of the love that supports our life even as the air we must breathe to live.

4:15
A fountain of gardens, a well of living waters,
And streams from Lebanon.

You are a garden fount, a well of living water falling from
   Lebanon.

Water was scarce in the semiarid biblical land of the Song of Songs. Every fount or spring made a small oasis garden flourish. Living waters were running waters, and hence fresh water from streams or underground springs. Some kind of a reservoir or well preserved any source of living water for gradual use in the dry season.

The spring thaw melts the pure snows in the mountains of Lebanon. Those streams make the desert bloom. His bride has indeed "come down from Lebanon" (4:8) and "winter is over" (2:11). The prophet writes: "The wilderness and the dry land shall be glad, the desert shall rejoice and blossom; like the crocus it shall blossom abundantly, and rejoice with joy and singing. The glory of Lebanon shall be given to it, the majesty of Carmel and Sharon. They shall see the glory of the LORD, the majesty of our God" (Is 35:1–2). For the lover the "sealed fountain" springs forth; the "enclosed garden" is all ablossom, and all the earth's delight is now at hand. "They are like trees planted by streams of water, which yield their fruit in its season, and their leaves do not wither. In all that they do, they prosper" (Ps 1:3).

The Bible opens and closes with mention of a river, the very waters of life that stream from the abundance of God. In the beginning "a river flows out of Eden to water the garden" (Gen 2:10), and in the ending "the angel showed me the river of the water of life, bright as crystal, flowing from the throne of God and of the Lamb" (Rev 22:1; see also Ezk 31:3–9 and 47:1–12).

The matchmaking servant of Abraham knows that Rebecca is the providential bride chosen to marry Issac by her way of drawing water: "there was Rebekah coming out with her water jar on her shoulder and she went down to the spring, and drew. I said to her, 'Please let me drink.' She quickly let down her jar from her shoulder, and said, 'Drink and I will also water your camels'" (Gen 24:45–46). To the Samaritan woman at the well Jesus says of the gift of his own life: "If you knew the gift of God, and who it is that is saying to you, 'Give me a drink,' you would have asked him, and he would have given you living water. . . . The water that I will give will become in them a spring of water gushing up to eternal life" (Jn 4:10, 14). Legend speaks of the annunciation to the Blessed Virgin Mary taking place beside a fountain.

We thirst for fresh water from the depths of our dry land. Even more we would draw waters of the spirit from the everlasting fountain of life that is God. Isaiah says: "and you shall be like a watered garden, like a spring of water, whose waters never fail" (58:11). And the invitation of Jesus to enter into the everlasting love of God is clear: "Let anyone who is thirsty come to me, and let the one who believes in me drink. As the scripture has said, 'Out of the believer's heart shall flow rivers of living water'" (Jn 7:37–38).

The psalmist imagines the absence of the divine beloved as a drought: "O God, you are my God, I seek you, my soul thirsts for you: my flesh faints for you, as in a dry and weary land where there is no water" (63:1). The impatient yearning of the lover to see the face of God is compared to thirst: "As a deer longs for flowing streams, so my soul longs for you, O God. My soul thirsts for God, for the living God. When shall I come and behold the face of God?" (Ps 42:1–2) The Song celebrates the vital presence of the beloved who pours herself out as a "garden fount." In the Song of Songs no image captures the effervescent vitality and outpouring love of the woman more clearly than the "well of living waters falling from Lebanon."

4:16
Awake, O north wind; and come, thou south;
Blow upon my garden, that the spices thereof may flow out.
Let my beloved come into his garden,
And eat his pleasant fruits.

Rise up north wind; come up south wind!
Blow through my garden that its sweet airs may commingle.
Let my true love come into his garden and eat of its hand-
    picked fruits.

With this invitation into the garden we are at the middle of the Song of Songs and the turning point of the courtship. He yearns to know his garden, and she responds eagerly. The allusion is to access, the access desired by the lover, sought equally and actively by the beloved, and now given in simple consummation.

The plea is for the winds to mingle and spread about the fragrances of the garden. The spirit of love is a wind that breathes life into the soul. In the pentecost account the Holy Spirit comes as a "mighty wind" that abolishes all divisions among humankind. In a reversal of the tower of Babel story, each person understands the speech of the other. From north and south, from east and west, from heaven and earth, from all quarters of the world let the wind blow. "The north and the south—you created them; Tabor and Hermon joyously praise your name" (Ps 89:12). The refrain in the Song, "Do not rouse nor raise up love until the time is ripe" is here fulfilled. Now is the acceptable time. The perfumed winds are invited to blow through the garden and to stir up love, because the awaited moment has come. Her voice breaks into his request to the winds: "Let my true love come into his garden."

In the Song the garden has functioned as a symbol for her body and by extension for their love together. In these climactic lines, therefore, to come into her garden is indeed to make love to her. Of a woman's consent one author writes: "Virginity is that small isthmus between a woman's no and her active yes, when *her* time has come, accountable to herself, her lover and God." To eat of hand-picked fruits implies a generous physical intimacy and a cornucopia of sensual delights. Gladly she is giving herself. Shakespeare writes: "Our bodies are our gardens, / to which our wills are gardeners" ("Othello," I,3,323–24).

The Song of Songs sings of the body and its solace. Lavish the fruits: apples (2:3), figs (2:13), pomegranates (4:13), dates (7:8), and grapes (7:9). In the garden of human love the fruits of the Spirit should also be included: "love, joy, peace, patience, kindness, generosity, faithfulness, gentleness and self-control" (Gal 5:22). Such fruits are not unrelated to the garden tryst in the Song nor to the garden of God that is the feast of paradise "in the beginning." The poet George Herbert writes of God's love as a feast: "Love bade me welcome; yet my soul drew back / . . . . 'My dear, then I will serve.' / 'You must sit down!' says Love, 'and taste my meat.' / So I did sit and eat" ("Love").

Human hope is for access to God. Human hope is to see God face to face and without any veil. John writes: "Those who love me will keep my word, and my Father will love them, and we will come to them and make our home with them" (14:23). Already in the Eucharist Jesus has given a pledge of that consummate and ultimate communion. "This is my body, which is given for you" (Lk 22:19). And to this astonishing promise might be added the words of the loving father to the elder son in the parable of the prodigal son: "And all that is mine is yours" (Lk 15:31). The final communion of God and humankind described in the Bible comes in the book of Revelation, which concludes: "'Surely I am coming soon.' Amen. Come, Lord Jesus!" (Rev 22:20).

5:1

I am come into my garden, my sister, my spouse:
I have gathered my myrrh with my spice;
I have eaten my honeycomb with my honey;
I have drunk my wine with my milk:
Eat, O friends; drink, yea, drink abundantly, O beloved.

I come into my garden, my sister, my bride;
I gather up my myrrh and my spices,
I eat my honey dripping from its comb,
I drink my wine with my milk.
Eat, friends, drink! Drink deep of love!

*F*rom the man's perspective, the central and the climactic line of the whole Song of Songs is this quiet exaltation: "I come into my garden." The scene is reminiscent of Adam's delightful discovery of Eve drawn from his rib during his sleep: "This at last is bone of my bones and flesh of my flesh" (Gen 2:23). Eight times in these lines the man speaks of *my* garden, *my* spouse, *my* honey. His welcome is always a surprise and ever a privilege. Now he knows how much she belongs to him. The woman has already spoken of his love as "sweeter than wine" (1:2) and the man of her love "sweeter than wine" (4:10) with milk and honey under her tongue (4:11). In her beauty she is the lily of the field, and in their communion she is the fruitful garden of intoxicating and vital spirits. Later in the Song her litany of the beauty of his body ends likewise in a garden (6:3), for she also comes into her own garden, because he belongs to her as well.

We become what we eat. Our food becomes our body. Food given as daily bread always reveals our dependence on another. Whoever feeds us gives us our life. Husband and wife exchange wedding cake with each other, giving and receiving, giving body and life to the other in comprehensive and intimate ways. Marriage is giving one's body as food. The shared wedding cake allows everyone to break bread with the bride and groom, and celebrates that exchange. Bride and groom must cut the first piece of cake together, and they place the cake in each other's mouth as if it were a sacred communion bread.

What they give one to the other as sweet and life-giving food will become their shared life given for each other. It is sacred and godlike to give life. Hence the significance of the marriage ceremony within the celebration of the Eucharist, so that the cup of married love is conjoined with the cup of divine love "given for all."

The "myrrh and spices" gathered up elaborates the man's acceptance of the woman's invitation to come into the perfumed garden and "eat of its hand-picked fruits" (4:16). The "honey dripping from its comb" is a further representation of the superb sweetness of embodied love. Overall the erotic allusions are multiple, revealing a reverent and grateful sensuality. The "wine with my milk" captures the intoxicating joy of the fruit of the vine and the intimate nurture of milk. Isaiah says: "Ho, everyone who thirsts, come to the waters . . . come, buy wine and milk . . . and delight yourselves in rich food" (55:1–2). On Calvary from the wounded breast of Jesus pierced with a lance there flowed water and blood, which in symbol are the sacraments of life-giving water in baptism and life-food in Eucharist, which is his body broken as bread and consumed as wine in the mystery of the sacramental love of God.

The final imperative to the "friends" to eat and drink deeply of love may be addressed to the lovers themselves in a kind of editorial aside expressing the sentiments of onlookers or bystanders, such as the "daughters of Jerusalem" (see 5:9). This command to partake in the feast of love may also be directed by the bridegroom to a wedding entourage, real or imagined. Wisdom personified invites her disciples to the feast: "Come to me, you who desire me, and eat your fill of my fruits. For the memory of me is sweeter than honey, and the possession of me sweeter than the honeycomb. Those who eat of me will hunger for more, and those who drink of me will thirst for more" (Sir 24:19–21). Matthew's Gospel also speaks of love's exuberance: "The wedding guests cannot mourn as long as the bridegroom is with them, can they?" (9:15). At the Cana wedding feast the wine ran dry, but Jesus changed water into wine. That final consummation of the love of God and the love of humankind is best portrayed as a wedding banquet and "blessed are those who are invited to the marriage supper of the Lamb" (Rev 19:9).

5:2

I sleep, but my heart waketh:
It is the voice of my beloved that knocketh, saying,
Open to me, my sister, my love, my dove, my undefiled:
For my head is filled with dew,
And my locks with the drops of the night.

I was asleep, but my heart still waked;
Lo, the love of my heart is knocking:
Open up to me, my sister, love of my soul, my dove, my
    perfection!
For my head is damp-wet with the dewfall,
My hair with the nighttime mist.

*I*n the garden scene above the man has his own song to sing. The following verses are now given over to the woman's inner music. Her reflections begin with a nighttime reverie (5:2–7) and emerge into a daytime litany of the charms of her beloved (5:10–16). For the man the turning point of the poem is his coming into her garden. For the woman the climax appears to be assurance of a bond with her lover that will endure. In dialog with the daughters of Jerusalem her song peaks in the poignant proclamation of the tender mutual love that she and her beloved enjoy. "I am my beloved's and he is mine" (6:3).

This nighttime reverie is an echo of an earlier similar episode. She loses and then finds her beloved in the dark (3:1–5). When our body is at rest in the night, then our soul is often most awake. Whether the woman be dreaming or whether she be fantasizing (daydreaming), her fear of losing him and her desire of finding him overwhelm her. Shakespeare writes: "all days are nights to see till I see thee, / And nights bright days when dreams do show thee me" (Sonnet 43). And of the perennial human yearning for the love of God, Isaiah simply says: "My soul yearns for you in the night" (26:9).

He addresses her with endearing names we have already heard. She is his sister (friend), the love of his heart, the love of his soul, his sole love, his shy dove, his perfection "nowise marred." She remains all given over to him. He knocks on her bedroom door. He asks her to open up to him, because he is "damp-wet with the dewfall," brought on by the warm days and cold nights of Palestine.

The woman in the Song is often situated in an enclosure. We find her in her bedroom behind closed doors, in her mother's house, in a vineyard that is fenced, in a sylvan bower, in the clefts of the rock, within the high mountains, in a carriage-bed, inside a walled city. She herself remains an "enclosed garden" and a "sealed fountain." Throughout the Song he approaches her, courts her, must come unto her despite the barriers. Earlier in the Song the lover, who is "peering in the windows, looking through the latticework" (2:9), hopes to find the beloved in her home and to invite her to come outside with him. Now, seeking to come inside, he knocks upon her bedroom door. In the book of Revelation the divine bridegroom of the soul says: "Listen! I am standing at the door, knocking; if you hear my voice and open the door, I will come in to you and eat with you, and you with me" (3:20).

5:3

I have put off my coat; how shall I put it on?
I have washed my feet; how shall I defile them?

I have taken off my clothes, am I to dress again?
I have bathed my feet, am I to soil them?

*T*o his request to come in from the damp-wet of the nighttime she hastily replies that she is already undressed. Such trouble to dress again. To walk across the dirt floor of her room to put on her clothes and let him come in would soil her feet already bathed for bed. In Luke's Gospel we read of the importuning knock of a friend seeking a favor at night: "Do not bother me; the door has already been locked, and my children are with me in bed; I cannot get up and give you anything" (11:7). In the Song could she be coyly testing him? Or is this a moment of fatigue or apathy in their relationship? Could she even be petulantly unwilling to bestir herself right now? Might she have "cold feet" to pursue an unapproved love affair in her family household? Feet in the Bible are often employed as a euphemism for the private parts of the body. More likely she is bantering with him, savoring a delicious withholding that his ardor must overcome in the age-old ways of romantic drama. Playing hard to get only increases the yearning of courtship. "Rarity gives a charm; thus early fruits are most esteemed; thus winter roses obtain a higher price; thus coyness sets off an extravagant mistress: a door ever open attracts no young suitor" (Martial).

After eating the forbidden fruit, Adam and Eve clothe themselves with fig leaves, because they are naked and ashamed before one another. From her point of view, she may feel vulnerable without clothes. Moreover, her feet are bathed clean. Who will wash them again? When Jesus goes to the house of Simon the Pharisee he is offended that the servants do not wash his feet as customary. Jesus defends the woman who with great love for him bathes his feet with her tears and dries them with her hair (Lk 7:36–50). Jesus himself washed the feet of his disciples (Jn 13:1–7). Ultimate trust becomes the issue.

A more spiritual reading might claim that clothes of the body are a protection for the soul. To take clothes off in the presence of a lover is to reveal not only the body but also the soul. To be naked before her lover is indeed to give herself to him. Lovers who know the body of their beloved will also be entrusted with the soul. Of divine love Paul writes: "For in this tent we groan, longing to be clothed with our heavenly dwelling—if indeed, when we have taken it off, we will not be found naked. For while we are still in this tent, we groan under our burden, because we wish not to be unclothed but to be further clothed, so that what is mortal may be swallowed up by life. He who has prepared us for this very thing is God, who has given us the Spirit as a guarantee" (2 Cor 5:2–5). Ultimate trust becomes the issue.

Throughout the Song the woman is often concealed. Her face may be hidden and her eyes veiled. We see her interior space through curtains, draperies, latticework, and locked doors. This night she lingers as a woman behind closed doors.

Clothing provides a covering for her body. Indeed we are first clothed in our skin. Though some veils can be lifted, the human body remains opaque. Clothes can be undone, but the flesh cannot be taken off. X-ray pictures reveal our bones, but we alone reveal ourselves. Self-disclosure is what we seek with the beloved. Such vulnerability, however, can be threatening even when desired. We would make our inner being available and we would give ourself away, and yet we may be hesitant. We alone can open the doors of our heart. Behold the lover in the Song stands at the door knocking. She is undressed for the night in bed. Her door is closed. Full of suspense, the outcome of this episode must be allowed to unfold.

5:4
My beloved put in his hand by the hole of the door,
And my bowels were moved for him.

My lover slipped his hand into the door slot.
My body trembled to its depth for him.

*T*hree interpretations of this line in the Song prevail: (1) In a literal reading
the man is trying to open the latch of her door. Slipping his hand into the
opening of the lock and trying to let himself into her bedroom in the middle
of the night, starts in her a shivering excitement. (2) His hand in the door slot
is a circumlocution for his initiating sexual intimacies with her, perhaps only
in her dreams, for he never enters her room and he is gone when she does
open her door (5:6). Thus she quivers at the first touch even in imagination
of her body's secret places. (3) The man is seeking the woman's willing
consent to know and love her in an intimate relationship broadly understood.
A rhapsody of body and soul is felt when she recognizes that the person now
at the door of her life is the destined love dreamed about and long awaited.
"The mandrakes perfume the air, and on our lintel's every delicacy; / A Fresh
and ripened harvest, O my heart's love, / I've held in keep for you" (7:14).

If one pictures a wooden door opening upon a bedroom one might imagine
the inner latch could be raised by a hand inserted from the outside. Others
have argued for a kind of spy hole common in Arab dwellings to this day.
Placed in the center of the door, the peep hole was covered on the inside
with a revolving disk that allowed one to look out without being seen. At the
sound of his attempt at entry or at his touch of her hand through the opening
of the door, her body trembles to its depth in her desire for him. She may be
so moved because she is about to give herself to him. She may be shivering
in anticipation of great joy. The knowledge that what has been so desired is
about to happen rivals the experience itself. Now is love's hour.

In the tenor of the whole Song the enduring human love story overshadows
any preoccupation with only an imagined romance of the night or merely the
regaling of the human body. All three readings, however, might be kept in
mind at the same time. Great poetry provides multiple meanings, and the
words support such simultaneous possibilities. The Song cherishes the human

body in all its sexual wonder, and the poem celebrates the ever-intriguing and beguiling courtship between a woman and a man. The even more mysterious love between God and humankind, known in the incarnation and embodied in the passion of Jesus, is thus described in John's Gospel: "One of the soldiers pierced his side with a spear, and at once blood and water came out" (19:34). And after the resurrection Jesus says to a doubting Thomas: "Put your finger here and see my hands. Reach out your hand and put it in my side. Do not doubt but believe" (Jn 20:27). A whole divine love story could be unpacked from these few words couched in John's masterful rhetoric.

5:5
I rose up to open to my beloved;
And my hands dropped with myrrh,
And my fingers with sweet smelling myrrh,
Upon the handles of the lock.

I rose to open to the love of my heart,
My hands suffused with myrrh slipping over the latch of the
    lock,
My fingers wetted with liquid myrrh.

*T*his line of the Song describes a universal human experience—the sweet excitement and the daring required to cross a line. One never knows what one is getting into. Ornate doorways and guardian gates heighten this passing through. The portals of a cathedral doorway are lined with statuary in tiers that usher one in stages into the church and gradually funnel the entrance into sacred inner space. Even without a door there is always an approach, a threshold, a liminal boundary. Imposing vestibules and elaborate courtyards serve a function of transition from fully outside to fully inside. Long passageways, corridors, or driveways through entrance grounds are often strategic and delightful delayed approaches and hence exciting anticipations. The moment of entry is always a time of privilege and of fear. Why should I be the one who is allowed to come in?

The woman earlier compared her lover to a "sachet of myrrh . . . all night between [her] breasts" (1:13). Myrrh was marketed in crystals sold in small sacks. When dissolved in oil the crystals became liquid myrrh. Later she will describe his lips like "lilies, gilded with glistening myrrh" (5:13). She may have anointed with myrrh her own hands, which now cover the door handle in her opening up to greet him. If somehow she is touching his hand through an opening in the door, he seems to be slipping away from her. If his hand was anointed, he may have left liquid myrrh on the door latch. Lucretius writes of insistent male courtship and disappointed swains: "But the lover, when shut out, often in tears covers the threshold with flowers and garland wreaths, and anoints the splendid doorposts with oil of marjoram, and the poor wretch plants kisses on the doors" ("De Rerum Natura" 4:1177–79).

One might read this text in conjunction with the preceding line as a veiled description of sexual intimacy. She is the locked door about to open; he is the hand that reaches into her. Accordingly, the liquid myrrh becomes a euphemism for the male or the female bodily fluids that accompany sexual lovemaking and provide lovers their own especial anointing. Engaging as the erotic reading may be, the larger context remains one of her eager and tender delight to let him enter into her room, which is her whole life. The scene evokes human love in all its dimensions. In her joyful and open immersion in his love brought to her, her whole body melts into sweetness. Now suffused with the delight of courtship love, her whole person opens out "to the love of my heart."

In this line one can see the tension of the entire Song encapsulated. Shall we read a physical eros or a spiritual agape? Shall we combine them both into a broad humanistic love, flesh and spirit, that takes each reality of the human condition seriously? Is it possible to avoid the limitation of physical love alone or spiritual love alone, and embrace a human bond that recognizes the physical without overlooking the spiritual? Perhaps the Song tells us when we are free of our fears, when we know ourselves truly loved and lovable, we will experience whole love—body and soul. Perhaps uniquely and only in the sacrament of the Eucharist is human communion fully spiritual and yet not disembodied—a foretaste of the resurrection of the body and life everlasting within the love of God, which is reflected in human love "as in a mirror darkly" (1 Cor 13:12).

5:6

I opened to my beloved;
But my beloved had withdrawn himself, and was gone:
My soul failed when he spake:
I sought him, but I could not find him;
I called him, but he gave me no answer.

I opened out to my lover, but my beloved had turned aside
   and gone away.
My heart went slack when he left me.
I looked for him but I did not recover him;
I called out for him but he did not respond to me.

*N*o courtship can force open a "sealed fountain" or an "enclosed garden," and lay claim. The door must always be opened from within. Love of body and of soul is a gift. With open door she now searches for him who was so impatient to come in, but he is now apparently nowhere to be seen. Has her lover gone away quietly without a word? Has he left her with some sharp reproach? Does her heart slacken because of his departure from her or because of his disappointment with her? She loses heart and becomes sad. The Vulgate Latin says it so poetically: *Anima mea liquifacta est ut locutus est* (my soul melted as he spoke). Is his departure perhaps his counter response to her teasing refusal to open her door? Is his departure the anger or the discouragement of a man who wins no welcome? In an erotic reading has he turned aside or withdrawn from sexual intercourse because his body has become impotent?

Human intimacy is both feared and desired. Enfolding arms are perceived at times as a restraint of freedom, but more often as a secure and comfortable enclosure. Sexuality in a woman is more readily a total umbrella acceptance, being touched all over, knowing the warmth of an enveloping love. Hence her devastation and her abandonment when her lover has gone away just when he most should have stayed. Women may take longer than men to respond, but their willingness once given lingers so much longer.

The woman in the Song is dismayed at the turn of events. She is frantic alone in the dark. Her lover is gone, she knows not where and she knows not why. She opens the door but he has come away. She searches but she cannot find him. She calls out but he does not answer her. Mary Magdalene in John's Gospel comes early in the morning seeking to anoint the body of Jesus entombed behind the rock in the garden grave where no body has yet been laid (Jn 20). She is desolate, alone, and yet deeply attached to him who healed her soul of its troubled condition (Lk 8:2). Mary Magdalene runs into a man she believes to be the gardener. The woman in the Song will encounter the nightwatchmen (5:7). Mary Magdalene seeks the one who knows her and then calls her by name. The woman in the Song also seeks the man who knows her and knocks on her door. The human soul seeks the God of love in the dark night. Mary Magdalene seeks at dawn Jesus whom she loved, who is risen from the tomb. Similar the story and tender the pathos of the human heart, which is created for an infinite and boundless love, and which searches in a vale of tears in the dead of night.

5:7
The watchmen that went about the city found me,
They smote me, they wounded me;
The keepers of the walls took away my veil from me.

The night watchmen came upon me as they went about the
    city.
They beat me and they hurt me.
They uncovered my cloak, those guards around the walls.

The dreamlike or nightmare quality of the present sequence (5:2–7) seems quite pronounced in this line of the Song. The woman has thrown a light cloak around her and rushed out of her home in search of her beloved, who has disappeared from her doorstep. A lone woman wandering the city streets late at night may well be challenged. She is exposed and defenseless, all on her own and without knowing where to turn. The nightwatchmen take advantage of her. Very likely thinking she may be a prostitute, they pull off her cloak or her veil to uncover her identity. Perhaps they wish to abuse her.

When Tamar sets out to impersonate a prostitute and to engage her kinsman as she believed to be her legal right, she "put on a veil and wrapped herself up, and sat down at the entrance to Enaim" (Gen 38:14). Judah "thought her to be a prostitute, for she had covered her face" (Gen 38:15).

Dark is the hour for the woman in the Song. The "enclosed garden" that was given as pure gift now has been taken for a loose woman who rents her body for a fee. She who would not put on her tunic is now stripped of her garment. She who cannot find her lover is now found out by the guardians of the city walls. In a spiritual vein one might think of Jesus who is stripped of his garments by the Roman soldiers on Calvary. Or one might recall the nighttime scene at the end of Mark's gospel: "A certain young man was following him, wearing nothing but a linen cloth. They caught hold of him, but he left the linen cloth and ran off naked" (14:51–52).

The visit of her lover to her room had been fraught with risk, and the uncertainty that all human love entails. One is vulnerable in all human relationship. To dare to love is to take one's life in one's hands and to have the courage to bestow it upon another, who may or may not cherish the gift as it truly deserves. Despite the risks she goes in search for him in the darkness, even though he has withdrawn, perhaps into himself where he is protected from the power of her love. To leave the security of one's house, to wander in search of a love that is lost, to struggle for one's independence, these are the underlying themes of this dreamlike yearning for the love of her soul lost in the night. There will be a happy ending to her search for her lost beloved. Though now there are obstacles and delays, the Song is a divine "comedy" not a tragedy, and lavish the love it celebrates overall. For the religious reader, "my soul waits for the Lord more than those who watch for the morning" (Ps 130:6). For the Christian reader, the resurrection follows the passion and death of Jesus.

5:8

I charge you, O daughters of Jerusalem,
If ye find my beloved, that ye tell him,
That I am sick of love.

Give me your word, daughters of Jerusalem,

Should you find my heart's love—speak of this to him;

Speak of my heartache for him.

*W*e have heretofore seen the daughters of Jerusalem. They function here as a chorus that allows the protagonist to speak her mind and to be overheard. They also allow the poet-author of the Song to move smoothly from the dream sequence (5:2–7) into the woman's litany of her beloved and his many charms (5:10–16). The woman may also be seeking their social confirmation in this crisis moment of her life. One could even imagine that the daughters of Jerusalem resemble the sisters of Lazarus in John's Gospel, who send a message to Jesus that the one "whom you love is ill" (11:3), but he comes all too late and they are disconsolate.

She has already spoken of being "so love sick I faint" (2:5). The bittersweet feeling of losing and finding brings tears of both sorrow and joy. Is the woman genuinely worried that her beloved does not know of her love for him? Some commentators have thought she is asking the daughters of Jerusalem not to reveal the truth of her slow behavior in the opening of her bedroom door? Or is her request to them merely a rhetorical question needing no answer? In short, who could believe that I would shut out my lover from my presence?

More likely she has misunderstood the courtship scene in the night, and she is lamenting the unfortunate outcome. She never intended by her delay that he should come away from her door. One can be too eager to say yes, but also too reluctant. She has been too slow, and the moment has passed. She is heartbroken—so near and yet so far. The axis of tragedy is just this poignant sadness about what might have been, had circumstances been handled differently. Think of the griefs of Romeo and Juliet, who miss each other's intentions in the dark of night by only a few moments—he in despair going to death just when she in hope was coming to life. Human beings are tangled lovers, and even the best intentions cause sadness at times rather than joy.

5:9

What is thy beloved more than another beloved, O thou fairest
  among women?
What is thy beloved more than another beloved, that thou dost
  so charge us?

Why does your love differ from anyone else, O most beautiful
  among women?
Why does your love differ from anyone else that you so
  entreat us?

*T*he daughters of Jerusalem pose the question of why the love between
the woman and her lover in the Song is special. How is he different than any
other man? Men are all alike. Women talk, and women confirm the same old
story. Why should they care if he is lost to her? Why is their love affair unique
and to be taken so seriously? In short, why should the daughters join the
search and carry a message for her? How shall they recognize him should
they be the first ones to find him, if he is only one among many? These
questions may be mostly rhetorical ones that enable her to give the eloquent
and heartfelt response that follows.

Their address to her, "O most beautiful among women," may be an ironic
echo of "most beautiful among women," which was his endearing description
of her earlier in the Song (1:8). Then she was roundly loved; now she appears
abandoned by him. The daughters probably intend, however, no freighted
commentary about the woman. Their role is one of thematic transition, as we
have seen before in the Song. The whole stretch of poetry that begins with
her voice taking over the Song in 5:2 and running to 6:3 is here punctuated
by her short dialog with the daughters. Perhaps the hand of a poet-editor who
last compiled the Song of Songs is most evident in this link between the dream
sequence (5:2–7) and the litany of his praises (5:10–16).

"Why does your lover differ from anyone else?" also invites another later question, "Where has your beloved gone?" (6:1). Between these two bookend queries
by the daughters, the text inserts the woman's very triumphal litany of the many
charms of her man. If the "daughters of Jerusalem" are construed as an original
part of the entire piece (5:2–6:3) rather than a later editorial seam, they then
provide a simple interlude, a dramatic delay that heightens the suspense.

5:10
My beloved is white and ruddy,
The chiefest among ten thousand.

My lover is fresh-shining and flesh-fair;
Eye-catching amid thousands.

We have already seen in the Song the man's litany of the woman's physical charms (4:1–7). She now responds with her own litany of his especial beauty (5:10–16). To the daughters' question in the previous line an answer is given that her lover is particularly beautiful to behold in color, form, and strength. Anyone who looks can see he is unique. If the body is in some way the reflection of the soul, then beauty without suggests beauty within. The Song describes without further comment the parts of his body and with a loving attention to detail. In the book of Revelation we read a similar litany: "Then . . . I saw one like the Son of Man, clothed with a long robe and with a golden sash across his chest. His head and his hair were white as white wool, white as snow; his eyes were like a flame of fire, his feet were like burnished bronze, refined as in a furnace, and his voice was like the sound of many waters. In his right hand he held seven stars, and from his mouth came a sharp, two-edged sword, and his face was like the sun shining with full force" (1:12–16).

To move the eye of one's imagination over the human body from head to foot brings suspense and an intense sense of excitement. These catalog descriptions are not unlike a staged beauty pageant. One is allowed to stare. The initiator of the litany of praise cannot say everything at once, and hence there is a piece-by-piece presentation of the body of the beloved in a visual cornucopia. The hope is to develop an intimate sight of the whole person by caressing the whole body bit by bit with delightful words that massage the imagination.

His face is radiant and reflects the light, "fresh-shining." His complexion is the color of bright healthy skin, "flesh-fair." Matthew writes of Jesus' appearance on Mt. Tabor: "And he was transfigured before them, and his face shone like the sun, and his clothes became dazzling white" (17:2). In the Song the man's skin takes on a ruddy hue, no doubt prompted by the vigorous circulation of blood in the young and healthy. The implication throughout is that he is strong and manly, full of vigor and vitality. The King James translation, "white and ruddy," may suggest skin tanned by the sun in some places but not overall. Yet, she loves him entire, and she knows what she is talking about. This is a bold statement. She likes what she sees and says so. Women supposedly do not notice or do not care. She does.

Of young and handsome royalty we read in Lamentations: "Her princes were purer than snow, whiter than milk; their bodies were more ruddy than coral, their hair like sapphire" (4:7). The man in the Song stands out in a crowd, "eye-catching amid thousands" (5:10). His beauty by his very presence remains conspicuous. King Saul's appearance is described: "There was not a man among the people of Israel more handsome than he; he stood head and shoulders above everyone else" (1 Sam 9:2). Young David watching the sheep in the back pasture and about to be anointed the new king by the prophet Samuel is aptly described: "he was ruddy, and had beautiful eyes, and was handsome" (1 Sam 16:12). In such a vein the man in the Song is lovingly portrayed.

5:11
His head is as the most fine gold;
His locks are bushy, and black as a raven:

His head is gold, fine gold;
His curls are fronds of palm, raven black.

*T*he woman lauds the captivating appearance of her beloved. He is precious and valuable to her. The image of a head of gold probably refers to shape more than to color. Small sculptures were preferably cast in gold because of all metals gold is the most malleable and allows fine definition. When possible, idols were cast in gold. In Exodus Aaron gathered the jewelry of the people and molded it into a golden calf. Daniel describes a great statue in Nebuchadnezzar's dream: "The head of that statue was of fine gold, its chest and arms of silver, its middle and thighs of bronze, its legs of iron, its feet partly of iron and partly of clay" (Dan 2:32–33). Of such golden statuesque form is the configuration of her beloved in the Song of Songs. His head is an artist's work, well modeled and well proportioned. His bone is of fine gold, gold refined by fire, gold without any dross. The golden background of the icons of Eastern Christianity speak of the holy, incorruptible, and eternal life of the sainted one held up for universal veneration. Gold was incorruptible. Indeed, golden was the greatest compliment.

His hair is abundant with luxuriant curls reminiscent of the ample folds of the palm frond. One thinks of Samson, whose uncut hair encrypted the secret of his unsurpassed strength, and whose exploits were legendary. Of Absalom, David's son, "in all Israel there was no one to be praised so much for his beauty" (2 Sam 14–25). He was a man without blemish in his appearance, but one brought to his death when his lavish head of hair entangled him in the limbs of a tree as he passed underneath (2 Sam 18:9).

With thick black curls his bright golden head is adorned. Raven-colored is his hair. More imposing than a crow, the raven is a large dark, black bird. Jet black hair is typical of Asiatic races, and Oriental peoples prize the color black. It is youth who have deep lustrous black hair. White hair is the color of old age, a reminder of death and mourning. Both the man and the woman in the Song boast of shiny black hair. Her hair is "deep lustrous like purple" (7:6), his "raven black." As the popular ballad sings: "Black, black, black is the color of my true love's hair."

The woman cherishes the full head of dark hair that crowns her beloved. One can imagine her combing his locks with her fingers. Jesus would remind his disciples: "and even the hairs of your head are all counted" (Mt 10:30). Therefore one should trust in the particular caring love of God, who notices each person as if there were none else. Love gives eyes with which to see. We are God's beloved, and we are known even to the hairs of our head. Young lovers delight in the bodily appearance of the beloved with rich and abundant hair. They recognize the beauty of God's creation, which reaches its apex in the human person whose head is crowed with lovely hair. The body in all its beauty speaks of God's love and engenders thankfulness for God's gifts in all those who appreciate them as shy tokens of a divine courtship, of which human courtship is the fine reflection.

5:12

His eyes are as the eyes of doves by the rivers of waters,
Washed with milk, and fitly set.

His eyes are as doves beside white running waters,
His teeth laved in milk, and set like gem stones.

*T*he comparison of eyes with doves has been a frequent metaphor in the
Song of Songs. Her eyes are called doves (1:15 and 4:1). Just as his eyes are
here set as doves beside white running waters, so later we read her "eyes are
pools in Heshbon" (7:5). His eyes are as shy doves along the bank of a stream,
darkling doves against a background of white running waters. His soft eyes
shine "beside white running waters," and lend sparkle to his countenance.

The connection between eyes and water may operate on many levels. The
eyeball itself is white and the iris of the eye in its darker color is set against
this watery background like a rock within a rivulet. The human eye is bathed
in water and the apple of the eye glistens on the surface where it seems to
float. Wet eyes reflect light just as sunlight sparkles off the surface of a stream.
The human eyeball itself is filled with water, and we look into the world
through a miniature sea. Henry David Thoreau speaks of an inland lake as a
"watery globe" and the "landscape's most beautiful and expressive feature . . .
earth's eye; looking into which the beholder measures the depth of his own
nature" ("The Ponds" in *Walden*).

The conclusion of this verse in the Song is not altogether clear in the Hebrew.
Unless the text continues to talk about his eyes, a likely conjectural reading
of this litany of his body would move down his face from his eyes. Thus his
teeth are "laved in milk, and set like gem stones." The metaphor does not
need much commentary. The beloved displays white and shiny teeth, set with
care and precision in his mouth like jewels in their crafted settings. Of jewel-
encrusted priestly vestments we read: "You shall set in it four rows of stones.
A row of carnelian, chrysolite, and emerald shall be the first row; and the
second row a turquoise, a sapphire, and a moonstone; and the third row a
jacinth, an agate, and an amethyst; and the fourth row a beryl, an onyx, and
a jasper; they shall be set in gold filigree" (Ex 28:17–20). With teeth shining
like gems the man no doubt displays also a sparkling smile and a quick laugh.

In her eyes the color of his mouth is rich white like milk, and his teeth glisten with light off polished stone.

5:13

His cheeks are as a bed of spices, as sweet flowers:
His lips like lilies, dropping sweet smelling myrrh:

His bearded cheeks are like spice beddings, rife with pungent
  blossoms.
His lips crimson lilies, gilded with glistening myrrh.

*M*oving down his face she describes his cheeks, shrouded we may assume with a full beard, which like cultivated spice beddings remains fragrant with perfume. Perhaps a scented powder was dusted on the beard, or a sweet pomade "like the precious oil on the head, running down upon the beard, on the beard of Aaron" (Ps 133:2). Perhaps his beard carries his own particular aroma. Spices are mentioned many times in the Song. Her love for him becomes in symbol "his garden" and her body "the beddings of spice" (6:2). She will prepare for him a "spiced wine, / The liquid blend of [her] own pomegranate" (8:2). At the close of the Song her gift of self is imaged as the "mountains of spices" where her lover is invited to romp like a young stag (8:14). Possibly it is her own fragrance that lingers upon his face.

"His lips crimson lilies." As in the first reference to her as "a lily of the valley" (2:1), we seek a springtime lilaceous flower native to Palestine and in this line clearly of a striking reddish color. Perhaps the crimson crown anemone or the wild red anemone would well fit the metaphor. The crimson tulip or the red tulip (*Tulipa sharonensis,* sometimes popularly called "rose of Sharon"), common to the coastal plains of Sharon between Carmel [Haifa] and Joppa, are also candidates.

His lips seem to her delicate crimson-colored labile tissue like lilies in bloom. Shakespeare writes: "These lily lips, / This cherry nose, / These yellow cowslip cheeks" ("Midsummer Night's Dream," 5:1:337). We speak with our lips and we kiss with our lips. We eat and we drink with our lips. We smile and we laugh with our lips. The color and shape of our lips are dominant features of our face. When lips are wet they glisten, and his ruddy lips appear to be crimson lilies gilded with shiny liquid myrrh like lip-gloss or the homespun honey-sweet moisture of erotic kisses. Sweet the touch and sweet the taste.

In the opening of the Song her first request is for the "kisses of his lips" (1:2). He is compared with a sachet of myrrh resting between her breasts (1:13). She is a garden of myrrh (4:14), and her hands on the handle of her bedroom door are "suffused with myrrh" (5:5). A "scarlet ribbon" (4:3), her lips "distill wild honey" (4:11). Her breasts are revealed as twin fawns of a gazelle that "nibble amid the lilies" (4:5). He comes to her garden and "he feeds among these lilies" (6:3). Browsing among sweet lilies lends fragrance to his lips. It does not take much imagination to think she too nibbles among the "crimson lilies" that are his lips "gilded with glistening myrrh."

5:14

His hands are as gold rings set with the beryl:
His belly is as bright ivory overlaid with sapphires.

His rounded arms are as gold adorned with precious stones.
His midriff is of ivory, smooth and veined with sapphire.

*B*oth the man and the woman in the Song speak mostly of the delight they find in the countenance of their beloved—hair, eyes, cheeks, lips, mouth, neck. In his litany of her physical appearance (4:1–7 and 7:2–7) the man does not call attention to her arms as the woman does for him in this verse. Perhaps the strength commonly found in the arms (and legs, see 5:15) of a man particularly appeal to the woman's sense of male beauty and attractiveness. Later in the Song she will ask: "Fasten me as a seal on your heart, as a seal on your arm" (8:6). With love she would be bonded to his heart and banded to his arm just as a ring encircles his finger.

Golden arms studded with gems may be a metaphor that is not to be construed with precision. The image suggests the surpassing beauty and value of the limbs of the beloved. "Rounded arms as of gold" may be a reference to tawny color as well as to the precious metal. In a quite literal reading of the line the Hebrew speaks equally of his *hands,* studded with precious stones, probably a reference to brightly painted finger nails or to rings. The fingernails of kings and queens were customarily painted royal gold or ruby red, and the "precious stones" may also be of an amber color, such as yellow beryl, yellow topaz, or golden chrysolite.

The logical descent in the Song is from head to arms to the lower chest, belly, or trunk—the midsection of the male body. The midriff is a vague bodily description, which corresponds to the uncertainty of the Hebrew text. His midriff flesh is probably both ivory-smooth and ivory-colored, and "veined with sapphire." True sapphire is uncommon and the reference here is probably to the azure blue mottled lapis lazuli, a rare semiprecious stone found in the mountains of central Asia. Pale and translucent skin not exposed to the sun might be compared to this peculiar stone. Elaborate statues to pagan gods were carved of lapis lazuli. One is reminded again in this verse of the statuesque quality of the body of the man.

Interpretations of "his midriff" have varied from a reference to a belt of ivory embedded with sapphires girding his clothing around his loins to a veiled euphemism for the blue-veined male phallus (Murphy, 72). The Song speaks of the genital organs of the body with great delicacy and indirection, if it speaks at all (see also 7:3). There is an innocence about the bodies of the lovers, and the half-said references to the pudenda both protect modesty and enhance the erotic appeal to the imagination. Human sexuality in its physical manifestation may appear to be both ridiculous and yet sublime, and the male sexual organs both ugly and yet beautiful. The story of "Beauty and the Beast" captures some of that strange sexual ambiguity that both repels and yet attracts.

Sculpted face of gold, sovereign arms and hands, regal fingernails of color, his royal body appears to her an exquisite work of art. She sings before its beauty. In the Song he is a living statue; she is a lush landscape full of life. He is royal temple, and she garden of paradise.

5:15

His legs are as pillars of marble, set upon sockets of fine gold:
His countenance is as Lebanon, excellent as the cedars:

> His legs are alabaster columns set down upon golden
>   pedestals.
> His stature is like Mount Lebanon, arresting as its cedars.

*F*rom thigh to ankle is the implication of the text: "his legs are alabaster columns." Alabaster is a translucent marble stone suggesting flesh-tone, smooth, thin skin. The golden footings that support the columnlike legs suggest the solid turn of his ankles and feet. He enjoys muscular strength in his legs, with fine skin, and he stands with stable and confident splendor. "Like golden pillars on silver bases, so are shapely legs and steadfast feet" (Sir 26:18).

His stature or figure is compared to the majestic beauty of the imposing cedars of Lebanon. Chosen the "prince of trees," the cedar towers in the high mountain forests north of Israel. Its wood is both strong and fragrant. For size and quality of timber no tree was more prized, and "no tree in the garden of God was like it in beauty" (Ezk 31:3–9). Her description of him ends with this image of his figure arresting as a cedar tree of Lebanon. His later description of her will close with an image of her figure supple as the date-palm tree (7:8).

The columns of the house of God in Jerusalem were carved from the timbers of the cedars of Lebanon. That magnificent structure contains all the precious materials used in the woman's loving litany of her beloved. Of the materials assembled to contract the temple of God, King David says: "So I have provided for the house of my God, so far as I was able, the gold for the things of gold . . . wood for the things of wood . . . all sorts of precious stones, and marble in abundance" (1 Chr 29:2). Throughout this litany in the Song the man has appeared statuesque and of heroic proportions. Here is a temple of beauty, a beauty touching on the divine.

In Shakespeare's "Tempest" Miranda enthralled with the overall glory in the appearance of her Ferdinand cries out: "There's nothing ill can dwell in such a temple: / If the ill spirit have so fair a house, / Good things will strive to dwell with 't" (1:2:457–59). For Paul the human body was also sacred. "Or do you not know that your body is a temple of the Holy Spirit within you, which you have from God, and that you are not your own? For you were bought with a price; therefore glorify God in your body" (1 Cor 6:19–20). And John says simply: "And the Word became flesh and lived among us, and we have seen his glory, the glory as of a father's only son, full of grace and truth" (1:14).

5:16

His mouth is most sweet; yea, he is altogether lovely.
This is my beloved, and this is my friend, O daughters of
Jerusalem.

His mouth is honey sweet; he is altogether delight.
Behold the love of my heart, the love of my soul, O daughters
of Jerusalem!

𝓕rom the very beginning of the Song the woman thought the "kisses of his lips" were "sweeter than wine" (1:2). He in turn proclaims her lips "distill wild honey" (4:11) and her "mouth is like a fine wine" (7:10). Of God the psalmist says: "How sweet are your words to my taste, sweeter than honey to my mouth!" (Ps 119:103). In this line of the Song the reference may well be to his words as well as his kisses. He speaks love to her. In the words of his mouth more than in the configuration of his body he is the love of her soul, her friend, "altogether delight." His whole person is lovely, not only what the eyes see, but also what the ears hear and the heart comprehends. Ronald Knox translates her words in the Song: "nothing of him but awakens desire." Similarly the man in the Song sings of her: "You are altogether beautiful, love of my soul, and nowise marred are you" (4:7). Mystics have ever sung of the ineffable beauty and love of God. Of the humanity of Christ, who embodies the infinite beauty of God, all the Christian world echoes the Song: "he is altogether desirable" (*totus desiderabilis* in the Latin Vulgate).

In his long litany of praise of her body (4:1–15) his description centers more on metaphors of fragrance and taste. She is his garden, her bodily love its fruit. Her description of him, however, focuses more on color and shape. His body is bold bright and well molded by a sculptor's hand. Gold color is prominent (head, arms, feet), along with cream white (teeth, white of the eyes, ivory and alabaster skin). His lips are crimson red, his hair raven-colored black, his midriff veined with sapphire blue. He is "altogether delight" to her eyes.

Of Simon who helped rebuild the temple of Jerusalem, Sirach writes: "How glorious he was, surrounded by the people, as he came out of the house of the curtain. Like the morning star among the clouds, like the full moon at the festal season; like the sun shining on the temple of the Most High, like the rainbow gleaming in splendid clouds; like roses in the days of first fruits, like lilies by a spring of water, like a green shoot on Lebanon on a summer day; like fire and incense in the censer, like a vessel of hammered gold studded with all kinds of precious stones; like an olive tree laden with fruit, and like a cypress towering in the clouds" (50:5–10).

The daughters of Jerusalem had asked her why her lover is any different than anyone else that they should be concerned with her at his disappearance into the night (5:8). Her words conclude that he is most beautiful because most loved. Thus "behold the love of my heart, the love of my soul." His handsome appearance might well be seen as the manifestation of the inner beauty that bonds them together. He is most beautiful in body because he is most loved overall. For that exceptional love and friendship between them, the daughters of Jerusalem must help her recover him. And well they may.

6:1 [5:17]
Whither is thy beloved gone, O thou fairest among women?
Whither is thy beloved turned aside? that we may seek him
  with thee.

Where has your beloved gone, O most beautiful among
  women?
Where has your love brought himself?
We would seek him with you.

*E*arlier in this exchange the daughters of Jerusalem had asked her why her beloved was so special (5:9). Given her very detailed response the daughters quite plausibly ask her where has such a beloved gone. The woman's litany of praise is framed beautifully by the dialog that the daughters provide in their pointed questioning about this man of hers at the beginning and now at the ending. In their verbal concern they may possibly be playing a polite role without sincere feelings for her, or even with some satisfaction that the "most beautiful among women" has become in her boasting quite undone. More likely, however, their concern stems from her loss, and their offer of assistance in her search should be taken at face value as sympathy following upon her eloquent song describing him whom she loves.

As a dramatic chorus, the daughters represent the audience who witness and empathize with the woman's distress. In the Song she appears distraught with worry, desolate at the flight of her beloved, and yet in her conversation with her companions she remains quite confident despite his disappearance. She knows that her love can never be truly lost. Their mutual commitment is perduring. Thus the woman in the Song keeps her composure, even though her heart is full of searching anxiety. A touching story is told of the human heart in its poignant caring:

> Once when Care was crossing a river, an ancient fable of Hyginus tells us, she saw some clay, and she thoughtfully took up a piece and began to shape it. While she was meditating on what she had made, Jupiter came by. Care asked him to give it spirit, and this he gladly granted. But when she wanted her name to be bestowed upon it, he forbade this, and demanded that it be given his name instead. While Care and Jupiter were disputing, Earth arose and desired that her own name be conferred on this creature, since she had furnished it with part of her body. They asked Saturn to be their arbiter, and he made the following decision, which seemed a just one: "Since you, Jupiter, have given it spirit, you shall receive the spirit at its death; and since you, Earth, have given its body, you shall receive its body. But since Care first shaped this creature, she shall possess it as long as it lives.

6:2
My beloved is gone down into his garden, to the beds of spices,
To feed in the gardens, and to gather lilies.

My heart's love came down to his garden, to the beddings of spice,
To meander in this garden and to browse among the lilies.

She speaks:

My heart's love came down to his garden, to the beddings of
   spice,
To meander in this garden and to browse among the lilies. (6:2)

I am my beloved's and he is mine.
He feeds among these lilies. (6:3)

$\mathscr{E}$arlier in the Song the woman invites the man to come into her "enclosed garden" (4:12–5:1). She is the "mountains of spices" (8:14). Let him come. In browsing among the lilies he will know her. She is the "lily of the valley" (2:1). Twice the Song relates that her lover "feeds among these lilies" (2:16, 6:3). She is lily-food to him, her "belly a mound of wheat rimmed with lilies" (7:3), her breasts newborn twin fawns of a gazelle "that nibble amid the lilies" (4:5). Shakespeare writes: "And give me swift transportation to those fields / Where I may wallow in the lily-beds" ("Troilus and Cresseida," 3:2:12–13).

In the Song of Songs a beautiful configuration of emerging images of their bonding flow intricately together and then separate. She is implicate in him and he in her. "I am my beloved's and he is mine" (6:3).

6:3

I am my beloved's, and my beloved is mine:
He feedeth among the lilies.

I am my beloved's and he is mine,
He feeds among these lilies.

$\mathscr{T}$he more pure the commitment of love, the less it is contrived and the more it is a yielding. Sebastian Moore writes: "My desire is whom I desire desires me." In a sign of their reciprocal love for each other the woman reverses the order of her previous exclamation: "my beloved is mine and I am his" (2:16). Later in the Song she will echo the present line: "I am my beloved's and his desire is for me" (7:11). This reciprocal love is the primary experience of the woman in the Song.

The woman delights in bonding to the man; he delights in access to her. His poem (4:1–5:1) speaks of access that all courtship deeply desires. It begins with an elaborate female litany and concludes with the opening of her garden to his entry. For the man entrance into the enclosed garden remains crucial (4:16–5:1). Her poem (5:2–6:3) speaks of bonding, that all courtship deeply desires. It begins with a resplendent male litany and concludes with her exaltation of the bond that they give to and claim from one another. Both poems end in the garden in each other's arms. Words to each other are unspoken, but the images speak of promises made in other words.

The bonding of human love implies a long time, indeed a life time. Hence sexuality must be persevering. The self-gift in love is vulnerable. Infidelity is so devastating precisely because so much of self in its irrevocable personal gift seems so readily trashed. A sexual relationship for a woman is intricate and far-reaching. A woman cannot engage in lovemaking without knowing in her bones the remote possibility of pregnancy, which gives to her sexual relationship a personal depth not as immediately felt by a man. She can be pleased by this reality or inhibited. Her capacity for life bearing includes a larger social world. For a woman sexual union implicates many things. Thus her involvement can hardly separate body and soul. Her part touches on the whole matter of life.

The woman at this moment in the Song knows that real presence can be spiritual presence. Though her beloved is physically absent and seemingly lost in the night, his presence to her is found in a shared heart rather than in a shared space. If she has his bond, the heart's desire of her beloved, she has him truly present to her. Something of presence beyond the tactile touch of bodies within the same space is what the woman claims of the bond with her beloved, even though she has not found him yet in her search in the night. In love her beloved dwells in her. And similarly for the mystic, God indwells in the soul of the one whose heart is set upon the divine beloved.

"He browses among these lilies." Eating and drinking are rich symbols of sexual intimacy. The ingestion of food and the intercourse of sex suggest certain parallels. How we ingest our food (loving nourishment) and how we engage in sex (nourishing love) are related. Neither activity is just biological or just functional; both are profound human ways that people touch the bodies of those whom they love. Ingestion is a paradigm of how we give the world access to our body. As we eat our food given to us, so we take in the various other intimate experiences of life. We are either reverent and loving toward the world that supports us, or we are rapacious and greedy, taking what we want or need without regard for the integrity of a whole way of life. The hungers of the body, whether for food or sex, reveal the even deeper and more poignant hungers of the soul. Ultimately food and sex are not just instincts of a body that hungers and a species that propagates, but transactions within a spirit that wants to live forever. She is imaged as a lily, but it is her love that is his food.

6:4

Thou art beautiful, O my love, as Tirzah,
Comely as Jerusalem,
Terrible as an army with banners.

You are lovely as Tirzah, my sole beloved, lovely as Jerusalem,
Awesome as an army on parade.

*T*his poem (6:4–10) within the Song of Songs is sectioned by the subsequent repetition of "awesome as an army on parade" (6:10). The text is perhaps fragmentary, because the verses that present a litany of the woman's eyes, hair, teeth, and cheeks (6:5–7) exactly repeat the description of her found earlier in the Song (4:1–3).

Both Tirzah and Jerusalem were capital cities, the former in the northern kingdom (Israel) and the latter in the southern (Judah). Tirzah was the capital of the secessionist kingdom from the reign of Jeroboam to Omri, some fifty years (circa 920–870). Tirzah was also considered to be a garden city, and the name etymologically means delightful. Jerusalem contained not only the opulent palace of King Solomon but also the sacred palace of the king of kings, the temple of the living God. Capital city of all capital cities of the world, Jerusalem in its overall loveliness is simply described as "the perfection of beauty, the joy of all the earth" (Lam 2:15).

An "army on parade" with weapons, banners, and insignia splendid in its array would be an awesome sight. King Solomon boasted of "fourteen hundred chariots and twelve thousand horses" (1 Kg 10:26). The Hebrew text here rendered as "awesome as an army on parade" has been a source of uncertainty among translators. The text could also mean she is seen by him "frightening as visions," such as night dreams. "The encounter of man and woman is never without some haunting vision that like a garment is cast over the body." Howsoever the Hebrew is rendered, she is admirable and astonishing in her appearance.

The woman is compared to a kingdom in its central manifestation of authority, status, wealth, and armed might. A capital city is adorned with much regal architecture and an army on parade is bedecked in all its splendid regalia. In the eyes of her lover she is spectacular in her beauty and lavish in her adornment. She is a prominent capital city; she is an army on parade with all its circumstance on display. From Tirzah to Jerusalem, from north to south, from top to bottom, the woman is extravagant. Her beauty is without compare. Pomp and circumstance but enhance her loveliness.

Both desire and awe meet in this line of the Song. The beloved is a woman of love and a woman of war. In sum, she is awesome, both terrific and terrible, and altogether wonderful in his eyes. She is a woman of mystery. One may recall the poignant and powerful scene when Dante sees Beatrice in paradise. In all her heavenly beauty she lifts her veil so that he may look upon the radiance of her face, which he had loved long before and lost sight of in the darkness of his earthly journey. Dante is overwhelmed. He cannot say more. "From that first day that I saw her countenance in this life until this vision I have never broken off the pursuit of my song, but now I must cease that pursuit of her beauty in poetry, as beyond the utmost every artist might do" (Paradiso 30:28–33).

6:5

Turn away thine eyes from me, for they have overcome me:
Thy hair is as a flock of goats that appear from Gilead:

Take your eyes away from me, for they make me wild.
Your hair is like a wave of goats flowing down the hill slopes
    of Gilead.

We think we can see into the person's heart by looking into their eyes. In Matthew's Gospel we read: "The eye is the lamp of the body. So if your eye is healthy, your whole body will be full of light; but if your eye is unhealthy, your whole body will be full of darkness" (6:22–23). Looking into another's eyes is a form of spiritual intercourse and may well serve as a preparation for a further intimacy. "My heart you have ravished, my sister, my bride! / You have melted my heart with one flash of your eyes" (4:9). Despite some discomfort with his ineluctable attraction to her, he is fascinated by her. Despite the danger of being overcome, the man still wants to look into the woman's eyes, "Those doves' eyes, / which can make gods forsworn" (Shakespeare, "Coriolanus," 5:3:27–28).

When excited by emotion, the pupils of the human eye expand. Cosmetic color can make the eyes sparkle against a dark background. Long eyelashes and delicate eyelids allow a fascinating game of now you see, now you do not. Female eyes may appear larger because the female skull is often smaller than the male. A woman's eyes create emotion altogether enthralling. His love for her is vastly complicated by the embarrassment of his insistent eye-to-eye desire for her. In short, her eyes drive him wild, a condition he both shuns and delights in. When Dante enters heaven to which he is drawn by the love of Beatrice, he first sees the figure of Christ, the Lord of all beauty, reflected in the mirror surface of her eyes.

"Your hair is like a wave of goats flowing down the hill slopes of Gilead" repeats verbatim verse 4:1. The ibex or wild goat of Palestine is coated with thick, long, soft, black mohair (see commentary 1:8 and 4:1). Mt. Gilead comprises the whole high mountainous region (3500 feet) of the Transjordan east of Galilee and Samaria where wild goats roam. The letting down of her hair in flowing waves renders an uncertain Hebrew text. The probable meaning is the moving motion of a flock of goats wandering down a hillside. In such undulating ripples he sees her hair shaken loose in its tresses, wave on wave moving like long black-haired wild goats in slow motion down a hill slope in mountainous Gilead.

Beautiful hair is a living part of the body even though hair has no feeling. Relics of the saints and lockets carried by lovers cherish a mere lock of hair. Alexander Pope's semicomic poem, "The Rape of the Lock," plays on the intimate yet seemingly trivial matter of cutting a lock of a woman's hair for a keepsake. Touching her hair without permission becomes suggestive of touching her whole body. Those we allow to cut or comb our hair enter into a certain intimacy with us. Samson gave up his wildness to Delilah whom he allowed access to his secret strength in the cutting short of his hair. The gospel woman who washes the feet of Jesus with her tears and dries them with her long, loose, unbounded hair has given something intimate of herself to him.

6:6

Thy teeth are as a flock of sheep which go up from the
washing,
Whereof every one beareth twins, and there is not one barren
among them.

Your teeth are like a flock of ewes at shearing time,
Come up from their wash,
All paired with twins,
No one of them uncounted.

*T*wice in the poem the well-formed and attractive teeth of the woman are praised with the same words. The reader is referred back to the previous commentary (see 4:2).

6:7

As a piece of pomegranate are thy temples within thy locks.

Your cheeks behind your veil rosy as cloven halves of
pomegranate.

*I*f the woman's veil is opaque and covers her face except for her eyes, it would be her cheeks that are well concealed. Earlier in the Song her cheeks were "laced with jewels" that veiled and decorated her face (1:10), and the identical pomegranate description of her cheeks is given earlier (4:3). Note also his "bearded cheeks," scented "like spice beddings" (5:13). The pomegranate simile may refer to the curved rind of the ripe fruit, which has a roseate tint like the rouge-colored skin of the woman's cheeks. The color also reveals feeling and emotion. The natural blush of a modest person in the play of courtship discloses the concerns of the heart. John Donne writes:

> We understood
> Her by her sight; her pure, and eloquent blood
> Spoke in her cheeks, and so distinctly wrought,

That one might almost say, her body thought.

("Of the Progresse of the Soule," 243–46)

6:8

There are threescore queens, and fourscore concubines,
And virgins without number.

Sixty the queens, eighty the concubines,
Nubile maidens without count.

*T*he lover in the Song compares all the women of the world to his one and only beloved, "one, only one is my dove, / So perfect" (6:9). She is unique and she alone is loved above all others. The numbers threescore (60) and fourscore (80) are circumlocutions for saying without score, without count, in effect, numberless. The woman in the Song is not just one among many; she is one in a million. Only she is his chosen love in all the world.

Concubines were wives of the king, but secondary wives in the social order. Large harems of attractive women belonged as property to patriarchal potentates of power and wealth. Of King Solomon we read: "Among his wives were seven hundred princesses and three hundred concubines" (1 Kg 11:3). Rehoboam, the son and successor of Solomon, possessed "eighteen wives and sixty concubines" (2 Chr 11:21). Harem girls or nubile maidens were chosen young women who were in waiting at the king's pleasure. In the book of Esther one reads of the large seraglio that King Ahasuerus assembles in order to choose a replacement for the recalcitrant Queen Vashti. With her surpassing regal beauty, however, Esther alone wins his heart in this queenly competition. In the story of *A Thousand and One Nights* a different woman is brought to the king each night and her life forfeited in the aftermath. As legend goes only Scheherazade manages to stay alive by spinning an ongoing tale that took endless nights in the telling.

The Oriental seraglio exploited women and reduced their humanity to a resource for male self-gratification. Although the harem of an oriental monarch was intended to raise up many children for the king's household and the consequent vitality of his kingdom, the dignity of women in such concubinage was surely compromised. These women were rarely given any genuine human freedom. The Song of Songs is clearly countercultural in its absolute prizing of the singular individual.

6:9

My dove, my undefiled is but one;
She is the only one of her mother,
She is the choice one of her that bare her.
The daughters saw her, and blessed her;
Yea, the queens and the concubines, and they praised her.

One, only one is my dove,
So perfect, the treasure of her mother, the dearest of her who
    birthed her.
When women look on her they rave about her;
Queens and concubines sing her praises.

To be a treasured only child is not the point of the declaration. The Song extols the beloved's unique quality. She remains beyond comparison. "My dove, / So perfect" is a reprise of his delight in her mentioned earlier in the Song: "love of my soul, my dove, my perfection" (5:2). The queens and concubines who sing her praises refer most likely to the women mentioned in the previous verse. The exaltation of a powerful woman is hardly unknown to the Bible. Of the triumph of Judith her people said: "You are the glory of Jerusalem" (Jdt 15:9). Of the graces of Mary of Nazareth her cousin Elizabeth said: "Blessed are you among women" (Lk 1:42).

In his dreams a man yearns to be the one and only, once-and-for-all lover in the life of a beloved woman. That woman remains to him the "enclosed garden" and the "sealed fountain," to which he seeks a unique welcome. In her dreams a woman yearns to hold just such a man. Men and women are not unalike at heart. Isaiah says it well: "Because you are precious in my sight, and honored, and I love you" (43:4).

A special bonding takes place with the first sexual partner of one's life. That experience is often underestimated in its power, because it is sometimes tentative and awkward. Because the yearning for sexual intimacy can be so overwhelming, the first person to give that consent deserves and receives an extraordinary gratitude. Hunger begets thanksgiving. One never forgets one's first love. First-time experiences are such a mixture of fear, wonder, and newfound joy. Friendships made during one's youth enjoy this same lavish measure of bonding and loyalty. Although people later in their lives make other friends, there remains a unique place for those first friends who filled such need, when one did not know if such friendship would ever be received. There is a unique bond of gratitude that unites a woman and a man because each has given to the other such hitherto unknown joy.

That the ideal human sexual relationship is the union initiated by virginal man and virginal woman, emotionally and spiritually mature in their love, remains to this day defensible. One total commitment, the profound gift of body and soul, would seem to take such energy and concentration that it cannot of its nature be altogether repeated. Second commitments may be genuine, but never quite as intense as the first love of one's life, that first gift of self without counting the cost, because one put no limits on the cost. Just as we can give our heart away once-and-for-all only once, so we can give our body away with that unique gratitude and appreciation only once. With no one else can there ever be quite that original thanksgiving, the awe and fascination of a first time, the dread and the wonder, all that was given in the primal experience of being known in such naked vulnerability. In James Joyce's poignant short story "The Dead," the woman's first husband, who has died, is unavoidably still present in the intimacy of her subsequent romance. The first one there in the heart is always there. No one else can fully take a first lover's place, as emptiness can never be so empty when once it was filled. The Song of Songs glories in such an awareness.

6:10

Who is she that looketh forth as the morning,
Fair as the moon, clear as the sun,
And terrible as an army with banners?

Who is this who appears like the dawn,
Resplendent as the moon, irradiant as the sun,
Awesome as an army on parade?

*T*he "queens and concubines [who] sing her praises" in the preceding line are probably the speakers here also. The interrogative we have seen before: "What [who] is this coming up from the desert?" (3:6), and this very query is echoed again at the end of the Song (8:5). The woman has been compared to the capital cities of Tirzah and Jerusalem. Now this brief poem celebrating her beauty is closed with a comparison of her to the reflected shine of the moon and the primordial fire of the sun. Female moon and male sun are both in her made apparent. Her glory is refulgent by night and by day. She rises from the shy shadows of rosy dawn to the blinding scintillation of high noon. In her epiphany she remains "awesome as an army on parade" (repeating 6:4). Of wisdom personfied in the Bible we read: "For she is a reflection of eternal light, a spotless mirror of the working of God, and an image of his goodness. Although she is but one, she can do all things, and while remaining in herself, she renews all things. . . . She is more beautiful than the sun, and excels every constellation of the stars. Compared with the light she is found to be superior, for it is succeeded by the night, but against wisdom evil does not prevail" (Wis 7: 26–27, 29–30). The woman in the Song shares such heavenly rhetoric.

One might readily imagine courageous women heroines, such as the biblical Jael who slays Sisera, and Judith who overcomes Holofernes, or the sea captain Artemisia of Herodotus, the brave Camilla of Vergil, or Joan of Arc, the maiden warrior of medieval France. One might further imagine an army of celestial stars in their divinely appointed parade across the heavens. In the book of Revelation in a text often appropriated as a reference to the Blessed Virgin Mary we read: "A great portent appeared in heaven: a woman clothed with the sun, with the moon under her feet, and on her head a crown of twelve stars" (12:1). Dante compares Mary, the mother of God, to the "torch of love's high noon" (Paradiso 33:10–11). The woman in the Song is seen as shining in the night with the reflected light of a full moon, and she appears warm

He speaks:

Spin around, spin, O Shulammite!
Spin, spin around, so that we may look upon you! (7:1)

How beautiful and how exquisite you are,
How dear, my beloved, my maiden of ecstasy! (7:7)

and bright as the noonday sun, the very source of light. Of Juliet, Romeo says: "One fairer than my love! the all-seeing sun / Ne'er saw her match since first the world begun" (I, 2, 96). And "But, soft! what light through yonder window breaks? / It is the east, and Juliet is the sun" (II, 2, 2–3). Elsewhere Shakespeare writes of the beloved: "Nor shines the silver moon one half so bright / Through the transparent bosom of the deep" ("Love's Labor's Lost," 4:3:30).

6:11
I went down into the garden of nuts
To see the fruits of the valley,
And to see whether the vine flourished, and the pomegranates
   budded.

To the nut grove I came down to look over the valley
   greening,
To see were the vines in blossom, were the pomegranates in
   bloom.

*T*he woman in the Song is here probably the speaker. Perhaps she is reminiscing about a previous rendezvous with her lover in the verdant spring-time (see 2:8–13). Perhaps the whole scene is a fantasy that introduces the reverie in the following verse. Later in the Song she again invites the man to "be off early into the vineyards; let us see if the vines are sprouting . . . and the pomegranates are in flower" (7:13).

In the Song the royal gardens of imagination include a lavish display of every exotic plant and tree. Orchards of fruit-bearing trees, such as date palms and pomegranates, flourish. What we call botanical gardens captures some of that ambiance. Providing cool shade in the sun, edible hard-shell fruit, and valuable wood, a grove of walnut trees would have been prized in Palestine. Those commentators who favor a cultic interpretation of the Song of Songs offer possible evidence that the Kedron valley was a sacred walnut-grove valley. There stand the tombs of the slain prophets, there also the pagan child-sacrifice abominations of Tophet took place, and there also in an adjacent olive grove Jesus underwent the agony in the garden of Gethsemani (see

Marvin Pope, 574–84). Nut groves may also suggest inner wisdom. The hidden kernel of the nut, which is hard to uncover, is a metaphor of wisdom discovered only with effort. In the Hebrew scriptures wisdom was personified as a woman of great beauty. The Song of Songs has been read as a courtship praise of lady wisdom.

Twice the man is drawn into the gardens to see whether the pomegranate trees are flowering (6:11 and 7:13). Twice her cheeks are described rosy like a "slice of pomegranate" (4:3 and 6:7). She herself is described as an "enclosed garden," indeed "a paradise of pomegranates" (4:13), of whose fruit he is invited more than once to partake. In her fantasy of bringing him to her mother's house for a lesson in lovemaking, she would have him "drink of spiced wine, / The liquid blend of my own pomegranate" (8:2). The "pomegranates in bloom" provide a scene whose fruitfulness carries overtones of ripened sexuality and a promise of future fertility.

6:12
Or ever I was aware,
My soul made me like the chariots of Ammi-nadib.

Before I was aware, my reverie carried me in a chariot beside
   him.

The Hebrew text of this line of the Song is much in dispute. The words are common enough, but the syntax is so elusive that many quite different translations into English have been offered. Perhaps the wording presents idiomatic usage that has been lost over time. There may have been emendations that remain uncertain in their intent. Perhaps the manuscript has been corrupted by errors in its scribal transmission. A number of translators simply acknowledge that the text is finally inscrutable (see Marvin Pope, 584–92).

Since no one is sure what this verse means, no one is sure who is the speaker. In the major biblical English translations of this verse in the Song, the speaker is presumed to be the woman. Generally it is thought that she acknowledges her emotional fascination and delights in some fashion in a royal chariot. Most translations lean toward one of three variant readings: (1) "the royal chariots of my people," (2) "the chariots of Amminadab," (3) "the chariots of the people of the prince." Amminadab is a proper name found a dozen times in the Hebrew scriptures, but never with any clear symbolism that connects it with the Song of Songs.

The New Revised Standard Version of the Bible assumes the woman is the speaker: "Before I was aware, my fancy set me in a chariot beside my prince." A few translations have construed the speaker to be the man. "I did not know myself; she made me feel more than a prince reigning over the myriads [chariots] of his people" (New English Bible). To sample free translations: "There I lost my sense, feeling like a chariot driven by a princess" (Robert Graves), or "Ecstasy: for there, / O my nobleman's daughter, you will give me your myrrh" (Peter Jay).

The very inadequacy of our understanding of what the words of this text mean serves well to remind us of the ineffability of the experience of human love. Love's fullness is finally a silence before a great mystery. How the love of human beings for each other stems from and ends in the love of God eludes our comprehension. The Song of Songs is arguably a woman's story, told from a woman's point of view, mostly narrated in her voice, and plausibly revealing how a woman understands a woman's love story. But though we understand each of the words, published commentators seem to lack the syntax to translate that love story into a pattern that does not take its dominant images from the love stories told more frequently and more familiarly by men. The grammar of a woman's courtship is less widely known in print than the grammar of a man's. Women were not encouraged to write. That ignorance is being dispelled even in our day in the only way that it can be. Women must tell their own story ever more openly, and they must forge the categories and the images that express the particularity of a woman's experience of human love.

This obscure verse in the Song is a fair reminder of the human condition. Men and women share the same words, but they do not use the same grammar of imagination and hence they may not tell the same story. Woman's story has been told less compellingly. The value of the Song may lie precisely in its being an early and biblical example of a woman's story told from within a woman's experience, but nonetheless a text that is not altogether readable until the overall mystery is more fully spoken.

7:1 [6:13] [2]
Return, return, O Shulamite;
Return, return, that we may look upon thee.
What will ye see in the Shulamite?
As it were the company of two armies.

Spin around, spin, O Shulammite!
Spin, spin around, so that we may look upon you!
Why would you look on a dancing Shulammite twisting
    betwixt two sides?

*I*n this poem of the Song the speakers would seem to be an entourage, just like the festive guests earlier invited to "eat, friends, drink! Drink deep of love!" (5:1). Or these onlookers may be the "daughters of Jerusalem," who now and again function as a chorus in the Song. They now wish to look upon the woman in her moving beauty. She may be dancing, or just turning around to be seen. She may be returning to the group from an absence. Howsoever, on all sides they want to see her. The woman in the Song wonders why they wish to single her out with their regard. Of the body and dancing one commentator writes: "Our spirits, our souls, our love reside totally in our bodies, in our toes and knees and hips and vertebrae and necks and elbows and fingertips. Our faces are painted on. We draw black lines for eyes, red circles for cheekbones and ovals for a mouth" (Toni Bentley). In his poem "I Knew a Woman," the poet Theodore Roethke writes: "She moved in circles, and those circles moved."

Shulam is a word otherwise unattested in the Bible. It may be a feminine form of the name Solomon. If it is a place, she is a woman from Shulam, a Shulammite. Shulam may be a variant spelling for Shunem, a small farm village in Galilee near Mt. Tabor. The prophet Elisha is given generous hospitality by a woman of Shunem, and in return promises that she will bear a son despite her barren years (2 Kg 4:8–17). When the boy dies, Elisha raises back

---

[2]In the King James Bible chapter six of the Song has thirteen verses, and chapter seven thirteen. The present line is verse thirteen of chapter six. In the Hebrew and in the Greek Bibles, however, chapter six of the Song has only twelve verses, and the present line is verse one of chapter seven, which has fourteen verses in all.

to life this only son of this good woman of Shunem (2 Kg 4:18–37). Shunem was also the home of Abishag, who was the beautiful young concubine provided for David in his old age to keep him warm in bed in his last days (1 Kg 1:3, 15). After the death of King David, Bathsheba, the mother of King Solomon, intercedes for Adonijah, who seeks to marry Abishag (1 Kg 2:17–22). If the woman in the Song is intended as a Shunemmite (Shulammite), an allusion in these stories to the women from Shunem would add overtones to the Song of Songs.

Considerable disagreement remains about what are the sinuous motions of the woman in this scene. Some commentators conclude either she is dancing between two lines of onlookers, or the two lines are dancing about her in some ritual formation, such as the dance of the *mahanayim,* the so-called dance of the two camps. Thus in some way she is turned about between them. To this day some Syriac weddings include a sword dance that requires the bride and groom to pass between two rows of dancers or daggers. One might imagine the sensuous dance of the daughter of Herodias before King Herod that merited for her a promise: "Whatever you ask me, I will give you, even half of my kingdom" (Mk 6:23). In tradition her name was Salome, which is a feminine form of the name Solomon and a cognate root of the word *Shulam.* Surely Solomon suggests the archetype of the extravagant lover and the Shulammite in the Song the archetype of the beloved. Overall the implication is that her gracefulness resides in her body and not just in her garments. "Dance is the only art in which we ourselves are the stuff of which it is made" (Ted Shawn).

7:2 [7:1]
How beautiful are thy feet with shoes, O prince's daughter!
The joints of thy thighs are like jewels,
The work of the hands of a cunning workman.

How lovely your feet in sandals, O prince's daughter!
Your thighs are so curvaceous,
Like contours sculpted by an artisan.

*T*his poem is the third and last of the litanies describing the beauty of the body that are so characteristic of the Song of Songs. This litany of the woman's body begins with her feet "lovely . . . in sandals" (7:2) and rises to the crown of her hair "deep lustrous like purple" covering her head "held high like Carmel" (7:6). The previous litany of the woman (4:1–7) began with her head and moved down to her breasts. The speaker of this poem (7:1–7) may be the onlooking crowd in the preceding verse, who on all sides want to see the woman. It is also plausible that the speaker is now the man, to whom alone the sight of the body of the beloved is given. In some Oriental courtship the deliberate viewing of the unclothed female body is held as the equivalent of a marriage promise. No other such litany of this scope is found in the Bible.

Sandaled feet, pointed toes, and a slender ankle furnish an image of the well-turned female foot. Speaking of nubile Israel in her youth, the Lord God says: "I clothed you with embroidered cloth and with sandals of fine leather" (Ezk 16:10). Of Holofernes beguiled by Judith we read: "Her sandal ravished his eyes, her beauty captivated his mind" (Jdt 16:9). Because the feet of women are usually small and the weight they bear often slight, most women move with a graceful lightness on their feet. The more delicate female foot by its very configuration prompts a natural dancing. Rhythm pervades the human body and we dance with our feet whenever we move them. Our choreography may be simple but our feet move in a signature footfall that flows from the song in our heart. We each march to our own drummer. The "feet" marked off in scanning lines of poetry testify to how closely related song and dance remain in the expression of the human soul. The appellation "princess daughter" is probably a reference to the dignity and poise of the woman's carriage rather than to her actual royal birth.

The Hebrew word for the *curves* of her thigh is another word otherwise unattested in the Bible. An exact translation is hard to ascertain because we have no other example of usage. If her feet are dressed in sandals it might be argued that her thighs are covered with clothes, "contours sculpted by an artisan." If, however, she is dancing, it seems more likely that the full shapeliness of her thighs is being revealed. In the rest of this litany, the focus remains on her body rather than on her vestment. Her motion discloses the symmetrical beauty of her thighs. Because of the wider hip bones of the female the upper thighs do have a generous feminine curvature, which is quite different in a mature woman and a young girl. Where the upper leg joins the pelvis also carries a strong erotic appeal. These contours of the female body are here described as the perfect fittings of a craftsman whose handiwork is shaped to a lovely curved form. Some kind of ornamental pelvic girdle may also be indicated in this verse of the Song.

In sum, sandaled foot and curvaceous leg move with gracefulness, and it
is this overall beauty of form and motion that this line of the Song captures
so well in this delightful figure of the woman. "Ah, when she moved, she
moved more ways than one: / The shapes a bright container can contain!"
(Theodore Roethke, "I Knew a Woman").

7:3 [7:2]
Thy navel is like a round goblet, which wanteth not liquor:
Thy belly is like a heap of wheat set about with lilies.

Your netherlands are a valley bowl,
Festal wine in sure supply.
Your belly a mound of wheat rimmed with lilies.

*T*he previous verse of this litany begins with the woman's beautiful sandaled
feet and moves to her shapely thighs. This verse concludes with a description
of her belly as a mound of wheat. Lying between thighs and belly her "netherlands" are included in the litany of her physical beauty. The Hebrew word in
its most literal meaning suggests the umbilical, and many translations speak
of her navel, further described as a bowl lacking no festal wine. Does the
Song intend the navel, whose shape might suggest a very small bowl? Does
this line with a modest reticence avoid direct reference to the woman's vulva,
which is a larger bowl whose excitation produces a love water that might be
poetically imagined as a festal wine? Such circumlocution is not uncommon
in the Bible. When going to sleep with Boaz on the wheat threshing floor,
Ruth is told with delicate modesty that she is "to uncover his feet and lie
down" (Ruth 3:4). To allow for wider meanings I chose "netherlands," by
which I have tried to indicate her lower abdomen, without specific reference
to her navel, her loins, or her genitalia. "Netherlands" retains the poetic context
and does not introduce an overliteral or jaringly clinical tone. The eroticism
in the Song is naive and innocent, which seeks to conceal as well as to reveal.
   These netherlands of the woman are shaped like a bowl, which is *rounded,*
a descriptive word that is otherwise unattested in the Bible. I have translated

it as "valley" bowl, in order to keep the landscape imagery of the whole line. While navel does present the image of an oversmall bowl, it does correspond well with the following mention of the belly like a mound of wheat. The navel also suggests an implicit relationship with the fruit of lovemaking, the infant attached by the umbilical to its mother's womb. Perhaps the navel includes the whole childbearing concavity of the woman.

In the varied sexual connotations of this rich and metaphorical verse of the Song we are reminded how female sexuality is always shaped by the joyful capacity and dangerous vulnerability of childbearing. In her body woman is always Eve, mother of the living. She remains the fertile field, and her belly the mound of wheat full of the seeds of life. To this day it remains customary in many places to throw rice seed as the bride emerges from the wedding ceremony. Thus the woman's netherlands are aptly described as a "valley bowl" where life may abound, "a land of grain and wine, a land of bread and vineyards" (2 Kg 18:32).

The physical fecundity of the female is almost incalculable. Although equally true of men, whose seed number as the sands of the seashore, men do not believe in their fertility as much as they believe in woman's. Men experience no new life inside their body. The fruitfulness of the female body would seem surely to be implied in the image of the wheat seed that will become oven bread. Woman is the golden bowl, the moon-shaped chalice, the holy grail that holds a precious blood-red life. Woman brings forth children in whose bodies the whole universe of the future is coiled as eggs within eggs within eggs, like the containment of a Russian Matuska doll. To Jesus, the bread of life and life-saver of the world, a woman would say of his mother: "Blessed is the womb that bore you and the breasts that nursed you!" (Lk 11:27).

The valley bowl full of *festal* wine introduces another word unattested in the Bible. A wine punch mixed with water and spices was not uncommon. Flavor could be enhanced. Guests could drink more and not become inebriated. Wine coolers in our own day bear a certain resemblance. Later in the Song the woman says to the man: "I would have you drink of spiced wine, / The liquid blend of my own pomegranate" (8:2). Here is a sweet and fruity wine, the happy joy of the vineyard and of the intoxicating ecstasy of love itself.

The rounded shape and tawny color of a wheat stack may have given birth to the image of the belly of the woman described as a mound of wheat. At harvest time the threshed grain is gathered into stacks that must be safeguarded from animals and thieves by a hedge of thorns or a barrier of some kind.

"When fire breaks out and catches in thorns so that the stacked grain or the standing grain or the field is consumed, the one who started the fire shall make full restitution" (Ex 22:6). The belly of the woman is rimmed with lilies. She is fenced in by flowers and protected not by force but by love's own symbol. These lilies carry overtones of a protective curtain surrounding the approaches to the mystery of the feminine. Lilies are like lace, like lingerie, replete with ruffles and pleats. Earlier in the Song we are told the man meanders in the garden of lilies and finds in her his food (2:16 and 6:3). Amid these lilies a delicate physical intimacy prevails. The flower is fragrant and colorful. Whether her body is veiled with gossamer, or her midriff bounded by an ornamental girdle around pelvic hips and loins, her body is well adorned and encircled with beauty. Hence she is the harvest wheat, the bread of new life, "rimmed with lilies."

In a Christian reading of the Song, Jesus compares himself to the gate for the sheep (Jn 10: 7). He is the good shepherd who lays down at the entrance to the hedged-in area where the sheep were gathered at night for safety. The thief or marauder would have to enter over his own body, which served as the very protective fence-door. When the crucified Jesus is laid in the grave they "rolled a stone against the door of the tomb." Life itself was closed off with a dark and heavy weight. But "strong as death is love" (8:6), and Jesus, who is the wheaten bread of eternal life, is truly risen.

7:4 [7:3]
Thy two breasts are like two young roes that are twins.

Your breasts are like a pair of fawns, the twins of a gazelle.

*T*his line of the Song repeats verbatim the praise of her breasts given earlier in the Song (4:5). In that line the "twins of a gazelle nibble amid the lilies." Was the lily-browsing a gloss added to the original line, which is given here? Or does the present line omit the developed description, perhaps because of the mention of lilies in the preceding verse?

In the present context the woman is very likely in motion, and probably dancing. The movement of her breasts under light clothing or unclothed may suggest some resemblance to fawns playfully gamboling. Adult and infant satisfaction here merge, erotic and maternal enchantment blend in the female breast with all its sensual fascination. Visual and oral pleasure combine with soft tactile satisfaction. The full and rich rotundity of the female here is celebrated. The scene is overall one of a pastoral idyll, wherein all life leans jauntily on the breast of mother earth in all her epiphanies.

7:5 [7:4]
Thy neck is as a tower of ivory;
Thine eyes like the fishpools of Heshbon, by the gate of Bath-
    rabbim:
Thy nose is as the tower of Lebanon which looketh toward
    Damascus.

Your neck a tower of ivory.
Your eyes are pools in Heshbon by the gates of Bath-rabbim.
Your nose a tower of Lebanon facing Damascus.

*T*he litany of the woman's beauty continues to move upward. This line of the Song describes her face and possibly her sidelong profile. Various translations do not agree whether the text intends to specify her nose, her eyebrows, her forehead, or the entire configuration of her face. The lovely curve of a slender female neck does strike even a casual observer with its gracefulness. The woman's large, dark, and moist eyes, "pools in Heshbon," convey the peace and calm of quiet deep wells of spring water. Her prominent nose harmonizes with her striking and pronounced facial beauty and enhances her overall attraction. In all this description sketched very quickly with a verbal brush much like the swift strokes of a water-colorist, the reader should see the total configuration of her countenance—the regal bearing of her neck and the liquid eyes separated by a straight-line nose. The paintings of women by Modigliani might come to mind.

Because the sequence of this litany proceeds from her sandaled feet to the crown of hair on her head, the sequence of this line may intend to move from neck to eyes to the brow, and to include the whole forehead, which faces forward like "a tower of Lebanon facing Damascus." All the features of her face appear richly endowed, prominent, and central in importance. They are associated with the capital cities of the Amorites (Heshbon) and the Assyrians (Damascus). Thus her facial features are commanding like a tower and dominant in their position overlooking the landscape below.

Her neck is described as a tower of ivory. Earlier in the poem her neck had been compared to the imposing "tower of David" (4:4). The ivory tower metaphor may imply the delicate curve of the ivory tusk. Perhaps the reference is to her neck circled with ivory-inlaid necklaces, a description parallel to "the tower of David roped with bucklers" (4:4). Very likely the line intends to delight in ivory smooth skin and the opaque cream color of her flesh. Perhaps the reader will hear an overtone of the inaccessible maiden preserved in a high tower, in order to safeguard what is valuable and to defend what is vulnerable. The neck not only connects the body with the head, it also channels the breath of fresh air into the life of the whole body. Food is carried through the throat to the body. Blood from the heart rises along the arteries on the outer edges of the neck to provide conscious life to the mind. All that is vital and fragile is gracefully yet precariously carried by this slender tower of ivory.

Her lover sees her eyes as "pools in Heshbon." Heshbon (probably Hisban [Hesban] near Amman in Jordan, north of Madaba) was a Transjordan city known for its deep wells and calm reservoirs. "Heshbon with its pasture lands" (Josh 21:39 or Num 21:26–30). Located somewhat east of Jericho along the Jordan river and one of its tributaries, Heshbon enjoyed abundant water and the luxuriance of an oasis. Ruins of a large reservoir remain to this day. These clear pools would probably be located by the city gates for easy access to the city water supply. Bath-rabbim remains an unidentified location, but plausibly one of the city gates of Heshbon. Bath-rabbim may mean "daughter of many," and hence a main gate (see Heshbon of the Ammonites and the "daughters of Rabbah" in Jer 49:3).

The "tower of Lebanon" may be an indirect reference to the well-defined mountains of Lebanon, which tower over the surrounding landscape. It faces Damascus in the east where the sun rises. Lebanon is derived from the word for the color white (laben), and the "tower of Lebanon" may also suggest the radiance of her face. The woman stands upright and stately, and from her direct regard there is no retreat. How the imagery all functions exactly we may never know. We do know the Song intends in this litany to pay compliments to the imposing beauty of her facial appearance.

7:6

Thine head upon thee is like Carmel,
And the hair of thine head like purple;
The King is held in the galleries.

Your head held high like Carmel,
And your hair deep lustrous like purple;
A king is tangled in its tresses.

From the bottom of her toes to the top of her head the Song has surveyed the beauty of the woman's body in the eyes of her beloved. Beauty may be in the eyes of the beholder, but the poet sketches her form with deft strokes that leave the observer convinced. One has seen with the mind's eye a vision of loveliness. Her head is "held high" like Mt. Carmel, which is the coastal mountain plateau that overlooks the contemporary port city of Haifa (the crusader city of Accra). Here the prophet Elijah called down fire from heaven to consume the holocaust and to destroy the false prophets of Baal (1 Kg 18). The mountain remains a holy place, and the ascent of Mount Carmel a short-hand for the laborious ascetic discipline of the spiritual life that leads finally to the mystic nuptials of the soul with divine Love (see the commentaries on the Song of Songs by John of the Cross and by Teresa of Avila).

In the Song the woman's hair is black (4:1 and 6:5) and fine like mohair. Her dark hair has a bright sheen, "deep lustrous like purple." A woman's hair places a luxuriant crown on her head. "Head held high like *Carmel*" (the geographic location) or carmil (the crimson-purple color) might be combined in a word play that claims both meanings. One might imagine Mount Carmel and "the purple mountains' majesty." On the coast of the Mediterranean Sea, Carmel was easily associated with the crimson-purple dye extracted at great expense from the tiny murex shellfish. In the Song we saw the palanquin of King Solomon, "its couch of purple weave" (3:10). This purple color was a dazzling mixture, which preserved the brilliance of the red and the intensity of the blue. It was royal purple, the color of kings and queens. "And Solomon made the curtain [of the temple] of blue and purple and crimson fabrics and fine linen, and worked cherubim into it" (2 Chr 3:14). Perhaps the woman in the Song rinsed her black hair with the reddish henna dye or the rich dye of the murex. Perhaps her black hair simply sparkled in the sunlight with natural highlights "deep lustrous like purple."

"Beauty draws us with a single hair" (Alexander Pope). A king is "tangled in its tresses." We have seen the man compared to a king earlier in the Song (1:4 and 1:12). The "tresses" of her hair remains an uncertain reading. The whole line seems to be an unusual tangent or editorial aside in the otherwise straightforward catalog of the woman's bodily features. Long loose hair flowing from a beautiful woman has been seen especially by men as a compelling physical attraction. Paul writes: "but if a woman has long hair, it is her glory" (1 Cor 11:15). A woman's hair unbound was also associated with the inspired trance of the sibyls and the women prophets. Loose hair carried an aura of wildness. A woman's hair out of control suggested some overwhelming emotion. To this day we speak of less responsible behavior as letting one's hair down. John of the Cross says that one strand of the beloved's hair is enough, because the divine king and lover of the human soul wishes to be captured.

In the Song a kingly power is enveloped in her queenly beauty, "robed in the long night of her deep hair" (Tennyson). A sovereign is held captive by her locks. One may readily think of the grand passion love stories, of Samson and Delilah, Dido and Aeneas, David and Bathsheba, Cleopatra and Antony, Romeo and Juliet. The man is entranced with the woman whose beauty and whose person overwhelm him. More often than not he remains unable to understand his fascination that becomes an entanglement much of his own making. Human beings are indeed often tangled lovers tied in tangled tresses, drawn powerfully to each other and yet often struggling to regain the equilibrium required for a friendship that continues both to intrigue and most of all to enable the lovers to be themselves.

7:7 [7:6]
How fair and how pleasant art thou, O love, for delights!

How beautiful and how exquisite you are,
How dear, my beloved, my maiden of ecstasy!

This line of the Song may well conclude this litany of her beauty (7:2–7). "How beautiful your feet" (7:2) and "how beautiful you are" (7:7) does seem to form boundaries enclosing her entire elegant description in its borders. Probably the man speaks her praises, though it is not impossible that onlookers voice them. He also speaks of his admiration for her (7:6c to 7:10a). She then picks up the dialog and pursues their courtship in the poem's remaining lines (7:10b to 7:14). More than a dozen times in the Song the word for beautiful is spoken of her or of him. More often than not she is the beautiful one ("beautiful among women" in 1:8, 5:9, 6:1; "beautiful you are" in 1:15, 1:16, 4:1, 7:7; "my beauty" in 2:10 and 2:13; "altogether beautiful" in 4:7; "lovely" in 6:4).

Salacious dancers also give access to the sight of their body, but they do not give access to themselves. Nudity is not nakedness, if by nakedness we mean self-disclosure. To look upon a person with lust is to turn the person into an object. To gaze upon the body with love and devotion is to confirm it as a subject of great value and as a mystery never known just by what one can see. One of the evils in lude dancing, besides the demeaning of women who perform and men who leer, is the illusion of privilege on demand. The voyeur entertains the fantasy that he can buy intimacy. Lewdness dulls the human capacity to look upon the body with integrity and to enjoy the revelation of lovers who want to see each other body and soul as they are.

The Song of Songs does not in these lines conclude a lascivious dance, but rather the text suggests the playful imagination of a lover who knows that the body of the beloved cannot be seen except with the eyes of the grateful heart and in the appreciative gift of a mutual love that respects the mystery of the human person veiled forever in the human body, where the flesh is an invitation to communion with the whole human person.

"My maiden of ecstasy" may well speak of the surpassing joys of physical lovemaking between man and woman. No other physical pleasure seems comparable to sexual union with its enveloping passion. The man may also be recalling his previous knowledge of the woman (for example, the garden tryst of 4:16 and 5:1). When Adam falls in love with Eve at first sight "the man and his wife were both naked, and were not ashamed" (Gen 2: 25). One easily imagines the delight of God as the father of the bride who presents Eve to Adam. As Adam takes his joy in Eve, so the man delights in the beloved woman of the Song, so she delights in him, and so God delights in each one us. To be faithful to that vision of love seen in the beloved and never fully grasped in this life is to keep infinite desire alive. Such a desire is finally a desire to see the face of God, who delights more in us than any human spouse delights in their beloved in this life, which so foreshadows a yet greater love.

7:8 [7:7]
This thy stature is like to a palm tree,
And thy breasts to clusters of grapes.

Your standing is like a palm tree,
Your breasts as date clusters.

A young lithe tall female figure compared to a palm tree may well seem appropriate to the imagination. "I grew tall like a palm tree in En-gedi, and like rosebushes in Jericho" (Sir 24:14). A desert oasis was typically shaded with palm trees, and Jericho with its plentiful waters was called "the city of palm trees" (Dt 34:3 and 2 Chr 28:15). Her bodily stature is stately like the royal palm tree—graceful, elegant, slender, and swaying in the breeze. "The righteous flourish like the palm tree" (Ps 92:12). In Hebrew the date palm tree is called *tamar,* which is a common female name. Apropos one might read the poignant stories of the two women named Tamar in the Bible (see Gen 38: 12–20 and 2 Sam 13:1 and 14:27).

Her breasts are described as date clusters hanging from the height of the date palm tree. Male and female palm trees are required for pollination, but only the female trees bear clusters of dates as their fruit. Dates are sweet food, dark and rich fruit, hanging close together in round-shaped clusters. She may be here imagined as a young high-breasted maiden—"Our little sister, she yet has no breasts" (8:8). Date clusters are also heavy fruits that weigh down as do the breasts of a mature woman—"my breasts are like towers" (8:10). In the next line of the Song her breasts are described as grape clusters.

The breasts of a woman are a natural symbol of food and drink, of abundant life. To see her and to touch her seems a special disclosure reserved for the beloved. We catch perhaps a glimpse of the unbounded glory of heaven in the shaped glories of this earth. "The longing to love the beauty of the world in a human being is essentially the longing for the Incarnation" (Simone Weil).

7:9 [7:8]
I said, I will go up to the palm tree,
I will take hold of the boughs thereof:
Now also thy breasts shall be as clusters of the vine,
And the smell of thy nose like apples;

Yes, yes, I will climb the palm tree and put my hands on its limbs.
May your breasts be like grape clusters
And your breathing as the aroma of apples.

*H*er figure slender as a palm tree and her breasts ripe as date clusters bring the man to an impatient exclamation. He will wrap himself around that palm tree and climb up to handle its fruits. The word for limbs or branches in the Song is otherwise unattested in the Bible, and we do not know exactly how the metaphor works. Clearly, however, the scene is quite amorous.

In the previous line the female breast is compared to date clusters. With grape clusters the imagery continues the erotic presentation of the breast as weighty fruit. Grapes clusters do have a shape that might be suggestive of the female breast. Moreover, wine from grapes makes the heart glad. From Palestine the Hebrew scouts return to Moses saying: "We came to the land to which you sent us; it flows with milk and honey, and this [large grape cluster] is its fruit" (Num 13:27). To cherish the woman's land is to draw from her heart a love richer than milk and sweeter than honey.

In painting, not infrequently the Blessed Virgin Mary nursing Jesus with her milk is shown seated in a grape arbor or with grape clusters in her hand. Jesus in turn gives his blood from the open wound in his side, the blood that the wine becomes in the mystery of the Christian Eucharist. Like a mother, Jesus feeds his disciples with food of his body and drink of his blood. Thus the grape cluster might come to symbolize both the female breast and the Eucharistic wine that mediate the mystery of a love that gives of its very substance to the beloved. We thirst for this draught of human kindness and this wine of divine compassion. Even Jesus thirsts and asks for a drink from the woman at the well (Jn 4). And she yearns for a living water, a water that will quench her thirst once and for all, and which Jesus who is Lord wishes to give to her and to everyone upon this earth.

Just as the body is our first environment, so the womb is our first total world. Tumultuous as our first tumbling arrival into our mother's womb may have been, the uterine world remains our first experience, however "remembered or impressed upon us, of a welcome into a world that we must find a place in or die" (R. D. Laing). We were then attached without intermission to our mother's uterine breast, the placenta itself a form of our lips holding tightly to the concave surface. It is quite possible that we never are quite reconciled with the loss of this our first mother's breast and the whole world that was focused upon supporting us with its life. Upon birth we are divided in two, irrevocably sundered by the sword from the gates of paradise where we once rested and lay our body upon the softest seas in a cosmos of delight.

Born into this world, we nurse milk at our mother's breast. It is to an infant a miniature globe, a universe of food and warm care. Thereafter we seek our living from mother earth, that round warm breast that yields grain and fruit in due season. Joining the uterine world and the cosmic world stands the figure of woman, part of both worlds, on whose breast, whether we were infant girl or infant boy, we hung for our food and our love for so long. Our mother's breast may be lost to us; a woman's breast may never be forgotten.

The man claims her breath is "as the aroma of apples." She has earlier compared him to an "apple tree in a dense woodland" (2:3). The color, fragrance, shape, and taste of apples all combine to make a fruit of perfect sensuality: "under the apple tree I roused you"(8:5). He wishes the aura around her may always be of apples, aromatic in the sun, apple blossom time come to autumn harvest. More literal readings have construed the breathing of the woman to be her kisses, perhaps some form of nose-kisses by which breath is shared. I prefer a reference to the continuing song of her mystery and the fragrant essence of her bodily presence. Of the ambient mystery of the divine we read: "I will be like the dew to Israel; he shall blossom like the lily, he shall strike root like the forests of Lebanon. His shoots shall spread out; his beauty shall be like the olive tree, and his fragrance like that of Lebanon. They shall again live beneath my shadow, they shall flourish as a garden; they shall blossom like the vine, their fragrance shall be like the wine of Lebanon" (Hos 14:5–8).

7:10 [7:9]
And the roof of thy mouth like the best wine
For my beloved, that goeth down sweetly,
Causing the lips of those that are asleep to speak.

Your mouth is like a fine wine
Smoothly running over [lips and teeth].

*E*arlier in the Song the woman has desired the "kisses of his lips" (1:2), "lips like crimson lilies" (5:13), and she exclaimed "his mouth is honey sweet" (5:16). Earlier in the Song he finds her "lips distill wild honey" (4:11). In this line he finds her mouth "like a fine wine." The image might refer to the words of their lips, but more likely their kisses, which speak a promise of a love "sweeter than wine" (1:2). Leanne Ponder's poem ("The Poet") captures the flavor of this passage:

"A page is no place for a poem," he said
laying down his pen
to write a sonnet with his tongue
on her
astonished
skin.

The dialog is thought to shift from his voice to hers as she completes his words with her own words: "smoothly running over lips and teeth." The verb is otherwise unattested in the Bible, and the meaning of her words remains uncertain. "Lips and teeth" are a reconstruction of a line too obscure in the

Hebrew to render with any certainty. The whole verse, nevertheless, carries the implication of sensual and intimate kisses.

Whether this line is about wet kisses given and taken, or intimate words spoken and heard, there is a commingling of body and of soul, of physical excitement and of personal communication. We give the words of our mouth to those whom we wish to give some access to ourselves. When we are truly indifferent to someone, we do not listen to them and we do not address even angry words to them. They simply do not exist for us, and by our silence we offer them no share in our life. To talk to someone is to give them a piece of our mind; it is to reveal what we intend and what we hold ourselves to be. A friend, a confidant, a mentor, a counselor, a teacher is given a privileged entrance into the soul of another. In our promises, moreover, we cup ourselves in our hands like water. We risk our integrity for better or for worse. We claim the truth as our witness.

In the words of our mouth we give an opening into our heart. The Latin word for wisdom is *sapientia*, which stems from the word to taste and to savor (*sapere*). Of the divine wisdom the Psalms speak: "O taste and see that the Lord is good; happy are those who take refuge in him" (34:8). In the biblical word of God we enjoy an undeserved intimacy with God. God has spoken to us of the inner life of the Father, the Son, and the Holy Spirit. In the word made flesh, who is the Son of God made man, God has given us everything. The word of God is the love of God, and the song of God is a love song.

7:11 [7:10]
I am my beloved's, and his desire is toward me.

I am my beloved's and his desire is for me.

*T*he woman joyfully proclaims: "I am my beloved's and his desire is for me." Earlier in the Song she says: "I am my beloved's and he is mine" (6:3). In the beginning of the Song this same sentiment is voiced by her in reverse order: "My beloved is mine and I am his" (2:16). The woman is full of confidence. She knows him with whom she has fallen in love, and she knows that he has fallen in love with her. She takes the initiative to declare their bond and to celebrate its mutuality. The courtship is regularly shaped by her gestures and justified with her words. The woman in the Song is assertive without apology and with the full freedom of a human being equal to her lover. Here is no male-generated stereotypical image of woman as a passive attraction able only to surrender herself to a man. Shakespeare's "Woman, thy name is frailty" would not become her. Jeremiah speaks in prophetic mystery: "How long will you waver, O faithless daughter? For the Lord has created a new thing on the earth: a woman encompasses a man" (31:22).

After the fall in the garden of Eden the Lord God tells Eve: "in pain you will bring forth children, yet your *desire* shall be for your husband and he shall rule over you" (Gen 3:16). Despite the consequent suffering, a woman's love for her man will dominate her. She has become dependent, if not upon him alone, then upon her own *desire* for him. The Song here uses the same Hebrew word in *Genesis* to mark a dramatic reversal. Her *desire* for him will no longer be one-sided and hence dependent. His desire will equally be for her ("and his desire is for me"). Their desire for each other will become mutual and supportive. I belong to him; he belongs to me. Theirs will be a dance of love where one leads and then the other, each knowing the rhythm and unspoken intent of their courtship. In the Song of Songs the happiness of the primeval story is regained, and man and woman love each other as the creator intended before they were driven apart by the divisive effects of sinfulness into roles of dominion and submission.

In giving her love to a man a woman gives her body and her soul. I believe men also love wholeheartedly, though culture influences them not to recognize and readily admit such a bond. Her commitment by its very nature implicates a future. If the man she loves turns away from her to another woman, her rejection is profound. She gave of her self, who she is and what she is. Though she has been given away, she has been set aside by an unfaithful companion. She is not enough. Yet she knows she must be enough, because she gave all she is. She could have given herself to another, who would have appreciated her for her self had she foreseen this disregard. In an unfaithful love she can hardly retrieve herself. She is given, and she comes to feel terribly wasted. Only in a faithful love is her gift recognized and is she treasured. Hence in the Song this line is a cry of such hopeful happiness. Her gift has been received. Her worth has been recognized. As the beloved who has given everything,

she is prized as she should be. She is "the pearl of great price." The man in
the Song knows what an awesome risk she has taken when she says "I am
my beloved's." The reception of her gift is revealed in her exclamation: "and
his desire is for me."

When Adam and Eve fall away from God as their heart's desire, they fall
away from each other. God speaks through the human heart's desire, and at
bottom every sexual desire is a spiritual desire for the knowledge and friendship of God. In the pristine world of the Song, the woman and man manifest
an innocent love, a love that leads to mutual respect and harmony with the
God who is love and who created human love in God's own image: "male
and female he created them" (Gen 1:27). The Song of Songs sings of a time
when there will be no conflict between woman and man, and none between
their love for each other and their love for the creator who made them. It is
of a paradise outside the past that the Song sings, a paradise to be claimed
in wisdom and prophetic vision, a human love coming to know sexual integrity
by the grace of God, who is creating "a new heaven and a new earth" (Rev 21:1).

7:12 [7:11]
Come, my beloved, let us go forth into the field;
Let us lodge in the villages.

Come, my heart's love, come into the fields,
Let us pass the night amid the villages.

*S*he invites him into the fields of the countryside. Let him spend the night
with her in the pastoral lands about the small rural *villages*. The Hebrew word
is uncertain, and *cypresses* or *henna bushes* have also been read. With an
elaborate metaphor of the body as a garden of paradise she had previously
expressed herself to him: "Let my true love come into his garden" (4:16). In
neither a wild desert nor a crowded city does she wish to be alone with her
beloved. She seeks the open fields amid the plentiful fruitfulness of the cultivated landscape of human husbandry. Outside court tradition and urban custom, they would be free to express with abandon the joy of their mutual love.

Out of sight they might spend together the whole night long. Earlier in the Song he invites her to come away with him into the springtime countryside: "Rise up, love of my soul, my beauty, come away! / Lo, winter is over, the rains are done and gone" (2:10–11). Again he invites her to come away with him: "Come down from Lebanon, my bride, come along with me from Lebanon" (4:8). Once again she summons him to come away with her.

Her invitation to come into the fields is an invitation given to him to come unto her. Sexual intimacy is ever a privilege given. Over no other part of our life do we guard the gate so exclusively. Even prostitutes who have given a rented access to their body will characteristically reserve some gesture of lovemaking, which token of themselves is not for sale. No other contact with the body is so intensely private. Intercourse gives access to the core of the body. No other intimacy reaches so far into the body of another. No other touch risks so much of personal vulnerability for heartache as well as long consequences of life and of death. Sex remains that peculiar bonding of human beings that is so enduring precisely because for a time two become one flesh. So profound a gift of love comes by invitation only.

> It's all I have to bring today—
> This, and my heart beside,
> This and my heart, and all the fields,
> And all the meadows wide.
>
> (Emily Dickinson, Poem 26)

"Let us pass the night amid the villages" amplifies "come into the fields." In the long night the dream of their unqualified communion will be befriended. In darkness there need be no boundaries to mother earth, to self-forgetfulness, to a love in the human body and in the human soul too deep and too mysterious to comprehend or to manipulate. Such measureless night whispers of the infinite love of God. At the end of the book of Revelation the bride of the lamb sums up the whole love story between God and humanity: "The one who testifies to these things says, 'surely I am coming soon.' Amen. Come Lord Jesus!" (Rev 22:20).

7:13 [7:12]
Let us get up early to the vineyards;
Let us see if the vine flourish, whether the tender grape appear,
And the pomegranates bud forth:
There will I give thee my loves.

Let us be off early into the vineyards; let us see if the vines are
  sprouting,
If the grape blossoms have opened, and the pomegranates are
  in flower.
There will I give you my love.

*E*laborating upon the preceding verse the woman continues the invitation
to journey into the fruitful countryside. It is daytime now, and she would lead
him into a vineyard of grapes and an orchard of pomegranates. She promises
him: "There will I give you my love." She chooses this bestowal because she
is the vineyard (1:6, 2:15, 7:9, 8:12); she is the orchard (4:12–13); she is the
fruit (4:16 and 7:14); she is the bowl never lacking a festal wine (7:3).

Jesus says" "I am the true vine, and my Father is the vine grower" (Jn 15:1).
In the marriage feast of Cana the water is changed into wine, lest the bride
and groom be embarrassed that the wine is in short supply. Never again will
profane love lack its invitation to the wedding feast of a sacred love that would
embrace and expand the human heart. In the Christian sacrament of marriage
the bride and groom, who have just exchanged wedding vows, join together
for the first time as a married couple in the mystery of the Eucharistic supper—
the bread of life that is the body of the Lord and the wine that is the blood
of the Lord given for them.

To see whether the "vines are sprouting" and "the pomegranates are in
flower" echoes earlier evocations in the Song: "to see were the vines in blossom,
were the pomegranates in bloom" (6:11; see also 2:12). This springtime effer-
vescence may reflect the intensity that her willing love arouses in him. The
Bible speaks of sexual relations as a profound knowing of another person.
"Now the man [Adam] knew his wife Eve" (Gen 4:1). Filling a space within
another and making a space for another remains the most intimate touch and
wonderful excitement of man and woman.

To arouse another human being is to mirror the creation awakening, when God is imagined to touch and breathe life into a waiting body. We are our bodies; our bodies express our souls. Human beings are enfleshed spirit and incarnate soul. To be in touch with another is to become vulnerable and revealed in soul as well as in body. There is no greater trust and no greater taming of what is wild within us than when two human beings communicate with their whole self, body and soul. Then their words, their service, their thoughtfulness, and all of what is theirs together as a couple culminates in the profound unity and joy that sexual intimacy can create. Such happy intercourse becomes the celebration of that seemingly banal human outercourse, which day by day forges a bond throughout a lifetime. In short, lovers stem from friends, and the fruits of the body ripen from the flowerings of the soul.

7:14 [7:13]
The mandrakes give a smell,
And at our gates are all manner of pleasant fruits.
New and old,
Which I have laid up for thee, O my beloved.

The mandrakes perfume the air, and on our lintel's every
   delicacy;
A fresh and ripened harvest, O my heart's love,
I've held in keep for you.

*M*andrake fruits are popularly called "love apples." The word for mandrakes in the Hebrew is related to the word for love that is frequently used in the Song. The appearance of the potatolike mandrake roots bears some resemblance to the human trunk and legs in an erotic configuration. Mandrakes were an ancient aphrodisiac. The small apple-shaped, yellowish, mandrake fruit with its purple veins was thought to stimulate sexual appetite and to enhance female fertility. In the Bible story Rachel conceives a child after bargaining for the mandrakes that Leah's son had found in the field: "she conceived and bore a son, and said, 'God has taken away my reproach'; and she named him Joseph, saying, 'May the Lord add to me another son!'" (Gen 30:23–24). From the fruit a narcotic wine was also made. Shakespeare's Juliet swallows a potion of *mandragora,* one of the "drowsy syrups of the world," that drugs her into the deep coma that is her feigned death.

"And on our lintel every delicacy." The reference may suggest the threshold to her house and the room where her mother bore her (3:4 and 8:2). Surely it will turn the reader's attention to the senses as the avenues of the body and the sensual feast that she is even now preparing as his welcome. Choice fruits will be displayed, and she herself the best of "every delicacy." Indeed, "Let my true love come into his garden and eat of its hand-picked fruits" (4:16).

The gospel claims that "every scribe who has been trained for the kingdom of heaven is like the master of a household who brings out of his treasure what is new and what is old" (Mt 13:52). "Fresh and ripened harvest," fruit both new and yet old, all speak of the woman's abundance. She is the cornucopia of the autumn season described so mellifluously in Keats' "Ode to Autumn." She bestows herself into the waiting arms of her lover with full knowledge that her gift of self is extravagant. She has gathered herself up. She has waited. She has chosen. She gives her self to him with a lavish and magnanimous prodigality. This scene in the Song takes on the atmosphere of a sacred ritual with food and drink. Their lovemaking is celebrated as a banquet of body and soul.

Ezekiel is prepared for his vocation as the Lord's prophet in a vision that commands him: "Eat this scroll, and go, speak to the house of Israel. . . . Then I ate it; and in my mouth it was as sweet as honey" (3:1,3). When we eat and drink at the table of the Lord in the Eucharist, his body fills us and transforms our body into that divine life that we have eaten. Beyond the host who provides food, homegrown and well prepared and gladly served, Jesus gives us a more ultimate bread. Jesus offers himself, his body given for us, the giver and the gift perfectly conformed. Of this divine love story the Bible concludes: "Let us rejoice and exult and give him the glory, for the marriage of the lamb has come, and his bride has made herself ready" (Rev 19:7).

8:1

O that thou wert as my brother,
That sucked the breasts of my mother!
When I should find thee without, I would kiss thee;
Yea, I should not be despised.

Would that you were my brother, given milk at my mother's
   breast!
Were I familiar with you in public, no one would think less of
   me.

𝒯he woman daydreams of a situation where her affection for the beloved could be expressed in an uninhibited way. There is no sign they are yet betrothed much less married. If he were her brother, one of her "mother's sons" (1:6), there would be no suspicion aroused by any familial expression of affection. If he were a brother, she could be to him a sister. She wants to touch him tenderly in front of everyone. The Song begins "may he kiss me with the kisses of his lips" (1:1). The bounded affection of sister and brother here merges with the unbounded love of wife and husband. We have seen in the Song how he readily names her "my sister, my bride" (4:9–5:1). We have seen how her love for him also risks public humiliation (3:1–5 and 5:2–8). In a spiritual reading, one might draw a parallel with the incarnation of Jesus the Christ, our brother, one with us in the flesh of the family of humankind and God-with-us.

For the child the mother's breast has been described as the primal state of grace, a condition timeless, effortless, and euphoric. To feed another is always a privileged access to their body and a singular intimacy. The woman who gives her breast feeds her child not just her milk but herself. The father who spoon feeds his children also knows a special closeness to their lives. Something of the "unqualified, boundless, helpless passion" of the child may yet linger in the adult. Human beings need love as much as they need food. Indeed, love is the food of the soul. The minister who gives out the communion bread or wine knows that he or she has been given entry into the spiritual life of another human being. To feed somebody the body of Christ, who himself feeds us his body and blood, is to share a spiritual intimacy.

Mother earth (*materia*) is the matter of all life. Eve is mother of all the living. From a woman we all come. In her we grow and of her we are fed.

A mother's milk becomes a mother's love. The child with its lips at a mother's breast and the lover with lips in a kiss share a resemblance. Need, affection, and love are sought. The gift of the body enlivens somebody. In human courtship lovers seek in their beloved some small reminiscence of that blissful union of two in one that every human being once knew in some way with a mother. A mother's love is an archetype of human love. Launched into existence because a woman carried us in, we yet seek as adults to have and to hold. "He asked when I fell in love with her. I said, 'The first time I saw her cry.' He asked, 'How did that remind you of your mother?' and I cried."

Throughout the Song the woman voices how she would be in so many ways a garden of shelter and a cornucopia of fruitfulness for her beloved. She would be wife and mother. His kisses would imbibe the milk of her love given for him. "Let my true love come into his garden and eat of its hand-picked fruits" (4:16). "A fresh and ripened harvest, O my heart's love, / I've held in keep for you" (7:14). The text remains, however, a song concerned not about the fruit of the womb but about the prior courtship. The body is delightful fruit, and it is fruitful because delightful. Thus the Song of Songs includes the immense fecundity of human love that is foreseen, because all love is diffusive by its very nature. "Love would be more if love it would remain."

8:2

I would lead thee, and bring thee into my mother's house,
Who would instruct me:
I would cause thee to drink of spiced wine of the juice of my
*   pomegranate.*

I would take you to my mother's house.
There you would enlighten me.
I would have you drink of spiced wine,
The liquid blend of my own pomegranate.

*I*n the ancient world of the east women had separate quarters, women's rooms or a woman's household (Gen 24:28). Naomi urges Ruth: "Go back . . .

to your mother's house" (Ruth 1:8). Some commentators think that it is the mother who raised her who would teach her the ways of love; others think it is the man who now would show her the ways of lovemaking. The Song may here tell a daydream of the woman, perhaps a fantasy similar to the two dreamlike episodes earlier in the Song (3:1–5 and 5:2–8). Whether in a reverie or not, she is apparently exploring her own sexuality. She desires to claim the full womanhood she shares with her mother. The woman in the Song is "the treasure of her mother, the dearest of her who birthed her" (6:9). In a previous verse the woman brings the beloved to her "mother's house, / To the room where she gave me birth" (3:4). Her mother's house may simply represent the female body. In all instances it seems a chamber of the heart and a special space.

She proposes to prepare a special drink, "of spiced wine, / The liquid blend of my own pomegranate." Lovers have ever wanted to drink each other in. They so eagerly melt and flow at heart into each other. Lovers would commingle. Because the oval-shaped pomegranate filled with seed (pome-granate means seedy apple) may readily suggest the female womb, some commentators have thought "the liquid blend of my own pomegranate" refers to the secretions of her body in its readiness for lovemaking. One commentator writes with some embarrassment that the imagery in the Song here "needs no explanation." Following the previous line it could be that the pomegranate is a reference to her rounded breast, and the liquid is the kisses her lover may now enjoy, "kisses . . . sweeter than wine" (1:2) or "honey dripping from its comb" (5:1).

The Song of Songs never loses its appropriate sense of mystery. The pomegranate drink the woman prepares for her lover carries many overtones. Love is always more than the body's chemistry. She is making for him a love potion with potent ingredients. Her love for him is what he must drink in, and her blend of pomegranate is the love of her heart of hearts beneath her breast. That draft of love will indeed enchant and transform him. One might bring to mind the role of love potions in the love stories of Aeneas and Dido, of Tristan and Isolde, and of Juliet and Romeo. All courtship stories have known that the sources of love are mysterious and magical. Dreams are the stuff sexual romance is made of, not bodily secretions. Her drink of pomegranate juice remains a secret, though its effects will be revealed.

The woman at the well is asked by Jesus "give me a drink" and told "if you knew the gift of God" (Jn 4:7, 10). In a spiritual reading, the holy Eucharist offers a special wine, and the sacrament invites those who drink into a union of love that far transcends the limits of the body, and is filled with the mystery of Christ's love that contains the very mystery of God. The word of God takes flesh in a mother's house. Jesus becomes the great teacher of love's ways. Though a mother may be everyone's first love, God is everyone's last love, summing up all other loves. Jesus promises that "those who eat my flesh and drink my blood have eternal life, and I will raise them up on the last day" (Jn 6:54). There is no more intimate communion, and no more ecstatic love song.

8:3

His left hand should be under my head,
And his right hand should embrace me.

His left hand cradles my head,
And his right hand stays me.

*F*ollowing upon the woman's promise in her mother's house to present her beloved a drink of a special pomegranate juice, the scene blends into one of physical intimacy. She tells again of being held in his arms. Most likely they are lying down together side by side. His left hand supports her head and his right hand is closed around her in an embrace that both enfolds her body and contains her movement. This line of the Song repeats an identical earlier description (2:6). As in this instance the lovers' embrace is followed by the warning refrain not to "rouse nor raise up love until its time is ripe" (2:7 and 8:4). In both instances the bodily intimacy is preceded by mention of a trysting place. "To his wine rooms he transports me" (2:4) and here she would take him "to [her] mother's house" (8:2). One might also note aphrodisiac foods in both instances: "raisin cakes" and "apples" (2:5) and "spiced wine, / The liquid blend of my own pomegranate" (8:2).

To the gardener's amazement, beautiful white roses flourish in a dunged bed of black earth. From a bed of blood, sweat, and tears fresh human life emerges in all its innocence. What is to be said of this human body, both embarrassment and ineffable revelation, both agony and ecstasy, an awful darkness that yields such an awe-full bright life. Sexual desire may encompass both an overwhelming dread and an enchanting fascination, both a shame and a delight, both a devouring lust and a self-bestowing love, both a frivolous itch and a deathless romance. The commotion of the flesh includes both the gravity of the body and the intimations of an ethereal soul, both a fevered sickbed and the gates of paradise. Around the human body the most ugly experiences have clustered and the most beautiful, the most hopeful and the most desperate. Human sexuality remains a great scandal and a great mystery.

That human sexuality is both procreative and life-giving in some way, as well as unitive and lovemaking in some way, only enhances its mystery. Sex serves both nature and language. We eat in order to live and we also live in order to taste that communion of soul enabled by table conversation. The life of the body must always be supported and the body of life must be celebrated. "His left hand cradles my head and his right hand stays me."

8:4
I charge you, O daughters of Jerusalem,
That ye stir not up, nor awake my love,
Until he please.

Give me your word, daughters of Jerusalem,
Do not rouse nor raise up love until its time is ripe.

*T*his fascinating and yet vague admonition is sounded in the Song for the third and last time (see 2:7 and 3:5). There is, however, no repeated urging of the adjuration "by the gazelles and the wild deer of the fields." These words are found in some manuscripts, but they are probably an echo of the previous formulations. All three instances of this refrain are preceded by a deliberate rendezvous. In chapter three this warning refrain, spoken by the woman, is followed by a question about who or what is coming up from the desert. In that instance it proves to be the carriage-bed of Solomon (3:6–11), and in this instance the woman herself "leaning against her lover" (8:5). The quest for pattern in the reading of the Song of Songs is supported by these intertwined theme songs that echo as refrains (2:6–7, 3:5–6, 8:4–5).

Here and now what does this line mean? One might think of the "mysterious unspeakable power of sex to leave us vulnerable to and connected with our partner." Love deep in the soul surely has its own timeliness. Love's donation cannot be rushed or forced to blossom. It develops according to its own nature and matures in good time by following its own inner wisdom. The arousal of love, moreover, may turn out to be "the awakening of a person's sense of being desirable, not (as commonly supposed) by being *desired* by another, but by being aroused by another to desire" (Sebastian Moore, 44). That awakening of desire needs to be carefully prepared.

We were made for consummate love, and we tend to settle for so much less. Hence this gentle and repeated warning of the Song. Do not rouse nor raise up love that is genuine desire until its time is ripe. Love is about enabling another to love, that is, to desire. It takes time. It is not to be taken for granted. In the Song this warning comes repeatedly, even though the lovers have previously given themselves in the garden scene (see chapter four). Perhaps because such commitment is so valuable the Song of Songs hedges it about with frequent admonition to ever take care of whomever one loves.

Should one wait on love? M. Esther Harding writes: "No woman as woman can plan her future. She can plan a career, but as woman she can only wait for the future to unfold itself. . . . A woman is always waiting—she may or may not conceive—she can only wait and see. Nine long months she waits, not knowing whether her child will be son or daughter, dark or fair, morose or gay, brilliant or a dunce." In an age without certain birth control, does this text urge prudence in the consummation of physical love? Is the presumption that the woman may be tempted too soon to yield herself, but knows her time has not yet come?

Jesus in the Gospel of John says to his mother: "My hour has not yet come" (2:4). The coming of love cannot be arranged. Love moves in the dark. In the myth of Psyche and Eros, she must not light the lamp and inspect her unknown lover. Paul Claudel says of woman that she is "a promise that cannot be held." Human love is not divine love, but it should lead to it. The ripeness of time is in the hands of mystery, for the gift of love is the gift of God. We await its coming as a lover the nighttime visit of the beloved (see 3:1–5 and 5:2–7). And in the end, only God can fill the infinite desire at the bottom of all our love affairs.

8:5

Who is this that cometh up from the wilderness,
Leaning upon her beloved?
I raised thee up under the apple tree:
There thy mother brought thee forth;
There she brought thee forth that bare thee.

Who is this coming up from the desert, leaning against her
lover?
Under the apple tree I roused you, where your mother
conceived you,
There you were quickened within her.

 he remainder of the Song of Songs (8:5–14) has been considered by many commentators to be an appendix of disparate verses. The continuity and coherence of these loose ends does seem more elusive, though there remain unifying echoes of previous lines in the Song. This particular verse may consist of two fragments, one describing an ascent from the desert floor and the other detailing a tryst underneath the apple tree.

"Who is this coming up from the desert, leaning against her lover?" is reminiscent of earlier lines: "What is this coming up from the desert like a cloud of smoke?" (3:6) and "Who is this who appears like the dawn?" (6:10).

In "under the apple tree where I roused you" it is not clear who the speaker is, though on first blush the woman "leaning against her lover" would seem to be. If the speaker is the man, the reference is then to the woman's mother with the erotic atmosphere of her "mother's house" (8:2) implied. Indeed, the mother of the woman is mentioned almost exclusively in the Song ("mother's sons" [1:6], "mother's house" [3:4], "the treasure of her mother" [6:9], and "my mother's breast" [8:1]). The mother of the man is mentioned only once in the description of the man "wearing the crown his mother gave him on his wedding day" (3:11). No mention is made in the Song of his father nor her father. If the Song of Songs is a universal love song it may here celebrate the world's first love, the mother who bears every human being into this world.

Shakespeare writes of mother earth: "common mother, thou / Whose womb unmeasurable, and infinite breast, / Teems, and feeds all" ("Timon of Athens," 4:3:177–79).

The apple tree may remind the reader of the sweetheart tree, the tree of love, with lovers' initials carved in the tree trunk. Apple trees suggest a certain romance, and the apple has been called a love fruit. As the popular song goes, "don't sit under the apple tree with anyone else but me." Earlier in the Song the man was described "as an apple tree in a dense woodland" in whose shadow she loves to linger (2:3). "Under the apple tree . . . where your mother conceived you" may remind the reader of the poignant story of Adam and Eve in the book of Genesis (chapter three). In one reading of the paradise story in Genesis, Adam consumes the fruit from Eve because he could not bear to be separated from the woman he loved. The reference here may also be to a sacred grove of fruit trees.

"Conceived" and "quickened" in the text provide an example of parallelism in Hebrew poetry. A previous meaning is echoed and thereby enhanced. The commotion of orgasm provides physical parallel to the experience of childbirth in that both experiences are overwhelming and experienced as inevitable once begun. Similarly, sexual love is an awakening from sleep that parallels birth as an awakening of life. The reference to the apple tree under which she/he was conceived parallels the mention of the room where her mother gave birth (3:4). By seeming chance human beings receive their initial life. By the serendipitous encounter of lovers and by small beginnings a human being who is truly miraculous, if not spectacular, comes to be conceived as love's fruitfulness.

In lovemaking when conception of a child is possible, a special kind of emotional bonding takes place between the man and woman who share that risk together. That bond may be the import of this line of the Song. An unwanted child, a deformed child, a woman at risk in childbirth, all these possible outcomes conspire to bond a man and woman in sexual union with an enduring loyalty to each other. When sexual intercourse is desired because a child is welcome and because the lovers each want deeply to recreate the beloved, who is enfleshed anew in this world, the merging of carnal procreation and joyful spiritual communion reaches the rarest fusion and culmination. The miracle of uterine life unfolding and the wonder of birth itself are hardly more indescribable than the love and desire from which these wonders spring in the human heart. If one adds the belief that new life is not only a miracle of nature but also a pledge of the new and everlasting life of a person born to see the face of God, then the bonding is awesome indeed. Faith in eternal life and the resurrection of the flesh elevate the tree of life and the fruit of the womb. With faith in the resurrection of Christ, eternity enters into time and divine love is yoked with human love in a sacred marriage.

8:6

Set me as a seal upon thine heart,
As a seal upon thine arm:
For love is strong as death;
Jealousy is cruel as the grave:
The coals thereof are coals of fire,
Which hath a most vehement flame.

Fasten me as a seal on your heart, as a seal on your arm;
Strong as death is love, perduring as the grave its bond.
Its flashings are flarings of fire,
A flaming forth of God (Yah).

The spiritual beauty of this verse reveals the very soul of the Song of Songs. An abiding union is what the lovers seek throughout their elaborate courtship. The popular idiom speaks of sealing a promise with a kiss, and Shakespeare calls the human kiss the "seal of love." Earlier in the Song the woman is portrayed as a "fountain sealed," which offers no opening to an outsider who has no welcome to the "garden enclosed" (4:12). A letter in ancient times was sealed with beeswax, and pressure was put upon the bonding with a signet ring on the finger or a sealing cylinder worn on a necklace. Such a seal was embossed in a particular way to serve as a signature of the owner. Pressed into the warm wax the signet fastened the ends of the document together and left the identification imprint of the owner in the soft surface. She would so abide upon his body with a endurance and a passionate ardor that will not be undone. Of Jesus, the beloved of the Father, John says: "For it is on him that God the Father has set his seal" (6:27).

He speaks:

Rise up, love of my soul, my beauty, come away! (2:10)

How beautiful you are, love of my soul, you are beautiful! (4:1)

When the evening breeze rises and shadows dissolve,
I will draw near the mountains of myrrh, the hills of incense.
   (4:6)

You are altogether beautiful, love of my soul. (4:7)

Bind me, the woman continues, "as a seal [worn] on your arm." The arm has been read as inclusive of the hand. Compare "his rounded arms [and fingers] are as gold adorned with precious stones" (5:14). In the Song the woman wishes to be herself the ring on his finger, the seal worn over his heart. Just as the ring worn on his finger she would be bound fast in love to him. His promise to her would be as a sealed signature, an indelible mark. Yahweh says of his faithful love: "See, I have inscribed you on the palm of my hands" (Is 49:16). In Haggai we read: "I will take you . . . and make you like a signet ring; for I have chosen you, says the Lord of hosts" (2:23). In the story of Tamar and Judah the signet ring is given as a pledge. She says: "'What will you give me, that you may come in to me?' He answered, 'I will send you a kid from the flock.' And she said, 'Only if you give me a pledge, until you send it.' He said, 'What pledge shall I give you?' She replied, 'Your signet and your cord, and the staff that is in your hand.'" (Gen 38:16–18). As events apparently turn out, that pledge is transformed into her "marriage" ring.

Death courts everyone and finally enfolds in a lasting embrace every single one of Eve's children. No one escapes death's silent and patient courtship. Love may indeed survive the death of the lovers, but their bodies do not prevail over the cold and the night. Love may be enduring as death, but love's body slips into the pit where the dead must lie. Affection might last forever, but all embodied love perishes at death. "The grave's a fine and private place / But none I think do there embrace" (Andrew Marvell, "To His Coy Mistress"). The immortality of the soul might be a consolation, but the shadowy body in Sheol knows no delight. That death of the body is inescapable. Death stalks everyone and death is inexorable, even if the bond of love remain "perduring as the grave." The Christian belief in the resurrection of the body does promise a new day, whose perfection may even surpass the physical joys of this earth, but the author of the Song of Songs did not know of such a hope.

Death is strong in its pursuit, and it perseveres to the end. If not today, then tomorrow. Death lurks ever in our blood and bones. The Song does not here just echo the promise of marriage vows to love "until death does us part." The claim here in the Song is far greater. Love will perdure even as death perdures. Death wins out over everyone. One can postpone death, but it is so strong that it will wear us down and triumph in the end. The dance of death, the "dance macabre," comes to include everyone. But, love is equally strong; love is strong as death. Love also wins out over everyone. One can postpone love, but it is so strong that it will wear us out and triumph in the end. The dance of love is a "light fantastic," and it comes to include everyone. Love thus courts and wins everyone in the end with the same perseverance as death. Love will not let go. Love fastens the lovers together with a seal, and that bond is not breakable. Love perdures with the same adhesion as death. Love is just as strong as death, just as bonding, just as insistent in its role within the human condition. Human beings can no more escape the exaltation of love than the body can escape the humiliation of death. The Song does not here argue love versus death, or that love outlives death, but rather claims both are relentless and both achieve their end. The call of love remains comparable to the call of death. Both voices are irresistible.

God is love; God is wisdom; God is strength. God is infinitely resourceful. Why should not God's love prevail in the end? And is this not the great human hope? As believers in such a God should we not claim such a hope? In fact, we do hope that love is just as strong as death, just as ubiquitous, just as able to touch everyone and in the end claim everyone. God's love will prove to be strong as death and will pursue everyone until love wins out. The wheat will outlast the weeds; the landholder will overcome the enemy. How God's love can be so resourceful we do not know, but can we not hope that God can turn around even the most evil behavior of human beings? I do not say that evil is not real, nor that sin does not have evil consequences, both for others and especially for those who assent to sin in their heart. I do say that we have reason to believe that God's goodness is stronger than sin, that love is just as strong as death. "For great is his steadfast love toward us, and the faithfulness of the Lord endures forever" (Ps 117:2). The Judeo-Christian God is a God of surprises whose creative energy is beyond telling, whose tender love enfleshed in a human body remains beyond imagination, and whose spiritual presence in this broken world of ours is as pervasive as the air we breathe, whether we know it or not, name it or not, claim it or not.

"His flashings are flarings of fire." One thinks of the solar flares on the sun or the lightnings on the earth. These outbursts of divine fire and enormous energy manifest the God who is "wrapped in light as with a garment" (Ps 104:2). One might think of that enormous primordial flaring forth at the origin of the cosmos. Love symbolized as an inextinguishable fire resonates in the poetry of the world. Passion is a consuming fire. The widowed Queen Dido in the *Aeneid* recalls courtship love again with these words: "I recognize the old flame." Her suicidal pyre speaks of the destructive conflagration of her unrequited passion. In the "Divine Comedy" the flames of desire become a curtain of pain that Dante must walk through in the last terrace of the "Purgatorio," where lust is finally purified into love by trial of fire. To Moses "the angel of the Lord appeared . . . in a flame of fire out of a bush" (Ex 3:2). The almighty God appears in the lightning on top of Mount Horeb and in the flames that consume the holocaust on the top of Mount Carmel. Upon the disciples at pentecost the Holy Spirit descended in "tongues, as of fire" (Acts 2:3). "And all shall be well and / All manner of things shall be well / When the tongues of flame are in-folded / Into the crowned knot of fire / And the fire and the rose are one" (T. S. Eliot, "Little Gidding," V: 42–46).

These flames of love are "a flaming out of God [Yah]." The Hebrew word, *Shalhevethyah,* ends with "Yah," the abbreviated form of the ineffable divine name [YHWH]. Some translations omit the divine name, because of a variant construal of the Hebrew, and they speak rather of a flame of surpassing vehemence such as might befit divinity. If the specific reference to God is kept in the translation, however, this verse of the Song becomes the unique mention of God and the climactic declaration that the perduring strength of human love, strong as death itself, derives its endurance from the boundless persevering love of God. After all, "God is love" (1 Jn 4:7). Human sexual love in its intensity is made in the image of divine love, the "Living Flame of Love," as John of the Cross proclaims. "The voice of the Lord flashes forth flames of fire" (Ps 29:7). Indeed, God is Light! "How precious is your steadfast love, O God! . . . For with you is the fountain of life; in your light we see light" (Ps 36:7,9).

8:7

Many waters cannot quench love,
Neither can the floods drown it:
If a man would give all the substance of his house for love,
It would utterly be contemned.

Bottomless waters cannot extinguish love, nor floodwaters overcome it.

Were anyone to barter all they owned for love, how it would
be ridiculed.

*R*unning water dissolves stones and carves grand canyons. Forest fires are
extinguished by rain, but the conflagration of love, both human and divine,
cannot be quenched by any amount of water, nor washed away no matter
the storm or flood. Come hell or high water true love will prevail. "The rain
fell, the floods came, and the winds blew and beat on that house, but it did
not fall, because it had been founded on rock" (Mt 7:25). The primal waters
of chaos cannot overwhelm love's land. Death does not overcome life, nor
does the night shadow the day. Nothing can drown the fires of love nor
dissolve the created bonds of love. "When you pass through the waters, I will
be with you; and through the rivers, they shall not overwhelm you; when
you walk through fire you shall not be burned, and the flame shall not consume
you" (Is 43:2).

In the story of Noah's ark the great flood of forty days and forty nights
drowned all life on the face of the earth in the waters of dissolution (Gen
9:9–11). "Many waters" is a phrase found over and over in the Hebrew scriptures. "Save me, O God, for the waters have come up to my neck. I sink in
the mire, where there is no foothold; I have come into deep waters, and the
flood sweeps over me . . . . Do not let the flood sweep over me, or the deep
swallow me up" (Ps 69:1–2, 15). Only the Lord God of creation, who hovered
in Spirit over the primal unformed waters, can overcome these troubled waves
of chaos. "The voice of the Lord is over the waters; the God of glory thunders,
the Lord, over mighty waters" (Ps 29:3). In the story of Exodus no watery
deep can stand between God and God's people: "Your way was through the
sea, your path, through the mighty waters" (Ps 77:19). To extinguish love's
flame not even "bottomless waters" suffice. Paul writes: "Who will separate
us from the love of Christ? Will hardship, or distress, or persecution, or famine,
or nakedness, or peril, or sword? . . . For I am convinced that neither death,
nor life, nor angels, nor rulers, nor things present, nor things to come, nor
powers, nor height, nor depth, not anything else in all creation, will be able
to separate us from the love of God in Christ Jesus our Lord" (Rom 8:35,
38–39). Indeed, love "bears all things, believes all things, hopes all things,
endures all things. Love never ends" (1 Cor 13:7–8).

"Were anyone to barter all they owned for love," both the buyer and their wealth would be ridiculed. Marriage can be arranged by purchase and contract. Sex can be bought. But love must be given. "The pearl of great value" (Mt 13:45) is worth giving all one owns to have it, and yet the pearl of love remains priceless. Love's value is beyond estimation. No bride price will prove enough. In wedding celebrations no expense is spared because the love of the bride and groom must be celebrated for what it is—invaluable.

"My bounty is as boundless as the sea, / My love as deep; the more I give to thee, / The more I have, for both are infinite" ("Romeo and Juliet," 2:2, 133–35). No one must count the cost of love beyond price. Paul writes: "I regard everything as loss because of the surpassing value of knowing Christ Jesus my Lord. For his sake I have suffered the loss of all things, and I regard them as rubbish, in order that I may gain Christ" (Phil 3:8). A superficial love might be reckoned, but not a mature love whose human decision cannot be measured. Love of a human person is never just a barter of body or soul. Human love at its fullest remains a gift of self. "For where your treasure is, there your heart will be also" (Mt 6:21). To try to buy such love rooted in the whole person is to attempt the impossible. Thus, such a misguided effort invites all around ridicule.

Moral advice is not found heretofore in the Song of Songs. Consequently, some commentators hold this short epigram about love's surpassing worth to be an interpolation, that is, a gloss or comment upon the previous line, written at first in the margin of the text and later incorporated into the received text of the Song of Songs.

8:8
We have a little sister, and she hath no breasts:
What shall we do for our sister in the day when she shall be
*   spoken for?*

Our little sister, she yet has no breasts.
What shall we conclude on the day she is pledged to marry?

"*You* grew up and became tall and arrived at full womanhood; your breasts were formed, and your hair had grown; yet you were naked and bare"

(Ez 16:7). The woman in this verse is yet a young girl and her breasts have not maturely formed. It is likely that the speakers are her brothers, though perhaps the woman herself is here recalling critical remarks of her "mother's sons" made earlier in the Song (1:6). The scene may be a flashback to an earlier time, because in their present courtship in the Song the man admires her woman's breasts, that hang like date clusters on a slender palm tree (7:8). Her brothers, however, are here worrying about the betrothal of their young sister, who in their eyes is unprepared. Custom often dictated that the marriage of a girl was arranged at an early age by her family for social and economic reasons. Their sister is not yet attractive to men, or in such a vein perhaps her older brothers wish to tease her. What kind of an espousal, therefore, can they hope to conclude for her?

The female breast gives milk for the child who needs it to live. In many cultures the female breast is not a source of erotic feeling. In equatorial climates tribal women often do not conceal their breasts. What is seen commonly becomes routine and does not arouse unusual sexual interest. In other cultures, the visual presentation of the female breast is surrounded with sexual eros. Perhaps what is revealed only in privileged moments carries emotional suspense. Such desire thrives on playfulness. Now you see, now you don't; look but don't touch. Male infatuation with a woman's breast ultimately defies a rational analysis. Perhaps the male eye is trained to find beauty in the female breast, which is draped with great care so as to show its ideal form. What is astonishing about this eroticization of a woman's breast is not that touch might arouse sexual desire, but that sight alone can do so. The shape of the female breast carries a mysterious beauty for men, perhaps all the more intriguing for its being a figure that dwells often in imagination. The dress of women attracts that imagination, and a great deal of thought and money has been spent upon the attractive presentation of a woman's breasts. The Song of Songs is ancient but not out of date.

The human story begins with the love of a woman, whose body bears us, forms us, and births us all. Her womb is the first breast the infant suckles. Her blood is changed into milk to feed the child at her breast. Human beings never quite forget having been a baby to whom any behavior was once permitted and for whom any service was gratuitously rendered. The weaning away from the mother's breast represents the human condition in miniature form. At the end of our adult life we must be weaned from the breast of this world. We must leave this earthly mother of us all. In a spiritual reading we are destined to be born into eternal life, and Christians believe that holy mother the church provides such a passage.

8:9

If she be a wall, we will build upon her a palace of silver:
And if she be a door, we will enclose her with boards of cedar.

If she be a wall, we shall armor her with silver;
If she be a door, we shall close her up with cedar board.

This line does not yield a certain reading. Most of literal readings of the Song see the contrast between the verses rather than a repetition. Earlier in the Song the woman laments her restricted activity: "My mother's sons were incensed with me. They tethered me as watch keep of the vineyard" (1:6). It would appear that the older brothers are here concerned about the proper conduct of their younger sister prior to the family arrangement of her marriage. Should she prove to be too indifferent in her welcome of potential suitors, they intend to adorn her appearance all the more to make her attractive. Thus, "if she is a wall" (inaccessible as a walled city), her family will dress her in fine clothes and "armor her with silver," jewelry befitting an eligible bride. On the other hand, "if she be a door" and welcomes men in her life (accessible as an open door), her family will restrain her and "shall close her up with cedar board." She must be neither backward nor forward in courtship. The men in the family want her malleable only according to their designs. Compare the knock on her door in the night and her hesitation to open the door as well as her eagerness to welcome her lover (5:2–7).

When men and women court without benefit of chaperone, the danger is that they will be carried away by passion and a child may be conceived. Since there is not yet a home for the child, courtship itself must not be allowed a loose rein. It is unlikely that in the near east the woman in the Song of Songs would have been allowed such intimacies with the beloved as the poem describes at length. In that sense the Song presents a hypothetical world of ideals, a future world of romance, a story world of a higher logic.

In a contemporary age where the conception of a child can be carefully planned, sexual intimacy has become more of a chosen language than a natural destiny, as much a mystery of new human love than a mystery of new human life. The function of courtship, nevertheless, would seem to remain to encourage and facilitate friendship. Personal intimacy is created by the sharing of talk, delights and embarrassments, hopes and fears, and every kind of mutual interest. If courtship excludes sexual intimacy, which is reserved for marriage, then the engaged couple will need to discover how to make love with their words, their thoughts, and their desires. Sex is an easy intimacy, on a superficial level at least, and early preoccupation with its intense fascination will crowd out exploration of those gentle and tentative sharings of heart and soul that create bonds among good friends as well as mature lovers.

Should sex be seen as a language, the value of fidelity need not be lost. The motive, however, is no longer only a question of responsible fertility and knowing to whom the baby belongs. Now it is a question of the profundity of what sexual intimacy says. If a human being gives himself or herself once and for all to another person, that speech is far more profound than the gift of self only for a time. It would seem to be lust that demands access to all of the body, no matter the why and wherefore. Love speaks in more careful words, giving what is precious only when it will be guarded and appreciated. With our body we can say something permanent and altogether profound. A diamond is a thing of beauty forever, and while it can be given as a superficial gift, it only sparkles when its true nature of reflecting an imperishable love is allowed to shine clearly for all to see.

Time for mature sexual relations includes a lifetime—gratitude and celebration of the past as well as commitment and anticipation of the needs and joys of the future. Both the inner-known risk of sexuality and its intense pleasure call for time-bonding, for engagement and commitment beyond just today. Hence the ultimate logic of human bodily love is the pledge of the future, even beyond time and space, a lasting marriage, "for better or worse, richer or poorer, in sickness or in health, till death does us part" (or rather in faith does us unite).

8:10

I am a wall, and my breasts like towers:
Then was I in his eyes as one that found favor.

I am a wall and my breasts are like towers;
And in his eyes I was a vessel of peace.

The young sister in the Song now claims the status of a grown woman. Her breasts have been formed and raised high. Her body remains a wall and her breasts its towers. She is now a mature woman. She makes peace and not war, and her city is not for the taking. She herself commands the city and opens the door.

The woman who gives her breasts to the sight and touch of a lover who knows her for the first time does enkindle in the man a debt of gratitude. Men rarely believe they deserve to be given welcome to the body of a woman whom they desire. Similarly, women are rarely convinced by themselves that their body is attractive and that they appear beautiful in the eyes of another. What is wonderful about the woman in the Song is that she celebrates her own body without hesitation. She is the ideal, the God-intended ideal, which is so often countercultural.

"And *in his eyes* I was a vessel of peace." To respect the modesty of another is to respect the mystery of that person. We use the phrase "to strip" someone of their dignity or wealth. To respect the modesty of another person is never to strip them, never to take from them what they do not wish to give, nor to deprive them of the cover they need. The body is a veil over the human being as mystery. The person is more than meets the eye. Human beings are not things; they are persons capable of knowing and loving God. The human being is enspirited flesh and enfleshed spirit. The human body thus both reveals and conceals the person. Human beings are never an object that eyesight can comprehend. We do not see a human being by looking at the surfaces and planes of their skin. We see them only when we look, not at their eyes, but into their eyes. We see them only when we see through them, lifting not just the veil of cloth that can be seen but also the veil of the flesh that can be touched. What we then know is the unique person, body and spirit, who will overcome death and see the face of God forever.

"And in his eyes I was *a vessel* of peace." The woman as "vessel of peace-fulness" may carry overtones of *shalom* (peace), and even of cognate words, such as Solomon and Jeru-*salem,* city of peace and the holy city. "Glorious things are spoken of you, O city of God" (Ps 87:3). Womankind remains at the heart of all peace. The hand that rocks the cradle is the hand that gives life rather than gives death.

"And in his eyes I was a vessel of *peace*." Our heart's deepest desire and God's love for us will some day converge. "In his will is our peace" (Dante). God does not impose on us or oppress us with a sovereign will opposed to our truest self. Our peace is doing God's will, because that turns out to be our own heart's desire. We may not know, however, what our deepest desire is. We may be confused by our many superficial, and hence false, selves. In truth, our deepest self wants to give our life away in love. We are made to be such lovers. And God wants nothing else for us than to be who we are. Nothing is imposed on us by God; everything unfolds by God's providence. God's peace is attained in us when we know that great divine love. The woman in the Song has known a great human love and in it she has known herself at peace. She has become a "vessel of peace," for human love points to divine love as the sacred marriage.

8:11
Solomon had a vineyard at Baal-hamon;
He let out the vineyard unto keepers;
Every one for the fruit thereof was to bring a thousand pieces
   of silver.

Solomon kept a vineyard in Baal-hamon.
He turned the vineyard over to caretakers;
A thousand silver coins the cost of its fruit.

*I*n the next two verses the overarching theme of the vineyard seen in the very beginning of the Song (1:6 and 2:15) reappears now at its closing. The quintessential story of Israel as God's own special vineyard in Isaiah (5:1–7) is echoed in the vineyard story of an unfaithful Israel told by Jesus, whose Father is the vine dresser: "'They will respect my son'" (Mt 21:33–41). Perhaps these vineyard verses are appended fragments whose original placement was not known to the final editor of the Song. Most likely the woman is the speaker, for in the next verse she proclaims: "My own vineyard is mine alone to give" (8:12). Earlier in the Song her body is the vineyard that she boasts she has not kept only for herself (1:6). King Solomon rents his vineyards and puts a price on his goods. In contrast, the woman in the Song bestows her vineyard and gives without counting the cost of her goods. Solomon displays a commerce; she manifests a gift.

Baal-hamon (Balamon), which may mean *Lord of wealth* or *Lord of multitudes,* might be located near Dothan in northern Israel (see Jdt 8:3). The vineyard of Solomon claims a monetary value: "A thousand silver coins the cost of its fruit." We thus know that the vineyard is extensive and the price expensive. "On that day every place where there used to be a thousand vines, worth a thousand shekels of silver, will become briers and thorns" (Is 7:23). The vast harem of Solomon, women kept and guarded, was counted even as a thousand. "Among his wives were seven hundred princesses and three hundred concubines; and his wives turned away his heart" (1 Kg 11:3). How contrasting in the Song of Songs, where the man boasts that his beloved is one in a thousand: "one, only one is my dove . . . the treasure of her mother" (6:9). In the Genesis story of King Abimelech's attempt to take Abraham's wife, whom he thought was the patriarch's sister, Sarah is untouched and her divine providence recognized: "'Look, I have given your brother a thousand pieces of silver; it is your exoneration before all who are with you; you are completely vindicated" (Gen 20:16). One might recall with sadness the account of the passion in the gospels when Jesus is betrayed by his friend and disciple for thirty pieces of silver. Between renting a vineyard or giving its flower and fruit, between taking a concubine or courting a beloved, there remains a great difference. The woman in the Song is not for sale (*mohar* or bride price); she is for love. Her body is hers to give, a gift that she alone bestows.

It is not possible to live without an exchange. We breathe in and we breathe out. We live the good life by an elaborate exchange of various goods and services. Our life is conceived, comes to birth, waxes and wanes, and finally dies, but always within a community of persons. That human community gives us the intellectual life that is language. Our friends bring our heart to life in the give and take of human love. From beginning to end our life remains related to others in a constant, necessary, and wonderful free exchange.

Such exchange, however, need not be a gift. A gift is always a human choice. Our choices define whom we shall become. In this freedom we adopt an attitude for or against life as a reciprocal give and take. Exchange, which remains unavoidable, becomes personal gift when I acknowledge the exchange as my choice, or when I receive someone else's gift and know it as their free choice. While I can hardly not breathe in and breathe out, I can breathe in the air that enlivens me as the creator's breath freely given to me, and I can breathe out my gratitude for life that is not mine to ignore but is mine to acknowledge as a loving gift gratefully received. Life at its fullest is the constant and ever-more profound giving and receiving of gifts.

Gifts are of many kinds. They come in different packages, and some are more valuable than others. Most treasured of all is the gift that most includes the giver. The "pearl of great price" is the gift that is the giver. When the gift is not just from the giver, nor just goods of the giver, but the gift is the very giver, and the giver is the very gift, then we have received all there is to give. We have received as in a source all the further gifts the beloved could possibly give. In their gift of love we have the priceless seed of all that they can do, can be, can hope ever to give us in the future. We receive not just the work of their hands and their heart, we receive their hands and heart as their gift. All love tends to such a gift, yearning for the identification of the gift and the giver, love and lover joined as a self-gift, given once and for all.

God loves with surpassing love. The gift of the Father is the Son, and the Son is the gift perfectly one with the Father giver. Together they give the Spirit of love, the gift of Father and Son, the gift that is one with the givers, one God gift and God giver, Father, Son, and Holy Spirit. Pure gift. Human beings made in the image of God imitate their creator. We would give ourselves away, although we never achieve in this life that perfect compenetration that reveals the gift and giver to be one, the lover and beloved to be united in a marvelous exchange, each alone and all together.

8:12

My vineyard, which is mine, is before me:
Thou, O Solomon, must have a thousand,
And those that keep the fruit thereof two hundred.

My own vineyard is mine alone to give;
The thousand for you, O Solomon,
And two hundred for the caretakers of the fruit.

This verse taken with the preceding verses seems to make a parallel with the earlier description of the woman who had not kept her vineyard as her brothers wished, but as she wished. One commentator notes that the whole length of the Song separates "my own vineyard is mine" (8:12) from "on my own vine I spent no care" (1:6). Throughout the Song the vineyard is metaphor for her body and her whole self (4:12–5:1 and 7:8–14, *passim*). "If nothing else, the Song tells of the discovery of oneself through love. In a sense the inversion of 1:6 and 8:12 encapsulates the total experience of reading the poem" (Landy, 156).

This verse makes explicit the preceding contrast between the commercial rental of the vineyard of Solomon and the loving gift of the woman's vineyard. Like the vineyard of Naboth that King Ahab desired at all costs (1 Kg 21), she is not for sale at any price. She is not the property of Solomon or her own brothers; she belongs to herself. King Solomon may take his thousand pieces of silver in profit from his own vineyard, and the caretakers may receive two hundred in wages, but her own vineyard remains priceless: "Were anyone to barter all they owned for love, how it would be ridiculed" (8:7).

Israel itself was the bride of God, the vineyard the Lord planted: "You brought a vine out of Egypt" (Ps 80:8). Jesus embodied the love of God, that is the self-gift of God's only Son given to humankind. Jesus said: "I am the true vine, and my Father is the vine grower" and "abide in me as I abide in you (Jn 15:1,4). The fruit of the vine becomes the wine, which in turn becomes the body of Jesus: "This cup that is poured out for you is the new covenant in my blood" (Lk 22:20). Unwillingness to acknowledge the consummate value of divine love given so gratuitously in comparison with human love in its calculation prompts Jesus to warn: "The queen of the south will rise at the judgment with the people of this generation and condemn them, because she came from the ends of the earth to listen to the wisdom of Solomon, and see, something greater than Solomon is here!" (Lk 11:31).

True gifts are not bought; they are given. In the gift we measure how much the giver has given, not how much they have spent. No price tags are included. We wish only to know what the gift cost the giver of himself or herself. The child that spends his or her whole week's allowance or the widow who gives her last copper coin to the temple treasury may have given gifts without much pecuniary value, but they have given expensively of themselves. It costs them. When we buy a gift, it represents at its best the gift of our time and talent to earn the money that we would have gladly spent on making the gift ourselves had we the time to spare and the talent to craft whatever we had chosen to give. God's handmade gift to us is the creation of humanity, formed from dust and spittle, shaped into the image and likeness of God, the work of God's hands, the clay in the potter's care. We are God's exquisiste handmade gift, the masterpiece of her hands, the summit of his personal involvement in the created world.

The woman who hand-sews a garment for her beloved puts warmth into the wool that no store-bought sweater can convey. Our presence enters our gift. Our present is this presence embodied in the many hours given of heart and hands to shape the garment to fit and to hold warm the body of the beloved. We know there is a difference between taking guests to a restaurant to eat and taking them home to share the food we prepare and serve them. More of us is given by the care to cook what they prefer and to make it special because they are special. Even more the gift if we have grown the food in our own garden. It is as if we add love all along the way as the seed turns into wheat, the wheat into bread, and the bread into the substance of their body, now given to them by us. In such gifts we give ourselves.

The gift of self cannot be counterfeited. When the body of another is taken rather than given, a lifelessness enters into the intercourse. Some form of violence replaces the sweet yield of genuine love. The exchange of man and woman becomes loveless, unloved and unloving, and most unlovely. Rape steals a body by force, but what is unwrapped is not the gift of self but the unwilling flesh caught in a hunter's trap. Prostitution rents a body for money or for barter, but what is unwrapped is the abuse of the body. Without love the gift of self is not given but taken back. Love affairs loan a body for romance, but what is unwrapped is the gift of self with reservations about the future and restrictions imposed by conflictual commitments of the past.

In the richest gift of self we give a gift that is carefully chosen, handmade and not bought, and given not for a time but forever. That gift is "my body given for you." I do not just have a body; I am my body. The gift of my body is thus the gift of my self. Sacred marriage identifies gift and giver so convincingly. One gives not just an episode, one gives one's self and one's time for all time, in and with and through one's body. In giving us the only Son, the word made flesh, God gave us not only the gifts of the creator but also the gift of God's very self. In giving us the beloved, God gave us everything. And human love is made in the image of God's love. The joy of the present in sexual union must be joy in the celebration of the past and in the pledge of the future. To the beauty that can be seen and touched must be joined the whole configuration of life that supports our human sexuality.

8:13
Thou that dwellest in the gardens,
The companions hearken to thy voice:
Cause me to hear it.

Garden mate, my companions are all ears;
Let me hear your voice!

Courtship is an ever-dynamic interplay of hide and seek, of lost and found. Here the man would have the woman reveal her heart in her words. The man's "companions" who want to listen to her voice may be his fellow shepherds mentioned earlier in the Song (1:7), or they may be a rhetorical device to invite her speech. Perhaps these companions wish to hear her confirm in her own voice the romantic attachment to the man that they have heard of only from his account. They may be teasing him about the veracity of his story of her devoted love. Possibly he does not wish them to overhear her voice in its intimacy intended for his hearing alone. Whatever the situation, she appears to be quiet as the shy dove "in the clefts of the rock, / In the crannies of the cliff" (2:14), who makes no sound when strangers approach. Throughout the Song the text is strangely quiet. There are no musical instruments, no sounds but the soughing and cooing of the mourning doves (2:12) and the poignant sound of the human voice singing the song of the heart.

Longfellow says that "the soul of man is audible, not visible," and that the human voice is a "celestial melody." Access to our voice is a gift we may choose not to give. Our words focus our mind and attention, and we can choose not to speak. Many European languages have special intimate forms of address (for example, *tu* in French, the equivalent of *thou* in English), which are reserved for speech that presumes the intimacy of friends, or of children and parents, or of human beings and their God. To hear the voice of the heart is a privilege not to be taken for granted.

Sören Kierkegaard tells a story of the love of God for humanity. A great king courts a humble maiden. Because the king does not want her dependence and endless gratitude to characterize their bond, he decides to abdicate his throne. As a common man, however, the once powerful king recognizes that his beloved may not speak to him at all. His love may not be returned. How shall even God "give without usurpation" and "receive without humiliation"?

In the story of Mary of Nazareth, God awaits the voice of Mary. She must speak that word of acceptance that can be heard around the world. She who is beloved must give God welcome. Augustine says that Mary conceived Jesus first in her ear, where the word of God was heard in the message of the angel, then in her heart, and only then in her womb. Because the overtures of courtship love can be spurned, the outcome of love is often in suspense.

To excommunicate a person is to deny them place at the common table. Friendship is confirmed in eating a meal together. Through the medium and exchange of food, we allow others a certain intimacy with our body. The Eucharist is God's bodily communion. The body of Jesus who is Lord becomes our food and drink. The Eucharist is the supreme sign of God's acceptance of us and of our approaching the divine. To sit at the table and break bread pledges unmistakable forgiveness. "Zaccheus . . . I must stay at your house today" (Lk 19:5). Jean Paul Sartre said that "hell is no exit," no escape from the other. I would say that hell is no entrance to the other. Alone we are not fed, nor touched, nor loved. Heaven, on the other hand, is total access, a full incorporation of the plenitude that is the goodness of God now loved with all our mind, all our strength, all our heart, and all our soul. When we welcome on earth the immigrant, the displaced person, the homeless, the stranger, the enemy, the unborn and unexpected child, we give access to what heaven is— a welcome loving exchange of life. We are at peace and become God's people when everyone, sinner and saint, is welcome together in an endless loving conversation. Hence in the Song, "Let me hear your voice!"

8:14
Make haste, my beloved,
And be thou like to a roe or to a young hart
Upon the mountains of spices.

Leap up and away, my own love,
Like a gazelle or a young stag upon the mountains of spices!

*T*he woman does not respond to the man with words to be heard but with deeds to be done. She invites him to come to her "like a gazelle or a young stag upon the mountains of spices." Just as the Song of Songs opens with her bold desire, "may he kiss me with kisses of his lips" (1:2), the poem ends with her insistence that the man be quick and lively about his lovemaking. The woman in the Song has no meek shyness about this courtship. She cherishes her sexuality and eagerly she asks for its fulfillment. Her imperatives urge him to run after her. Her body is the "mountains of spices" just as her body is the garden of delights, where the sweet airs are everywhere. She is the perennial landscape, the space where he may always come. She will show the way, and about her he will have running room to romp upon fragrant mountains above ample valleys. The proverb says: "he who hesitates is lost." Let him be as enthusiastic in his love as she remains urgent in her willing pursuit of him.

Love is a dance and the dance goes on. The ballet of God's creative love is graceful as a gazelle and lovely as a ballerina. Earlier in the Song she describes his excitement with similar imagery: "here he comes bounding down the mountain sides, springing over the hills. / My beloved is like a gazelle, a young hart" (2:8–9). And yet again: "turn back to me, my heart's love; / Be like a gazelle or a young hart on the mountains of Bether" (2:17). Both divine love and human love employ the same imagery of the wild and graceful deer of the mountain highlands: "God, the Lord, is my strength; he makes my feet like the feet of a deer, and makes me tread upon the heights" (Hab 3:19). The ascent of the mountain also symbolizes a mystical love. We will be joined together with those we have loved most in the communion of saints. "Come Lord, stir us up and call us back, enkindle and grasp us, be our perfume and sweetness. Let us love. Let us run" (Augustine *Confessions* viii: iv). "The Spirit and the bride say, 'Come.' And let everyone who hears say, 'Come.' And let everyone who is thirsty come. Let anyone who wishes take the water of life as a gift" (Rev 22:17). "Leap up and away, my own love, / Like a gazelle or a young stag upon the mountains of spices!" "Amen. Come, Lord Jesus!" (Rev 22:20).

Concluding Perspectives

The Song of Songs is the Language of Love

THE BIBLE begins with the promise that woman and man will become in their love two in "one flesh" (Gen 2:24). The Bible ends with the wedding feast of the lamb of God wherein all graced humanity together enjoys the love of God forever (Rev 19:7). Jesus' first miracle changes water into wine at the wedding feast in Cana (Jn 2), and his life concludes with the resurrection of the body, now married unto glory in the garden of Joseph of Arimathea. Indeed, the Bible is God's love story, and "strong as death is love" (8:6). The Bible speaks lyrically of the divine love story, the source and the end of all human love stories. Here is an outspoken love, the very word of God, a long divine love letter writ with human words. "You shall be my people and I will be your God" (Ez 36:28).

Divine love and human love are twin loves, just as the twin fawns that symbolize the twin breasts of the beloved in the Song of Songs. Sacred and profane love are united in the biblical song, whether the text is read primarily as divine love or primarily as human love. The biblical song is always a twin melody, the heartfelt tones of the double-reed oboe d'amore, the longed-for consummate harmony of body and soul, of man and woman, of human and divine love in a sacred marriage.

In the Hebrew tradition, the sacred tetragrammaton (YHWH) is not pronounced. God's name, and by implication God's love, remains ineffable. When reading the Bible in public, the reader substitutes a more generic word for God, such as *adonai* or lord. The Song of Songs is the divine love in a form that can be humanly spoken. It is biblical love as a spoken love, and a sung love. One might even think of the reading of the Song as a performance of a melodious musical score. One is given notes and some directions, but there is no one vocal rendition. As we sing the music we disclose ourselves as well as the lyrics of the Bible. "Sound is not the craftsman of the singing, but it is submitted by the body for the singer's soul to make into song" (Augustine, *Confessions*, xii:xxix). The Song of Songs belongs in the company of the great biblical songs, such as the song of Deborah (Judges 5), the song of Hannah (1 Sam 2), the song of Mary (Lk 2), and Paul's song to love. "Love is kind, love is patient. . . . It bears all things, believes all things, hopes all things, endures all things." (1 Cor 13).

· II ·

The Song of Songs is an Envisioning Love

The world of creation and the world of the beloved are seen with new eyes in the Song of Songs. Sight is enhanced by love itself. Love may be blind and beauty may be in the eye of the beholder, but love also sees more than meets the eye. If sin blinds, love sights us. If sin numbs, love sensitizes the human being. Those newborn eyes of the lover remain at the heart of the Song. The lovers' rich and varied description of the flora and fauna reveals how generously they see each other. The lovers' ample and tender description of each other tells how they see, touch, and taste the world itself.

The contemporary author Thomas Moore writes: "The ensouled body is in communion with the body of the world and finds its health in that intimacy" (*The Care of the Soul* [San Franciso: Harper Collins, 1994]). The descriptive litanies of the Song relate to the human body as the noun vocabulary of human poetry relates to the whole created world. "A high culture of flowers and spices is a powerful way to ensoul the world." This outercourse is the rehearsal of the intimacies of intercourse. As one incorporates the world through the senses, so one will welcome the body of the beloved. The cumulative affirmation of creation thus sets up the delight and reverence for the beauty of the beloved, and vice versa. In the Song, the imagery in the beautiful litanies of the body of the beloved seems even more poignant than the physical body itself. Here is a cornucopia of vitality, the blessed vivacious world of creation which is the gift of God. These litanies in the Song show how the lovers see as well as how they look (I am here much indebted to Michael Fox). The new eyes of love provide a new world order, "a new heaven and a new earth," touched by eros tenderly. It remains a world animated by human love and by the "love that moves the sun and stars." All is grace; all is gift; all is blessing. The world appears as it truly is—the body of God's love. Indeed, "the message of the Song could be expressed as 'God is love, perceived in the beauty of the world'" (Landy, 178). Though the world may not yet have arrived at such a vision, it will come to it.

· III ·

The Song of Songs is an Unveiling Love

Once upon a time there was an enchanted garden in a golden age. When we are loved by another, we suspect we are loved by yet a greater love. Indeed, we hope we are the beloved of God. Indeed, our natural delight in our self, our conviction that our life matters, and our desire that our love for another should be celebrated, reflect God's pure delight in us. Human beings are God's beloved. "All life is courtship of the hidden love we ever seek, who made us and who delights in us with infinite love" (Sebastian Moore, *The Inner Loneliness* [New York: Crossroad, 1982]).

The Song of Songs tells in spoken words and in body language the simple truth about the human condition. All embrace of the lovely limbs of the children of God is rehearsal, foretaste, pledge, and advent of the ultimate mystery of God's love, that royal "road of the beloved, searching for the Lover in the full confidence that the Lover, whose voice has already been heard, is waiting for me" (Sebastian Moore, *The Inner Loneliness*). The whole world sings because of the embodiment of God's love in the human being of Jesus Christ. The word of God becomes a body language. Human love is unveiled as an image of a divine love.

· IV ·

The Song of Songs is a Remembered Love

We read the Bible lest we forget to remember from where we came and to where we are going. What God has wrought must be recalled every day anew, lest we forget how much our God has loved us. The Bible is the memory of a people. The Song of Songs is the memory of the human heart. Lynda Sexson writes: "Memory is not just the storing of the past, it is the storying of the present" (*Ordinarily Sacred* [New York: Crossroad, 1982]). And memory is the inventing of the future. The Song treasures human courtship as a shy token of the great and everlasting love story of the God who made us in order to belong to God in pure friendship.

"Perhaps one of the functions of love is for the lover to perform the intimate task of wrapping another within that chamber of memory, to carry and feel the love" (Lynda Sexson). Human love that the Song so joyfully celebrates may provide us with the most keen "intimations of paradise" that we are likely to know on the earth—lest we not remember.

· V ·

The Song of Songs is the Bond of Love

The Bible's Song sings of the bond that human affection creates between two human beings in love. That bond is extraordinarily strong and extremely joyful.

The Song is about that bond. It is not about sexual morality, religious marriage, or children and family. The Song, of course, is nowise opposed to these moral and social values. Its concern is with the bond of affection that precedes all else and which is presupposed by all subsequent social values. Morality without the inner attraction for the beloved becomes the difficult keeping of an extrinsic law. Marriage without mutual affection becomes the fulfillment of a contract rather than the heartfelt song that carries life along. Children without the love of their parents for each other are never fully aware of the beauty of the world of love. In the Christian tradition marriage is a sacrament that confers grace. That grace is first anticipated in the very wonderful bonding of woman and man in courtship love.

Being in love whatever the circumstances is always a treasure in and of itself. It is awesome; it is magical; is spirit-filled; it is an epiphany of the divine in the body of the human. So strong is this bond of human affection that an entire lifetime can be built upon it. It is so strong that unrequited love in courtship or a divorce in marriage can break the human heart in so many pieces that it may never be put together again. Courtship love is a miracle glue, and the Song sings of its very wonderful bonding. All else that is good about the human family receives a bonus and an enormous support from this bond. We presuppose its presence and its strength in almost everything we do with the human body and its passion.

· VI ·

The Song of Songs is a Love Strong as Death

No other verse in the Song of Songs speaks of ultimate meaning as well as the oft quoted "strong as death is love" (8:6). Just as death is persistent and in the end claims every human being, so love is perduring and in the end gives meaning and life to every human being. God's love is not outdone by death, and human love is in the image of God's love. Of Jesus it could be said: "The disciples saw that his intimacy with God, his emotional equality with God, his freedom from the original guilt, was a reality stronger than death which seemed to have rendered it a mere aspiration or dream" (Sebastian Moore, *The Inner Loneliness*). We least want to die when we most feel alive. The innocent love of man and woman in the Song prefigures the innocent delight of Jesus of Nazareth in the vitality and goodness of all human life. When we are filled with love's yearning, death is then altogether unwelcome, almost unthinkable, judged to be an outrageous contradiction. Hence arises the tension between love and death, a mystery that is felt deeply at the end of the Song of Songs. Shakespeare's Romeo says: "I dreamt my lady came and found me dead—/ Strange dream, that gives a dead man leave to think!—/ And breathed such life with kisses in my lips, / That I revived, and was an emperor" (5:1:6–9).

Christian death at one level is a reluctant departure from the innocent beauty of this life, but at another level it is an eager flying into the arms of the Beloved who awaits us with the consummate communion that we have all along desired. We have but seen a glimpse and known a foretaste of that joy in the loving embraces of anyone in this life who has held us to their heart. "Strong as death is love" and so the sacred marriage of the Song of Songs never ends.

> A damsel with a dulcimer
> In a vision once I saw:
> It was an Abyssinian maid,
> And on her dulcimer she played,
> Singing of Mount Abora.
> Could I revive within me
> Her symphony and song,
> To such a deep delight 't would win me
> That with music loud and long,
> I would build that dome in air,
> That sunny dome! those caves of ice!
> And all who heard should see them there,
> And all should cry, Beware! Beware!
> His flashing eyes, his floating hair!
> Weave a circle round him thrice,
> And close your eyes with holy dread,
> For he on honey-dew hath fed,
> And drunk the milk of Paradise.
>
> (Samuel Taylor Coleridge, from "Kubla Khan")

Afterword

BY NICHOLAS AYO

THE QUESTION "who will love me" has been put many ways. Who cares for me? Am I important to anyone? Who will meet my many needs, both physical and spiritual? There is perhaps no other question so important from our first breath as a baby to our last breath before the grave. Indeed, the question is most poignant at the moment of death. Do I matter to anyone forever? Or, am I just matter, a speck of dust on a cooling stellar cinder in a vast and cold universe of a billion galaxies in flight from each other at the speed of light. Human beings may be more than just their body, but no one can communicate without their body, nor ever be truly indifferent about the welfare of their flesh. The body is our first and last garment, a sacred matter wrapped in a white baptismal robe at our beginning and in a white funeral pall at our ending. One might phrase this one momentous human question in this way: "Who will cherish my flesh"?

In the birth of a child we recognize a parental love, the love that is reminiscent of the creator's love for our own existence. It is an unconditional love, a gratuitous love, the only "free lunch" given in this universe. "Can a woman forget her nursing child, or show not compassion for the child of her womb? . . . Though a mother forget her child I will not forget you. See. I have inscribed you on the palms of my hands" (Is 49:15–16). A baby cries for attention. To cherish its flesh is to give food and to hug its body. Its dependence on another to attend to its body is a matter of life and death. As much as a baby wants food, the human being also wants meaning. A child seeks a response, a relationship, a mutual smile of recognition and acceptance. It would say—I know you who now cherish my flesh. The question even from infancy remains this. Who will cherish my flesh?

The archetypal story of Romeo and Juliet is perhaps the model of adolescent love seeking the beloved. None else but this unique beloved will serve, and such a love must be forever. So intense is the luminosity of young romantic love that life and death hang in the balance. Romeo and Juliet give all for love, even their life in order to cherish the heart-wounded flesh of the other. So dear have they become to one another, two become one flesh, that they will die for each other. They know who will cherish their flesh! In the human love story it is indeed the spouse who most cherishes the flesh of the beloved. Most human beings are convinced they are loved because of the intense emotions of courtship and lifetime commitment. In adult love one is old enough to choose and free enough to give as much as possible. Lovers of every stripe know who will cherish their flesh! And, it is human love that prepares us for divine love.

To us all, old age will come, and the same question returns. Who will cherish my flesh, especially when it is tired and subject to "the thousand slings that mortal flesh is heir to"? It is a time when human beings are tempted to despair. I must die. Who then will cherish my flesh? How the decay of the grave is terrible to accept. The Christian promise of the resurrection of the flesh lays claim that the God who created me, body and soul, shall cherish my flesh forever. I shall see the face of God and live. The promise is not just for the survival of an immortal but bodiless soul. I shall know "the resurrection of the body and life everlasting." The Song of Songs becomes finally a prayer for God's saving love, a prayer couched in poetic words and a prayer lived in a passionate body—that exquisite God-given instrument of song and dance filled with the life of the Holy Spirit, that sacred marriage longed for from the beginning of time.

> Prayer the Churches banquet, Angels age,
>> God's breath in man returning to his birth
>> The soul in paraphrase, heart in pilgrimage,
> The Christian plummet sounding heav'n and earth;
>
> Engine against th'Almightie, sinners towre.
>> Reversed thunder, Christ-side-piercing spear,
>> The six-daies world-transposing in an houre,
> A kind of tune, which all things heare and fear;
>
> Softness, and peace, and joy, and love, and blisse,
>> Exalted Manna, gladness of the best,
>> Heaven in ordinarie, man well drest
> The milkie way, the bird of Paradise,
>
>> Church-bels beyond the starres heard, the souls bloud
>> The land of spices; something understood.
>>> (George Herbert, "Prayer")

Afterword

BY MEINRAD CRAIGHEAD

The Mystery of the Threshold

IN THE SUMMER OF 1996 I accepted the invitation to create a series of paintings which would accompany Nicholas Ayo's rendition of the Song of Songs. In the early winter evenings of that year, I began the search for the images. I recited the Song into the fire which burned in my wood stove, then, painting, I watched as the words of the lovers unfolded into the nonverbal landscape of their ancient love song. As I painted, the lovers entrusted me with their intimacy and led me into their sacred trysting place.

Soon the spirit animals, two of them the threshold guardians of that sacred space, made their appearance. The threshold marks the invisible place of transition between the world of the secular and the world of the sacred, the point where one is judged worthy or unworthy of entry. The threshold guardians divine our intent; they may allow us passage or they may repel us, if our intentions are profane, if we are unready or unworthy to participate in the story. If they allow us passage, we look across the red threshold and cross into the secrets of the enclosed garden. By giving us their permission, the spirit animals allay our discomfort and vaguely voyeuristic curiosity and free us to enter the sacred space with confidence and to share in its energies. We are allowed into the moment, the place of rendezvous, because we understand the sanctity of the sacred rite and wish to worship at this mystery. The lovers and the animals give us permission to participate in the holy drama. We are welcomed.

Spirit animals may be summoned but, more often, they arrive unbidden, as did the young Hart, the first animal to appear in this group of paintings. Suddenly, there he was, ancient symbol of virility and renewal, the young Lord of the Hunt, looking at me through the latticework, inviting me into the story, into the mystery of the hunt. With his arrival, the hunt for images which would accompany this story had begun.

Next appeared the Dog and Crow, guardians of the threshold. The Dog is the watcher at gates, rivers, and crossroads, at places of transition and at crossover times; he is the soul's eternal guide and guardian. In these paintings he participates in the love scenes; in one of them his tail is erect with the energy in the garden, pouring from the conjugal embrace. The Crow, like the hart, presages death of the old and birth of the new, a change in paradigms. She stands unmoving at our vulnerable moments of transition.

The red threshold and the two threshold animals appeared simultaneously, and they were to do so in all eight paintings, but in some of them Dog and Crow would eventually disappear and sink into the subcutaneous layer, invisible, but still present as energy just below the surface. A "finished" painting is like a skin over deep layers of buried imagery. The dynamics of a painting in process are as complicated and mysterious as those of a life story in miniature: ever in flux, the painting may, at any moment, shapeshift, finish, or continue. Images rise out of the artist's creative imagination, remain or pass, may return again and vanish again. But the energy of the images, be they animal or whatever, is permanently embedded in the very fabric of the composition. Even unseen, these layers continue to pulsate in the hidden life of the painting.

Select Bibliography

THE BIBLIOGRAPHY of the Song of Songs would comprise a book in itself. Marvin Pope's *Song of Songs* (New York: Doubleday Anchor Bible, 1977) lists two hundred pages of references. Hardly any other single book of scripture seems to have enjoyed such popularity and drawn so many commentators in the Patristic period as well as in the Middle Ages. The Song of Songs tells us of the love of a woman and a man, a love that through the centuries was understood as a sacred sign of God's love and its most everyday embodiment. For an exhaustive and encyclopedic review of the bibliographical literature about the Song of Songs Marvin Pope's work deserves special recognition. For a more recent wide-ranging listing and an evaluation of this copious literature I recommend Roland Murphy's *Song of Songs: A Commentary on the Book of Canticles or the Song of Songs* (Minneapolis: Augsburg Fortress, 1990).

For summary information on the history of interpretations of the Song of Songs see Christian Ginsburg, *The Song of Songs: Translated from the Original Hebrew, with a Commentary Historical and Critical* (London: Longman, Brown, 1857), pp. 20–126. See also Marvin Pope cited above, pp. 89–229, and Roland Murphy cited above, pp. 11–41.

G. Lloyd Carr, *The Song of Solomon: An Introduction and Commentary* (Leicester, England: Inter-Varsity Press, 1984) offers a short and balanced treatment of the Song. Althalya Brenner, *The Song of Songs* (Sheffield: JSOT Press, 1989), is page for page a most succinct quality review of the Song. Dianne Bergant's short and thoughtful commentary on the Song in the *Catholic Study Bible* edition of the *New American Bible* (New York: Oxford, 1990) is very judicious. Michael Fox, *The Song of Songs and the Ancient Egyptian Love Songs* (Madison: University of Wisconsin Press, 1985) gives a readable and insightful survey of the collateral love poetry surrounding the Song of Songs. Francis Landy, *Paradoxes of Paradise* (Sheffield: Almond Press, 1983) presents a most imaginative reading of the Song. Roland Murphy's work cited above remains the single most helpful resource and commentary that I found in surveying a great number of books on the Song of Songs.

Christian Ginsburg and Marvin Pope present a survey in their book introductions of both Jewish and Christian allegorical readings of the Song. For the Middle Ages where many of the commentaries on the Song will be found, see the comprehensive scholarly survey of E. Ann Matter, *The Voice of My Beloved: The Song of Songs in Western Medieval Christianity* (Philadelphia: University of Pennsylvania Press, 1990). For a wide-ranging and devout spiritual reading of the Song of Songs as a mystical treatise upon the love of God for humankind, I would suggest Blaise Arminjon's *The Cantata of Love: A Verse-by Verse Reading of the Song of Songs* (San Francisco: Ignatius Press, 1988). This quite readable survey of the many commentaries through the centuries on the allegorical meaning of the Song of Songs includes excerpts from such authors as Origen, Gregory of Nyssa, Theodore of Mopsuestia, Cyril of Jerusalem, Ambrose, Augustine, Gregory the Great, Bernard of Clairvaux, William of Saint Thierry, Ruysbroeck, Tauler, Catherine of Siena, Teresa of Avila, John of the Cross, Francis de Sales, Andre Chouraqui, and Paul Claudel.